Six Causes

Six Causes

The Vedic Theory of Creation

Ashish Dalela

SHABDA
PRESS

Six Causes—The Vedic Theory of Creation
by Ashish Dalela
www.ashishdalela.com

Published by Shabda Press
www.shabdapress.net
ISBN 978-81930523-3-4
Second Edition

Dedicated to His Divine Grace A.C. Bhaktivedanta Swami Prabhupāda. His books saved me from the darkness of ignorance and showed me that truth is simple but not simplistic.

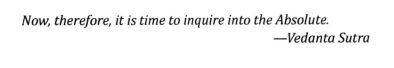

Now, therefore, it is time to inquire into the Absolute.
—Vedanta Sutra

Contents

List of Figures

Preface

The rise of science has created a fierce debate between creationists and evolutionists[1]. The evolutionists argue that the material universe came to its present form step by step over billions of years, while the creationists claim that it was created by God all at once. Creationists and evolutionists also differ in their claims about the age of the universe. But perhaps the biggest difference lies in the role they attribute to consciousness. Consciousness, in the evolutionist account, has come late in the existence of the universe, while consciousness in the creationist accounts existed prior to matter. In fact, in Vedic philosophy, consciousness creates objects *from* matter.

Science presently has no clear explanation for consciousness, but the evolutionist claims that we will get to that account eventually, based on advances in neuroscience and brain biology. This brings up questions about what in matter will explain consciousness, and the many types of experiences it generates, such as meanings, feelings (such as pain), emotions, intelligence, free will, personality and the sense of identity. There is also the question of whether experiences are entirely subjective or they have objective counterparts in matter. If there are counterparts, then how are the mind and body related? Note how these questions are not merely of interest to creationists, but also constitute central problems within mainstream science. A solution to these problems, however, requires a different view of matter than what is prevalent in current science.

Attempts to bring alternative perspectives on matter into science have failed. There are serious questions about whether an alternative account will significantly alter the manner in which matter is currently described or will merely reinterpret its concepts. Thus far, alternative approaches have only offered reinterpretations, sometimes claiming that scientific concepts were foreseen by religious philosophies in the past. This isn't very helpful to the cause of either science or religion. As far as the more dramatic revisionist approaches are concerned, they have never really taken off.

In this regard, Vedic accounts of creation are particularly helpful because the Vedic theory describes matter in a radically different way. Unlike science which describes matter in relation to other material objects, Vedic theories describe matter in relation to the observer's capabilities of perception. While current science describes the world in terms of quantities (measurements of quantities such temperature, mass and speed), the observer perceives the world in terms of types (sensations such as color and taste, concepts such as yellow and bitter, actions such as walking and talking). The types that exist in nature, in Vedic philosophy, are the types that consciousness can potentially perceive. Thus, the Vedic theory does not derive consciousness from matter but matter from consciousness. This viewpoint is not just different from current science, but it weaves mind and matter together in a more coherent way than other religious traditions or scientific theories currently known.

In the Vedic account, mind, intelligence, meanings, emotions and sensations are all material, although they are different types of matter than the things that we can see, touch, taste and smell. These material varieties are further distinct from consciousness, which creates these categories. According to the Vedas, these different varieties of matter are created by reflecting the abilities of consciousness into matter. For instance, the material world consists of concepts and actions in just the manner that consciousness can know and act. The material world contains truth and other judgments in the manner in which consciousness can judge. Matter reflects intentions in just the way we experience intentionality. Many other aspects and abilities of consciousness are similarly embedded in matter during the process of creation. Vedic philosophy states that an eternal primordial matter is differentiated into several objective categories when abilities in consciousness are reflected in matter.

Consciousness however is eternal and is never created or destroyed. Primordial, undifferentiated matter is also eternal, although the differentiated categories in matter, which arise due to the reflection of the abilities of consciousness in matter, are not eternal. Material categories are objective and can represent things, ideas, meanings and mental states, but the soul is subjective. The soul represents the ability for choice which becomes embedded in matter as various types of information. The soul is therefore the source of information and differentiation and without the soul matter is undifferentiated. The ability for choice cannot be reduced to matter although the effects of choice can be observed within matter. In that sense, the study of matter can indicate properties of consciousness while not reducing consciousness to matter. All known scientific theories portray a picture of reality devoid of choice. They argue that choice is emergent, epiphenomenal and a post-hoc explanatory addendum to changes that happen automatically according to the laws of nature. In the Vedic view, choice is fundamental and cannot be reduced to matter. In fact, consciousness divides and organizes matter through its choices. Nature is governed by moral laws of choice which current science abstracts as physical laws of matter by eliminating the observer out of the study. This elimination creates explanatory gaps which current science has been unable to fill. The study of laws related to conscious choices and how choices create material objects represents a complete theory of material nature.

There are several differences between the Vedic view and that of modern science in how they approach the question of origins. In modern science, the universe is the outcome of a big bang, and galaxies are created when the universe expands and cools down. In the Vedic account, God creates the universe by reflecting meanings in His consciousness into matter. Creation is described in the Vedas similar to the creation of artistic products like books and paintings. The universe is the product of a creative urge in the creator by which He externalizes His personality into matter. Notions of God's personality and His nature therefore precede the existence of the universe.

The Vedic account of reality resonates with modern scientific accounts in many places, though these two accounts have very different conceptual foundations. With some effort, the similarities in these two accounts can be clarified and Vedic ideas can be used as intuitive grounds for new scientific theories. The Vedas also describe theories of mind, intelligence and personality, which are emerging fields in current science, and represent somewhat new domains of study. The

Vedic account can prove useful in building scientific theories about the mind, but it requires one to subscribe to a semantic view of matter different from the current physicalist view. Vedic theories of creation give us an alternate account of the relationship between mind and matter, which is based on semantic rather than physical properties in matter. Matter itself is described semantically in the Vedas, and these differences highlight the possibility for a new type of material science and technology, which is based on the manipulation of meanings rather than matter.

The Vedic view weaves notions about the ethics and morality of conscious choices within the theory of matter because, ultimately, all objects are created due to choices of consciousness. The choices of consciousness represent its free will but this will is not without responsibility. The relation between a choice and its consequence is studied within science as the relation between state preparation and measurement. But this scientific study of choice only relates to the effects produced by our actions, not to any moral consequences associated with the actions themselves. Thus, there is nothing good and bad, or right and wrong in modern science. Science deals in the judgments of truth, not the judgments of rightness or goodness.

The Vedic view incorporates moral judgments in its descriptions of matter because it directly studies choices and their effects not just on matter but also on the actor. This moral 'science' is different from material science, but like material science, it is empirical and has effects that can be studied scientifically. The Vedas apply a threefold distinction in consciousness—existence, activity and pleasure—to the study of matter. Descriptions of existence are true or false, actions are right or wrong and pleasure is good or bad. This broader philosophical framework in Vedic philosophy allows us to integrate questions of morality with an objective study of matter.

Unlike material laws that act upon objects, the moral laws act on consciousness. Like physical force transforms objects, our actions transform our experiences and the abilities for experience. This is intuitively well-understood even today, although there is no scientific theory that explains the consequences our actions have on consciousness and its abilities to know and enjoy matter.

Vedic philosophy on creation is not always easy to grasp and its expositions have often been confusing to the lay person. These confusions are caused by a multitude of difficult concepts which tend to overwhelm the novice. I have, in this book, tried to address this by using everyday intuitions, Western philosophy and commonsense ideas to explain Vedic concepts. This book shows how Vedic descriptions constitute a cohesive and coherent theory of reality spanning questions of matter, mind, intelligence, the unconscious and consciousness. This hopefully makes the book useful to those who may have been puzzled by Vedic descriptions in the past.

The Vedas describe the material creation as a two-part process. The first part concerns general *principles*, which I will cover in this book. The principles illustrate key philosophical views on the nature of the world, its relation to the creator, God, and how the universe originates when meanings in God's consciousness are reflected in matter. The second part concerns the actual creations, such as planets, species, and things, which I will not cover here. The Vedas describe that the material creation is comprised of multiple "universes," which differ not in the general principles of the universal creation, but in the type of material objects, namely, galaxies, species and things that exist in them. In this sense, while principles transcend particular universes, creations in them are unique. In this book, I cover principles, and defer the study of actual creations to a later work.

All spiritual philosophies distinguish between a material and a spiritual reality; the Vedic philosophy is no exception. In Vedic philosophy, God plays a preeminent role in both these realities. He is said to be the controller and enjoyer of both worlds. However, there is a considerable difference in the nature of His control and enjoyment in the two cases. While the Vedas are monotheistic, different 'expansions' of God are said to control and enjoy the material and spiritual realities. This book is almost exclusively about the material reality. Unless otherwise explicitly stated, all references to God are meant to refer to His form that controls the material universe.

The idea that God creates the material universe poses difficulties for many theologians who struggle with the following apparent paradox. The paradox is that if God is benevolent and beautiful then why would He create a universe containing ugliness and suffering? The atheists argue that if God creates the ugly and painful world then He must be ugly and sadistic, and thus He could not be the benevolent and beautiful creator that the religionists claim Him to be. If, on the other hand, God is only beauty and kindness, then what is the origin of the ugliness and pain so pervasive in the material world?

In Vedic philosophy, the spiritual and material worlds are created due to two different kinds of needs in God: the need to know Himself as He *is* and as He is *not.* These are complementary forms of knowing a thing, and they constitute the complete understanding of God. However, the negative aspect of knowledge is not considered the primary form of knowing. The material creation is the outcome of God's negation, and it does not always exist. This negation is perceived as the opposition and strife between different things in the material universe. The differences in the spiritual creation are, however, not opposed; they are merely different alternatives. God is said to be the origin of all diversity, but this diversity exists as oppositions (or duality) in the material world while the same diversity is perfectly reconciled (as non-duality) in the spiritual world.

Impersonal interpretations of Vedic philosophy treat non-duality as non-diversity while personal interpretations view non-duality as non-contradiction. This book adopts the personalist viewpoint, and describes shortcomings in the impersonal view.

The pain and strife in the material world is therefore an outcome of traits in God, but it is not a true reflection of God as He *is* because the diversity is created due to a negation in the process of creation. The material world represents everything that God is *not.* What God *is* and what He is *not* are in one sense aspects of the same person, and yet they are expressed in two different ways. The Vedas state that these two forms are like milk and yogurt; yogurt is also milk but it has been transformed from sweetness to sourness. Except for this subtle difference, the material and spiritual worlds are created according to the same principles, and the study of the material world can enlighten us about the nature of the spiritual world.

The important takeaway from this viewpoint about the two types of creation is that the material world can also be understood as God's expression of knowledge and pleasure, although it represents God's self-negation and self-denial. Like an inverted tree, whose roots are above and the leaves are below, the material creation is an inversion of the spiritual creation. We cannot fully understand the inverted tree without understanding the upright tree, and in that sense without using the language of the spiritual creation, we cannot understand the manner in which the material creation comes about. This also means that the same language must be used for both descriptions, although with the caveat that the material creation is inverted. This viewpoint explains why the universe has strife and suffering, although God is benevolent and beautiful.

The writing in this book is philosophical—in a specific Vedic sense. Philosophy in the West takes worldly facts to be a given, and builds theories of worldly facts. Philosophy in the Vedic sense takes the Vedas to be the given and builds theories to explain Vedic statements. Western and Vedic philosophies therefore differ in their starting point or what they regard to be the "given." Nevertheless, the Vedas touch upon everyday experiences as evidences for the constructed theories. Those familiar with the philosophical study of the Vedas know that there are six main schools of Vedic philosophy, each based upon references from the Vedas. These are called *Sāṅkhya, Yoga, Vaiśeṣika, Nyāya, Vedānta* and *Mīmāṃsa*. Each school or sub-school is a theistic interpretation of the Vedas and employs the Vedic aphorisms to build an encompassing outlook and consistent ideology about the universe. Each of these six schools focuses upon a specific aspect of the Vedic philosophy. For instance, *Sāṅkhya* focuses on a theory of cognition, *Vaiśeṣika* on a theory of atomism, *Nyāya* on logic and methods of argumentation, *Yoga* on mediation, *Vedānta* on the nature of truth or reality and *Mīmāṃsa* on ritualistic practices. I will be doing the same for the process of creation in the Vedas. Although this practice of philosophy is dissimilar to practices by the same name in the Western world, they are the continuation of a now somewhat broken Vedic tradition.

1

Why Creationism?

There was neither death nor immortality then. There was not distinction of day or night. That alone breathed windless by His own power. Other than that there was not anything else. Darkness was hidden by darkness in the beginning. All this was an indistinguishable sea.

—Rig Veda, Creation Hymn

The Problem of Origin

A key philosophical question related to the problem of creation is "Why should something be created?" or "Why is there something rather than nothing?" Philosophers who ask this question may not necessarily doubt that the world presently exists, although solipsists during Greek times did question it. They are instead looking for rational grounds for something to be created into this present form of existence. We know that the world around us is changing. Things are created and destroyed. The nations, communities, cultures and organizations to which we presently belong were created at some point in time. Could it be that this gigantic universe was also created at some point in history? If yes, *how* was the universe created?

It has been customary to treat the problem of creation as a problem of change taken to its logical extreme. We see that new things are created through a process of material change. The philosopher therefore supposes that there must be some change in the beginning that caused the creation of matter and the universe. But, if the present universe is comprised of everything that exists, then what existed prior to

1

the universe? If the visible universe is everything that exists, then the universe must come from nothing.

Greek philosophers were aware of this problem and the question of origin was debated in this context for nearly two thousand years without much of a useful outcome. In recent times, therefore, the question has changed. Now, we don't ask "How was matter created?" We rather ask "What caused the universe to appear in its present *form*, given that matter in some form already existed?" This approach preempts questions about the origin of matter and focuses upon giving matter a form—its current form. Matter in this view is eternal and not created. Matter is, however, given a form. The idea that matter is eternal arose along with the development of science when Newton wriggled himself out of nearly two millennia of paralyzing Greek questions concerning the origins of material existence by saying that science should study *changes* and not *existence*. Newton's point was that we cannot debate the origin of matter and energy. We can only speak about the changes to matter and energy given that these already exist in some form in the universe.

From what we can know from within the universe, questions about changes to form can be tackled better than questions about the origin of matter. And yet, questions about the origins of matter are very tempting for some. Indeed, this is one primary area of methodological and ideological conflict between scientific and religious views of creation. In science, matter and energy are eternal, although they can be interconverted. The appearance of the universe is a transformation of energy, not its creation. Most religionists however think that God created the universe, which involved the creation of matter or energy. They are therefore involved with the question of what precedes matter and causes matter to exist.

I will not debate whether matter is eternal or not, because the eternality of matter is assumed in Vedic philosophy. Similar to the scientific view, in the Vedic view matter is transformed from an 'unmanifest' or 'dormant' stage to a 'manifest' or 'active' stage. The primary difference between scientific and Vedic ideologies is how this transformation takes place. Scientists today hypothesize that matter acquires a form through a random fluctuation in empty space-time, which is, by itself, originally formless. In other words the creation of form is a chance event. The Vedic view says instead that the forms in matter have an origin in the fundamental capabilities of consciousness to sense, use, know, judge, intend and enjoy. Consciousness embeds its abilities to know and act *into* matter. The primary difference between these two viewpoints is that consciousness arrives late in the scientific view, after billions of years of matter developing into sophisticated forms, while in the Vedic view consciousness exists from the very beginning and creates forms.

In modern times, the question about the origin of form has been debated for several decades between design creationists and evolutionists. The design creationist says that the laws of nature hold sway over matter—in exactly the same way that current science has discovered—but the laws of nature allow many phenomena to occur, not all of which are determined by the physical laws of nature. Biological species, specifically, are underdetermined by the laws of physics. For these species to arise in the form that we see them, enormous amounts of information is needed, which cannot be created randomly. This information, the creationist maintains, is an element of design by God[2]. The design takes place within the laws of nature, and overcomes the information gap needed to create complexity. The evolutionist rebuttal to this argument is that our universe is a rare event. It is highly improbable but given enormous universal timescales, anything—even a small probability—becomes reality. A stronger version of the design argument, therefore, sees the hand of God in the laws of nature themselves. Physicists know that the formation of atoms, molecules and other complex structures depends on the values of natural constants. If these constants were even fractionally different than what they are, things that we see in the present universe would not exist. The values of these constants, the design creationist claims, are not random occurrences, but an element of design by God. The materialist rebuttal to this view is that material properties and laws appear through a step-by-step symmetry breaking in a multi-dimensional space. The design creationist however asks how that multi-dimensional space came into being. Such a complex mathematical structure is, after all, not "nothing" and the information needed to create such a mathematical structure had to have had a source. In recent times, this problem has become further compounded by the postulate of multiple universes which differ slightly in terms of natural constants. The values of natural constants, the materialist claims, are an accident of our present universe; in another universe, these values would be different.

The debate between creationists and evolutionists rages on because they appear to interpret the same facts—namely, empty space-time, physical laws and natural constants in these laws—in two different ways. The evolutionist says that these facts about nature are a coincidence of time and infinite possibilities allowed by modern mathematical theories, but the creationist claims that they are elements of God's design. It seems to me that this debate cannot be settled without bringing additional ideas to the question itself.

The key missing piece in this debate is a lack of clarity in how we conceive information. The manner in which science conceives information is different from how observers perceive it. Science describes object states in relation to other objects while we perceive these states in relation to our minds and senses. For instance, science will measure temperature using a thermometer and produce values such as 50°C while the senses will measure the same temperature and produce types such as hot or cold. The mind and senses attribute to the world *semantic* information rather than physical states. The fundamental difference between these two notions about information keeps cropping up in all debates about chance and information, but they are never adequately explained. Before we get into the creation-evolution debate, therefore, let us try to define the difference between physical and semantic information. What is semantics and how is it different from the physical states? Semantics can be broken down into at least three distinct ideas.

First, it is the ability in matter to hold information about other objects; the human world is characterized by the existence of thinking minds which hold information about the world. But minds are not the only stores of information. Books, paintings, music and sciences, which are descriptions of other things, also store information and our commonsense view says that we can hold information about other things within matter. However, no physical theory supports this idea. In all physical theories, matter provides information about itself, not about other objects. Thus, books, music, and theories of science are meaningless physical entities, to which we attribute meaning. But how can we attribute meanings to things if we are also material? The *aboutness* of semantic information is one key area of difference between semantic and physical information.

Second, the manner in which sciences postulate the existence of reality is different from how we perceive that reality. Science says that reality is mass, charge and frequency, which we perceive as taste, touch and smell. Semantic information pertains to how we *perceive* the world, which is different from how current science describes reality. Our commonsensical view attributes our perceptions back to reality. For example, if the apple is perceived as red, round and sweet by us, we must be able to talk about the apple in terms of how we perceive it rather than as physical concepts of mass, charge, energy, momentum, etc. which we don't perceive. In performing physical measurements, what we perceive is detector clicks and pointer movements, which are different from mass, energy or momentum. Every physical concept must be mapped to perceptions for science to be empirical, but the language used to describe matter and perceptions are quite different. Science employs the language of perception while describing our observations, but discards this language during theory formation and reality attribution. Matter, in current science, must be described in terms of its relation to other objects, not in relation to observers. This gap between theory and experiment within science has never been bridged. We see pointer movements and hear detector clicks, but interpret them to be indicators of energy or mass. Mass as a property can be applied back to reality but the sound of the detector click cannot be applied to reality. Every perception is typed, but science converts these types to quantities. For example, a sound may be loud or soft; they are two different types. In science, there is only one type—frequency—which has two different values that correspond to our perception of loud and soft. The gap between physical and semantic information is whether we describe nature in terms of types or quantities.

Third, science studies the properties of individual material objects but the everyday world attributes new properties to *collections* of such objects which can't always be reduced to the parts themselves. For instance, a plank of wood becomes a leg only when it is part of the chair, but not when outside of it. Biologists habitually describe the living body in terms of organs with functions while the materialist sees it as nothing more than atoms, molecules and their states. In the way that a plank of wood is not a leg outside the whole chair, chemicals are not organs outside the whole. While the physical states studied in science are states of the individual objects, the functional concepts we apply to them are properties of the collection of objects. Physical information is always about the individual parts while semantic information is generally about the relation between a part and the whole. Thus, meanings are defined collectively: something is a car only in relation to a driver, a road, a place to go, and the desire to go. Something is food in relation to a stomach, the desire to eat food, and the will to survive and lead a healthy life. Thus far, we know how to measure physical properties of individuals, but we still do not know how to associate these individual physical properties with meanings in the context of whole systems. This is another important area of semantic vs. non-semantic difference.

Semantics requires information to refer to other objects, to employ types rather than quantities, and to carry meanings which arise in contexts but not in individuals. These are problems not of religion, but of how matter is described in science. Accordingly, the roots of the debate between materialism and creationism lie in everyday intuitions about how the mind refers to things, cognizes the world in terms of types and sees new properties in collections, while science studies things-in-themselves, describes them in terms of physical quantities, and reduces collections to parts. The apparent conflict between these two descriptions would disappear if nature indeed had referential properties, could be described by types and had new properties that arise in collections. Since all these are within the scope of science, the answer to the question of whether religion has anything to offer to science is positively yes. What religion has to say is that there is another way to describe nature, namely in terms of *references*, *types* and *collections* with which we are familiar from everyday experience, but which does not exist in current science. The formation of theories that describe nature in new ways would not be any less empirical. If these theories make new predictions, beyond the reach of current science, then they would change our view of reality from things to meanings. A meaning can be objectified in matter, but its origin cannot be settled without reference to consciousness. In that specific sense, the origin of the universe requires the existence of consciousness which objectifies its choices as objects, by embedding meanings within matter.

The Physical Basis of Meanings

One of the problems in semantics is that concepts by which objects are described individually differ from concepts by which they are described collectively. Material objects acquire new properties when aggregated into collections. These new properties are not just features of the whole system; rather, they are features of the individuals within the whole. Whether or not an object is part of a collection makes a difference to that object. The most important question at this time is: What do we mean by a collection? In current science, matter is situated in space-time, which does not have boundaries. Science loosely uses the concept of a system, which is a bounded area of space-time, but the concept of a boundary does not enter physical *theories* in any meaningful way. Objects inside and outside the boundary are the same. If there are no boundaries in space, and all matter exists in an infinite expanse of space-time, then how can we speak about systems in physical or even biological sciences?

This is a new facet about information that has gone unnoticed and undetected in both creationist and evolutionist accounts. Let's suppose for the moment that there is nothing material about the boundary that divides matter into systems. Let's say that these boundaries are properties of the observer that divide matter into macroscopic objects. Once matter has been aggregated into collections, each member of the collection has new properties that did not exist prior to the drawing of the imaginary boundary. The ability to draw boundaries in space-time therefore has real physical effects, even though you may not perceive the boundary itself. This basic insight forms the basis of an elaborate theory of mind-body interaction in Vedic philosophy. The mind conveys its choices by drawing boundaries, which creates new properties within matter. The boundary cannot be seen, but we can speak of it objectively.

In Vedic philosophy, mind and matter interact through the subtle element called Ether. Mind does not control matter directly. Rather, it changes 'forms' in Ether, which in turn change properties in matter. One of the fundamental aspects of the mind is that it divides the universe into parts. We commonly encounter this fact in our efforts to know the world where we break complex things down into parts, until we can comprehend the parts. This division of the universe into parts is somewhat arbitrary and governed by our ways of thinking and using the world. There is no reason for me to think that the table in front of me is a unitary object, which I can use for reading and writing, different from the air that surrounds it. For the ant on the table, the table may not be a unitary object and table drawers can be seen as different from the table. For me, the meaning of the drawer is given in relation to the table as a whole. Our ability to attribute concepts to matter depends on our ability to divide matter into *macroscopic* objects. The parts get their meaning from the nature of the whole, which is also a part within a bigger whole, etc.

If the observer's ability to draw boundaries in space has an effect on reality, then the existence of functional parts and wholes can be attributed to the observer's ability to draw those boundaries. These boundaries cannot be seen, although their existence has physical and empirical consequences. By drawing boundaries in different ways, matter is aggregated into macroscopic objects in different ways. The properties of the parts are a consequence of how the mind has drawn the boundary. Now, the fact that something is a table leg is not an accident. It is rather the product of drawing a boundary between the table and the rest of the world, and dividing the table functionally into different types of parts. Scientists often describe macroscopic objects as systems, although object boundaries have no role in current scientific theories. By adding the notion of macroscopic boundaries—that exist in space, and yet are invisible to observation—it is possible to bridge the current gap between semantic and non-semantic ideas about matter. Semantic units arise when matter is divided by boundaries and aggregated into wholes. Without boundaries, matter is just non-semantic particles.

That semantics arises inside closed boundaries is an idea that can be applied to ordinary macroscopic systems and to the universe as a whole—a closed universe must be a semantic system. Like a human body is divided into a set of functions, which make sense collectively within the boundary of the body, Vedic philosophy divides the universe into functional parts. The universe as a whole is thus sometimes compared to a *virata-purusha* or cosmic person. Although there is no single consciousness that inhabits the cosmos like a soul inhabits the whole body, the cosmos is still treated like a single 'body.' The notion of a cosmic person is an extension of the idea that every closed system is divided into semantically distinct parts and becomes a functional system because of this division. If the universe is a closed system, then, like every closed system, it must be comprised of functional parts. Parts of the universe will be distinct like the head, throat, heart, stomach, hands and legs in a human body. This functional treatment of the universe hinges on the idea that closed systems are semantic systems, and meanings arise automatically within closed systems. The only assumption we need in order to treat the universe semantically is that the universe is closed.

The notion of closed systems and the fact that they give rise to semantic properties leads us to a new view of space, different from the one used in current science. In a non-semantic space, a location in space denotes a different object, but not necessarily a different *type* of object. In classical physics, for instance, all particles are identical types of objects. Current science distinguishes matter as different existents, but not as different types. In this science, we see two particles, and say that they exist in different locations, although they are of the same type (i.e. they are both particles). This view has its roots in the notion that locations in space identify different existents, but not distinct types. The causal laws of nature too are defined for each *type* of object and not for every individual existent. Thus, the same law applies to a very large number of objects. Contrast this with a semantic space, where each object is a different existent *because* it is a different type. For instance, each object can be different because it denotes a different concept—e.g., a table and a chair. This would imply that no two objects within a system can be exactly identical. Since the laws of nature are associated with different types of objects, each object must obey different laws. To do science, we need to associate the law with the type of object. A science that subsumes many types of objects under the rubric of a single type of law will be causally incomplete as compared to a science that associates a unique type of law with each distinct type of object.

Two objects in separate locations in non-semantic space can have the same type. But two objects in a semantic space are in separate locations because they have different types. If something has a distinct type, then it must also be a separate existent. Type distinctions are therefore stronger than existence distinctions. Semantic space simply means that all things in a space are distinct not just as existents but also as types. There are as many types in the universe as there are locations in the universe. The law governing each object is relative to the type of object. Since each location is a unique type, there are as many unique laws as there are locations. In a semantic space, the laws of nature are tied to locations in space. Unless two locations are semantically analogous, objects at that location will have different behaviors. In current science, all locations in space are identical, and the notion of universal law is achieved by dropping the type distinctions between locations. Of course, in many cases, it is possible to partially ignore the type distinction amongst objects; for example, we can treat all humans to be of the same type. If we now draw laws of human nature and attempt to predict human behavior based on these laws, we will find that that these laws describe human behaviors to some level of accuracy, but, ultimately, these laws are incomplete because the universality of the law hinges on the idea that all humans have the same type, which is false. Laws of human nature will be incomplete, because they ignore type differences between humans. Similarly, in a semantic space, any theory that subsumes a variety of things into a single class of objects, regardless of the object's location within space, will be incomplete.

It is well-known that almost all areas of modern science are incomplete. These include mathematics, computing, physics, and biology. It is however less widely known that mathematics and computing are incomplete because completeness requires the ability to distinguish between things, names and concepts although names and concepts cannot be distinguished from objects in physical space. At the root of this problem is the fact that mathematics treats space non-semantically, and entities in this space are different identities but not different types. The assumption that two different objects in the same space denote different types contradicts the idea that all locations and directions in space are essentially identical.

Physical theories in particular are based on the idea that there are a few types of things in the universe and hence a handful of laws that apply to these few types of things. Different physical theories are conceived in different types of spaces. To reconcile these theories, we must first reconcile the spaces of different objects.

Unfortunately, this reconciliation has been very difficult because science believes that the only way two types of things can exist in a single space is if they are described by a new single type. This is often called unification in science where two diverse types of phenomena are explained as 'surface' symptoms of a deeper type. To conceive a more general type of thing, scientists postulate spaces with a greater number of dimensions than the dimensions needed for spaces of the individual phenomena. This has led to incredibly complex multi-dimensional theories of nature and scientists assert that these other dimensions are very small and therefore not commonly perceived. That also makes empirical verification of such theories highly problematic, if not impossible. The semantic space approach changes the landscape of how different types are supposed to exist in the same space. In this new view, we don't require additional dimensions in space to incorporate additional types. We only need to treat locations in space as denoting different types of things. There are thus not additional dimensions in space to incorporate different types of things. Rather, location itself represents a type.

In current scientific theories, laws represent types of things, and physical properties represent existents. Their distinction arises because we suppose that there are many things in the universe but only a few types of things and eventually our laws will reconcile everything to a single type. But what if there were as many types of things as there are things so that we can drop the divide between things and types? If the distinction between existence and type is dissolved, there is room for a new kind of science that does not have the incompleteness that exists in almost all areas of science today. This is because we will no longer subsume many things into a fewer type of things. Since laws are associated with types, by allowing as many types of things as there are things, we will allow as many laws as there are objects. The law is now a function of the type. To predict the behavior of a thing, we must first know its type. This shift requires a change in current notions about space-time. Now, two objects in different locations are different types of objects.

There are four kinds of space in Vedic philosophy called *vaikhari*, *madhyamā*, *paśyanti* and *parā* and they correspond to four kinds of experiences—waking, dreaming, deep-sleep and transcendent. Locations in these spaces create semantic distinctions between bodies, minds, personalities and souls, respectively. This means that different bodies, minds, personalities and souls are not just different existents, but they are also different *types* of existents. Distinctions in *parā* are manifest in *paśyanti* which are manifest in *madhyamā* and eventually manifest in *vaikhari*. Thus, material creation manifests the pre-existent, eternal distinctness between souls first into the distinction between personalities, which is then manifest into distinct minds, subsequently manifesting distinct bodies. The body, of course, denotes distinctions between bodies, but it also represents distinctions between minds, personalities and souls. To see these distinctions, new ways of interpreting the bodily states are needed. Accordingly, the body can be described in many ways, representing a type of object, a type of mind, a type of person and eventually a type of soul. Note that the distinction between types implies a distinction in identity, but the distinction between (physical) identities does not always imply different types. The type distinction includes the identity distinction, although the reverse is not true.

My body and your body are not just different bodies, but different *kinds* of bodies. The difference between our bodies is based on different types of matter that makes them up, but also indicates different types of minds, personalities and souls. To distinguish different bodies, we need to understand type differences amongst the bodies. If a body moves from one location to another, it is transforming from one type of body to another. This view changes many fundamental notions about motion in current science. Motion in classical physics is a change in location without change in identity. Thus, a particle moves without changing its type and the law at earlier and new locations is the same law. Motion in a semantic space is however a change in types.

The cause underlying this change is the cause that changes type not just location. If the object changes type during motion, then laws at earlier and new locations are different. The laws of the body at present are different from the laws that were applicable in the past and will be different in the future, because the laws are tied to the types and the body is changing its type.

If space-time is semantic, then everything currently constructed in science is incomplete. This is because, in current science, we subsume many distinct things into limited classes of things, which have limited usefulness. The resulting scientific description is incomplete and leads to the impression that matter is non-semantic. Non-semantic views of matter now conflict with everyday semantic notions of matter, including the idea that we have minds which sense, conceive, judge, intend and enjoy. To fix this erroneous view of matter within science, science needs to revise its current notions of space-time. A shift in how we view the nature of space-time has the potential to resolve the conflict between semantic and non-semantic languages, and eventually the conflict between scientific and religious viewpoints. This resolution is based on new scientific notions, and not on faith. The ideas towards this resolution are indeed drawn from Vedic philosophy which is considered revealed knowledge rather than researched knowledge. But, hopefully, in the search of truth, we wouldn't care where the truth comes from.

Vedic notions about space-time have many scientific consequences, which I will not discuss in this book. These are discussed at length in my book entitled *Sāṅkhya and Science*. The brief expose of Vedic ideas above, and its relation to science, is meant to show that the debate between creationist and evolutionist ideologies depends on some simple scientific questions. Does the observer's ability to draw boundaries in space have real effects in matter? Do distinctions of locations in space represent real physical properties? Are objects fundamentally point particles or extended forms? Are all directions in space and time equivalent? Depending on how these questions are answered, there can be a new science in which matter will be described in a new way. This book does not discuss the scientific implications of Vedic ideas, how they can lead to new theories, and their new empirical consequences. This book assumes that the Vedic viewpoint is correct, and describes at length—in a lay person's language—the intricacies of this viewpoint.

What Western philosophy calls the 'mind' has many parts in Vedic philosophy which correspond to different kinds of meanings. The senses have sensations, such as color. The mind holds concepts, such as white. The intelligence cognizes objects such as a table. The ego perceives intentions, such as the idea that this is *my* table. Consciousness associates morality to intentions. These different types of meanings arise in relation to different aspects of the observer and they create different properties in matter. Thus, there are many kinds of semantic properties in matter, which can be understood through a deeper understanding of the observer. Various ways of dividing, combining and relating semantic objects pertain to the ways in which consciousness uses its choices. The properties and capabilities of consciousness can thus be studied in matter through the ways in which meanings are formed by divisions, combinations and relations. Consciousness does not reduce to matter, although it has material effects by which its nature can be understood.

The conflict between creationist and evolutionist viewpoints hinges on different notions about space, time and matter. Although detailed scientific implications of these differences are not explored here, I hope that the reader can see that these differences are not a matter of faith. They rather represent different material ideologies which can be used to develop alternative scientific theories. The semantic viewpoint indicates a science based on the capabilities in consciousness, rather than the properties of objects as they exist independent of consciousness. This book aims to describe the Vedic ideas on matter and creation. I would refer the readers interested in the implications of these ideas to modern science to other books, such as *Sāṅkhya and Science*, *Quantum Meaning* and *Gödel's Mistake*.

Why Is Semantics Necessary?

Current debates on evolution and creation are based upon a conflict between two types of languages—scientific and semantic. Everyday languages describe the universe using semantic concepts, which get their meanings in relation to other concepts and observers. Science describes the world using non-semantic concepts which can be reduced to measurements of properties using measuring instruments. Measuring instruments are also part of everyday language but they pertain to a part where we measure matter in relation to other material objects. In measuring matter in relation to other objects, we draw a context-independent description of reality. Aside from this, there are also context-dependent properties in objects. Take, for instance, the red light at a street intersection. It has the property of redness, which can be measured universally against a color chart that acts as a standard for defining colors. But, at the street intersection, the red light also has a contextual meaning that indicates drivers to stop. In other contexts, the same red color will have different meanings. For instance, red can denote passion, danger, war, etc.

There are two ways in which a red light is perceived. First, when we see red, we attribute the property of redness to the streetlight. Of course, in science, the streetlight is not red although it is *perceived* as red; light is a frequency. Physical sciences forego the idea that objects have color, taste or smell by choosing to measure mass, length, time, etc. which science believes are primary properties. All these properties are objectivized from secondary properties in experience; for instance, the property of mass is objectivized from heaviness, length from the experience of extension and time from the experience of duration. But science claims that these properties are inherent in the object as compared to color, taste and smell, which are only in the observer. Second, we also perceive context-sensitive meanings in objects—e.g., that red light at a street intersection implies the drivers must stop—which are not used in science because science measures reality universally. The red light at the street intersection has an additional context-sensitive meaning, which changes from one context to another. Universal descriptions discard contextual meanings and hence their effects as well.

Nearly all the problems of modern science arise because we describe matter in terms of physical quantities rather than cognitive types. These types can be possessed properties or contextual properties. Accordingly, the causality is based on types rather than quantities. Once matter is described in terms of mass, charge, position and momentum, and color, taste and smell have been discarded, successive types such as concepts, propositions, intents and pleasure—which depend on the perception of color, taste, smell, etc.—must also be discarded. We cannot say that someone indeed knows, judges, desires, or is happy. They just appear to us as knowing, judging, desiring and happy, but these are just perceptions and not reality. Now, the study of the observer is simply the study of how the cognitive world is created as a mirage and illusion. The way we perceive the world has no causal role within the world itself. This view of the observer contradicts our basic intuitions about how the world is controlled by our choices, how some observer's identity persists even though their bodily and mental states changes, and that our perceptions of the world are really about the nature of reality.

We have the choice to stick to current science thereby undermining our basic intuitions about ourselves or revise science in a way consistent with these intuitions. The revision requires us to see matter as meanings rather than as things. Its causality depends on relations between types rather than forces between things. And its laws pertain to how meanings are created through choices. The divide between creationist and materialist accounts of nature hinges on the divide between semantic and non-semantic views of matter. The divide can be talked of rationally and without reference to faith. It is empirical and intuitively embedded in our everyday world. The question is simply: Do we recognize everyday intuitions sufficiently to formulate predictively successful scientific theories with them?

The Cognitive Realism of the Vedic View

In Vedic philosophy, the universe is temporary, but it is not an illusion. That means that everything we experience can potentially be applied back to reality. This includes color, taste, and smell, but also concepts, propositions, intents and pleasure. Every aspect of the observer is reflected in matter. We can *know* about someone's sensations, concepts, beliefs, intentions and pleasure by studying their body, although we may not have the same *experiences*. We know someone's mental state because we infer it from their bodily state. The knowledge of the bodily state itself comes from sensations. In other words, we try to infer the mental state in terms of the sensations it produces. That is an indirect way to know the mental state, and does not constitute the observer's experience. The Vedas state that we can experience the mental state if the mind directly associates with the mind of the other person, not indirectly acquainted by sensation. The mental state is therefore also real, although it requires a different type of sense—in this case, the mind—to perceive it. The body affords knowledge of the mental state by objectifying that state in a message that others can decode. Matter is a medium of communication between minds, and everything that exists in the mind can exist in the body, but minds can also exist disembodied. Furthermore, the body—being an expression of a mental state—is developed as a manifestation of the mind. The mind precedes the body, and determines the properties in the body. Once the body has developed, changes in the body can also influence the mind, just as the mind influences the body. The basis of this influence is that both mind and matter have the same kind of information, although the information in the mind and the body exist in two distinct ways.

This idea can be illustrated by the following everyday example. Imagine that you are reading a travelogue. The symbols in the travelogue are representations of the mental states of the traveler. By reading the description, you can know the mental states of the traveler, and thus the travelogue serves as a medium of communication between the author's and the reader's mind. The travelogue is however not identical to the author's experience of travelling, although every experience obtained by the traveler's mind can be potentially objectified in the travelogue. The expression of the travel into the travelogue is optional for the author, who may have the experiences without expressing them in a travelogue. The traveler must however write the travelogue if he or she wishes to communicate about his travel. The symbols used in the travelogue are symbols of mental states, although they have been objectified in matter. This means that the traveler objectifies in matter what he or she sees, tastes, touches, thinks, judges, intends and enjoys, and this objectification is not limited to describing his or her trip in terms of mass, charge, momentum, energy, etc. You can, of course, measure the travelogue in terms of the physical properties used in current physics, but that way you will fail to obtain knowledge of the traveler's experience.

In a similar fashion, the body objectifies the meanings in the mind but current physics studies it as length, mass, charge and momentum rather than as symbols of meaning originally in someone's mind. Although we possess the ability to see matter as symbols of mental meanings, we choose to view these symbols as objects, discarding their meanings, and thus we are only left with their physical properties. In everyday life, however, we don't just measure the height and weight of a person. We also know that he or she perceives, conceives, judges, intends and enjoys. How? We have learnt to read the body language of living beings and we see that body language as symbols or signs of their mental states. This does not bar us from measuring the body in terms of height and weight. But, by only measuring the height and weight, we will not get to know the mental states. We will know about the body, but we will fail to communicate with their minds. Our ability to read the mental states from the bodily states does not reduce the mind to the body. Rather, the body serves as a medium of communication between minds.

Current science measures bodies using kilograms and meters, which don't have a mind. Obviously, the kilogram and the meter cannot 'read' the symbolism of the physical states. And by pursuing the study of matter based on the measurement of kilograms and meters, science fails to draw out the meanings that exist in matter, because they cannot be deciphered by meters and kilograms.

To know meanings in matter the observer needs to learn the language that encodes mental states into physical states. When physical states are interpreted according to this language, the observer can draw out meanings from matter without changing the observable itself. For instance, if redness denotes danger, then to know danger we don't need to sense anything beyond red, although we need to know the language in which redness denotes danger. The problem of semantics is thus not one of changing what you are measuring. The problem concerns the instruments in terms of which we are measuring. If the measuring instrument only measures length and weight, then it cannot know meanings. New types of measuring instruments are needed to know meanings. The senses and mind in the living being are these observation instruments. The author of the travelogue converts meanings into words, and the reader transforms words back into meanings. If the meaning is red, then the word encodes redness. The ability to encode meanings into matter implies that we can call the symbol of mental redness also as 'red' although the sign 'red' and the meaning red are distinct. The same words can describe both mind and body, but these words mean different things. In current science, every word means something physical, but not mental. In everyday language, the same words apply to both experiences and material objects.

Therefore, we can say that our experience of redness corresponds to something red in the external world, although the external world is a sign or symbol of the mental meaning, not its experience. The sign of redness cannot be understood purely in terms of length and weight, and we need to postulate new types of material descriptions of ordinary objects, that allow us to use the same words to describe reality and its experience. These new material properties are primary properties, because they exist in matter, even when we don't experience them. But they are distinct from the types of primary properties currently used in science. Semantic primary properties constitute a language of signs in which matter encodes meanings. Many people can look at a red apple and will see it as red. Their perception of redness hinges on the fact that they have similar types of senses and mind. That means the redness can also be treated as an objective property in matter although in relation to senses, not in relation to objects that cannot sense. By treating the red object as a symbol of the meaning of redness, we can describe matter in a new semantic way without reducing mind to matter. These new concepts will obviously produce a new science.

If apples are indeed red against a universal color scale, then we can also speak about the meaning of the red color at a street intersection. The difference between scientific and semantic languages now becomes obvious because the behavior of people—namely that they stop at a red light—is a new causal effect, that cannot be explained based on the frequency of light in a universal fashion. Stopping at the light is a real effect in the world, which is based on the perception of red, which is, in the current science, only in the mind. Why people stop at red lights now requires a mind-body interaction such that our perceptions can play a causal role in the world. This interaction has two problems: (a) how physical states become mental states—e.g., how frequency becomes color and (b) how perceptions of color lead to causal effects in the world—e.g., stopping.

The Mind-Body Problem

Many scientists believe that if mental states are encoded in matter, then there is no separate mind. This is based on the belief that current theories of matter are complete. A brief analysis however tells us that if matter encodes mental states, then we already have an important problem in current theories of matter. The problem arises because we cannot reduce *symbols* of secondary properties to currently known primary properties. If the brain represents color and taste, but matter itself does not have color and taste, then we need a new class of primary properties that can symbolize color and taste in the brain. These new properties will in turn require new kinds of physical theories of matter. Seen in this way, the mind-brain correlation is not a crisis for the existence of the mind; it is a crisis for current physical theories of nature which were founded on the premise that matter is primary properties and a thing-in-itself while minds were supposed to be things-about-other-things. Now, if brain states are correlated with sensations of color and taste, then the brain encodes symbols of secondary properties. The encodings of secondary properties in the brain do not constitute the experience of color or taste, but they constitute the ability to *symbolically* denote color and taste using primary properties. The fact that minds are correlated with matter implies that matter itself has to be described in a new way. The cornerstone of this description is that matter is a symbol of the mind, and that meanings that exist in the mind can exist in matter as symbols. Mind and matter are related as a sign and its meaning. We can know the meaning from the sign, and similarly, we can know someone's mental state from physical states.

This establishes a relation between mind and body without reducing the mind to the body. It argues for a new view of matter which is empirically testable, because the view applies not just to brains but also to any material object whatsoever. We can attain the distinction between mind and body without the problems of mind-body interaction. The distinction is needed because there is nothing in present science that can explain experiences, such as sensations.

The scientific journey needed even to make the brain a symbol of the mind requires enormous strides in a physicalist view of nature. Most scientists who profess mind-body identity often do not see the difficulties that the mind-body identity thesis poses for physics and mathematics. Just so that primary properties can symbolize secondary properties, physics needs to reconceive primary properties in a new way because the current set of properties in physics cannot be symbols of secondary properties. In fact, the current set of physical properties cannot be symbols at all[3]. The revision to science must begin with the ability to recognize symbols. To describe these symbols in a mathematical language we need a semantic mathematics that can distinguish red apples from the symbols of red apples without creating logical contradictions[4]. The complex configuration of primary properties cannot be seen as symbols of secondary properties because the mathematics we use to describe nature itself cannot deal with meanings. No amount of complex arrangements in this mathematics will represent meanings. And this is when the brain is only a symbol of the mind, not actually the mind. That is, the brain is a computer that has symbols of smell and taste, but not qualitative sensations or experiences of smell and taste. The difficulties would increase manifold if the brain was actually the mind.

If the mind and brain are correlated—and we know that they seem so—then matter itself must represent color, smell, touch, and other higher mental constructs. We know that these properties cannot be represented in terms of current physical properties, and we also know they exist in matter. It follows that current theories of matter are inadequate to describe all of the brain's features. To describe these states, we need new theories and concepts. These theories will be drawn from our understanding of the observer. For example, if an observer says he sees red, then the physical state must be a symbol of redness. Similarly, if a person is anxiously pacing the room, this bodily state can be described using the mental concept of being anxious. Mental experiences and their linguistic descriptions therefore help to formulate the symbols in terms of which matter must be read and interpreted. The same symbols can also form the basis on which matter is changed or manipulated. The resulting technology will not change length, weight or time. It will rather manipulate matter in terms of symbols of mental states.

A different view of the mind, therefore, implies a different view of matter as well. This different science of matter in turn indicates a new kind of technology. Beliefs in a semantic view of nature are not simply beliefs without an empirical consequence. These beliefs rather imply a radical shift in describing matter. Commitment to a religious paradigm involves a far more radical shift in our scientific paradigm than either scientists or religionists have seen thus far.

Flaws in Creationist Theories

The flaw in current creationist views about nature is that most creationists do not dispute fundamental issues with scientific theories, but offer resistance to science in regard to soul, God and afterlife. Most creationists will not argue with an evolutionist on the issue of whether the apple is indeed red, or just appears to us as red. They will however argue that when we experience God, the experience is real and not merely an appearance. It is not difficult to see that if the experience of redness is an appearance created by some non-red reality, then the experience of God is also created in the same way. If you admit the idea that the apple is not red, but only appears to us as red, then you must also admit that there is no God, although we may imagine God. Both the perception of the apple and the perception of God involve the same kind of theoretical explanation.

The main issue in the creationist-evolutionist debate is not whether God created the universe. The issue is about which parts of ordinary language we are prepared to allow for describing experiences. In current science, all parts of language, except those words whose meaning can be expressed in physical measurements, are forbidden. This includes words we use to describe sound, sight, touch, taste and smell. If we cannot apply words like yellow, sweet and soft back to reality—when almost everyone agrees on what these words mean, and we have direct perceptual acquaintance with these ideas—then we cannot also consider God and the soul to be real. In current science, an apple may appear red, but redness has no causal role. Similarly, the creationist may experience the presence of God but that does not mean that God has any causal role in the universe. Most creationists do not recognize that their view about God is no more meaningful in current science than postulating that my perception that the world is red means that redness is real and plays a causal role. As a perception, God is as unreal as the redness of apples. The problem is, however, not just about the perception of God's existence. The problem is that every perception—including the perception of red—is essentially unreal in science.

From where scientific knowledge stands today, the next step is to reintroduce the idea that there are other parts of ordinary language (which science doesn't use today) that can be real. The simplest of these consists of words that describe sensations of color, taste, touch, smell and sound. This involves a fundamental methodological shift in science. Rather than describe matter in terms of concepts derived by looking at material objects, we will describe matter in terms of the concepts in terms of which we perceive them. If these descriptions are successful, then it means that matter embeds properties that we know through sensation, and therefore sensed properties such as red, round and sweet can be potentially real. It now follows that the senses precede the creation of matter because matter carries properties in just the way that senses can know by sensation. By describing matter in terms of sensation-words, we can assert that the sunset is yellow, and it will be real, not just my perception. We can also conclude that senses are prior to sensation.

Once the idea of concepts—e.g., red, round and sweet—is real, the notion of propositions—which connect different concepts logically to form meaningful objects—comes into question. This can include the idea that something red, round and sweet is an apple. Today, for instance, a scientist will argue that an apple is comprised of such-and-such chemicals which react with so-and-so other chemicals in the body producing this-and-that effect, which we colloquially perceive as better immunity and good health. There is, however, no direct causal connection between the apple and our body as objects, because these objects themselves are unreal. The scientific view does not recognize that an apple is a collection of percepts (e.g., red, round and sweet) structured in a certain way. If we cannot reduce redness to physical properties, then we certainly cannot reduce apples to atoms and molecules. If, however, we have come to the point where we treat an apple and a body as real concepts, then we can talk about the causal interconnections between them. This is a new kind of causality than causes in current science. Now, matter does not evolve due to causal forces between atomic particles, but we can talk about the causal effects of apples on the body's health.

At this juncture, some scientists may be content that we have incorporated sensation, concepts and causal relations between concepts within science. Science does not need any more of the ordinary language. But, like the previous descriptions were incomplete, the causal description in terms of concepts and percepts is incomplete without the idea that we want certain outcomes, and our intentions use the causality inherent in matter to achieve those results. For example, apples may be good for health but I may not eat apples because I dislike their taste. The effect of the causal connection between apples and health also hinges upon my intention to keep good health. Intentional notions such as ownership of property, or the fact that we attribute creations to creators (e.g., that some writing is Shakespeare's plays), now become candidates for the next wave of realism. In a sense, we already live in an intentional world, because democracy and liberty attribute us choices and intentions. But these notions hardly have any role to play in scientific theories (they do have a role in scientific practice, in so far as science claims to be an 'open' enterprise). The question of whether choices make a difference in the world and whether these choices have consequences for their actors make way for a new type of realism. In the realism of conceptual causality, apples are good for health. But in intentional realism, we eat apples because we want to. The goodness of apples doesn't ensure that apples end up in my stomach. I have to make efforts and choices to acquire and eat apples.

Intentions however do not sufficiently explain actions. I may have the intentions to hurt someone but acting on them may not be justified. This raises questions about the morality of actions and the moral consequences of our choices. In current science morals are not real, just as sensations, concepts, propositions and intentions are also not real. Intentional actions create outcomes in matter, but these actions are in turn constrained by morals. The materialist and religionist are motivated by different kinds of moralities. A soldier is morally right in fighting for his country but a civilian is not morally right in hurting other fellow citizens. A mother is morally responsible to discipline her children when they are kids but not responsible to discipline them when they have become adults. We have various contextual notions about what is morally right and wrong, and these rules change with roles, statuses and phases of life.

In the commonsense view of life, our sense of morality drives our intentions, which changes our thoughts, which alters our actions, which change objects. But this commonsense view has no scientific counterpart today. The commonsense view of a person spans across several parts of everyday language, but this language has no role in modern science. The conflict between creationist and evolutionist accounts of nature cannot be solved without incorporating greater portions of everyday language within science. That inclusion, in turn, requires treating sensations, concepts, propositions, intentions and morals as entities that exist within reality. The study of creationism is valuable because it brings more aspects of the observer's experience into the study of reality. But, to progress on this path, creationists too have to revise their view of nature. They have to see that constructs of choice and happiness are built upon other semantic constructs like object-concepts and sensations.

The Role of Consciousness in Creation

The multi-tiered view of reality has its roots in the nature of consciousness as described in the Vedas. In Vedic philosophy, the living beings have a gross body, which reflects the state of their 'minds.' This 'mind' is, however, not a monolithic thing as in Western philosophy. Rather, the 'mind' is deconstructed into five parts, namely, senses, mind, intelligence, ego and consciousness. The senses generate and acquire sensations like taste, touch, smell, sound and sight. The mind generates and acquires concepts such as yellow, sweet and pungent. The intelligence combines these concepts and creates objects. The ego perceives intentions and ownership, like someone who desires apples. And finally, consciousness perceives and creates morality, such as the goodness of eating apples. Senses, mind, intelligence, ego and consciousness are thus creators and consumers of different classes of meaning. All these kinds of meaning and their experiences are temporary and causally governed in the material universe. The soul is 'behind' these five kinds of instruments, and remains dormant even when there is no experience.

Those who are somewhat familiar with Vedic philosophy will quickly recognize the descriptions of senses, mind, intelligence, ego and consciousness from Vedic literature. They may not as easily recognize the idea that these instruments are both creators and consumers of meaning. It is even more difficult to immediately see that the ability to create and consume meaning implies that all these forms of meaning are real, because meanings can be externalized as symbols of meaning in matter. The Vedic tiered view of the observer implies a tiered realism, in which the capabilities of the observer are reflected in matter, and create different kinds of properties. The tiered view of the observer is relevant to modern science because it implies that matter has many more properties than conceived in current science. Thus, there are properties in matter that correspond to sensation, concepts, propositions, intentions and morals.

The tiered semantic view of matter in Vedic philosophy is intimately tied to how consciousness controls matter through its choices. Recall that matter in Vedic philosophy is eternal but undifferentiated. Matter presents the possibility to be various kinds of objects, which are created by combining matter with information. Information is originally the collection of choices for consciousness and it is embedded in matter as objects which are perceived as sensations, concepts, propositions, intents and morals. Consciousness therefore interacts with matter through choices. Choices or information represents an intermediate level of reality that can exist both in consciousness and in matter. Ultimately, all information originates as choices of consciousness, but once these choices have been externalized, they can be seen as individuation of material objects.

The relation between information and choice can be seen even in physical information where binary-state bits encode objects. These bits quantify information but lack the qualitative features of semantic information. The choices of consciousness are more sophisticated, because consciousness defines *modes* in which it knows, uses, thinks, judges, desires and enjoys matter, and therefore has qualities. Indeed, what science describes in terms of quantities—e.g., frequency of light—can also be described in terms of qualities such as red, blue, yellow, green, etc. An elementary language of types already exists in consciousness, and this language is embedded in matter to create various types of things. The modes of experience are various types of information that create physical, sensual, mental, intellectual, intentional and emotional objects. If consciousness withdraws from experiences, information is destroyed and matter loses form. By withdrawing, consciousness ceases to experience, and the universe ceases to have form. Matter then changes state from differentiated objects into a state of undifferentiated oneness.

In Vedic philosophy, therefore, consciousness is the cause of creation and it creates the universe simply by willing. Consciousness does not materially cause the creation because matter is eternal and never ceases to exist. Rather, it causes the creation by externalizing its choices as forms which combine with matter to create objects. The universe comes into existence not from nothingness, but it is divided into objects from the prior state of formlessness. The Vedas state that the first thing to be created is the alphabets of a primordial language called *śabda-brahmān*. These alphabets are elementary choices that consciousness can make. All forms, and hence all objects, are ultimately mutations of the language of choices. This language manifests itself at various levels, successively objectifying the choices of consciousness first into an unconscious causal realm, then into a waking and dreaming experience and finally into physical objects. I will discuss these various types of information in this book.

Since the universe begins by externalizing choices into matter, the material universe is sometimes called the 'external' energy or *bahiranga-śakti* of God. The essential import of this idea is that material objects do not enter consciousness. Consciousness rather comes in contact with matter through its choices. This choice is seen as 'attention' when we focus on some sensation, thought, proposition, intent or moral value. By withdrawing attention, the experience ceases to exist. Consciousness is therefore not bound by material conditions and it can withdraw from matter by removing its attention. But the withdrawal depends on consciousness distinguishing itself from its experiences, which are products of matter. Everything we currently consider waking and dreaming 'experience' is a product of material elements called senses, mind, intelligence, ego and *chitta* or contaminated consciousness. These are mirages of the choices of consciousness reflected into matter. These experiences are not 'inside' consciousness; they are outside consciousness and to which the observer pays attention. For instance, when we sense or think, the sensation and thought exist in the senses and mind, not within consciousness. Consciousness however contacts these objects through its choices. All material experiences are outside consciousness and the observer can withdraw whenever he wishes to.

The Vedas, however, state that there is another type of experience in which objects enter consciousness and become part of the observer's consciousness. The concept of 'attention' doesn't exist anymore because there is nothing outside consciousness for it to pay attention to. The concept of attention arises when the objects of experience are different from the observer. But when the objects enter consciousness, the knower and the known have identical choices; they are intentionally united. This type of experience is called *antaranga-śakti* or internal energy in Vedic philosophy and it constitutes the mystical and spiritual aspects of Vedic philosophy.

The ideological clash between science and religion is greatest with regard to their theories of creation but the clash is based on different presuppositions about what is more fundamental in nature. Science claims that matter is fundamental while consciousness is emergent. Vedic philosophy claims that both matter and consciousness are fundamental, but material objects emerge through the choices of consciousness. In science, creation is the outcome of natural causes and, in religion, creation is the outcome of choices made by consciousness. The clash of these ideologies cannot be resolved at the level of experience alone (e.g., by assuming that religion allows the communion with God that science forbids). They instead require a prior formulation of theories that explain and predict the experiential differences. That is, before we look to reconcile science and religion at the level of experience, we must seek to reconcile them at the level of conceptual foundations. This book aims to develop an alternate theoretical and conceptual foundation based on the Vedic view on creation. This foundation can also start a clearer dialogue between the conflicting ideologies of science and religion.

From Knowability to Knowledge

In the Vedic view, conscious experience is the only phenomenon, as this phenomenon covers all the others as special cases; the creation of the material universe is the creation of materials. The world exists as a phenomenon. All phenomena are real in a specific sense—they exist at the point of observation, but they are not eternal. The phenomenal universe therefore exists but it is not permanent. What is permanent in the universe is the *language* of symbols from which everything is constructed. This language as noted above is called *śabda-brahmān*. The language is never created or destroyed but the words and propositions created by mutating the symbols in the language are created and destroyed. The limits and bounds of the universe are the limits and bounds of experience. God generates the universe as various types of ingredients that consciousness *can* experience; these include sensations, concepts, propositions, intents and morals. However, to experience this creation, individual souls must *choose* these experiences. The universe is therefore the combination of the choices of God and the individual living beings, and their choices play different roles in creation. God is the primary soul and He makes the universe available for other souls to experience.

But what happens when no one is experiencing reality? Does the world disappear if I close my eyes? This is one of the famous paradoxes of Idealism in Western philosophy. Idealism suggests the primacy of the observer and contrasts with Realism in which the objective world is the primary substrate for experience. Philosophers object to Idealism because it seems to imply that if something isn't observed then it must cease to exist. So, I might suppose that my room disappears when I go out of it, like a burrowing animal that buries its head into the sand under the belief that if it doesn't see imminent danger, the danger doesn't exist. George Berkeley—one of the founding fathers of modern empiricism (but an Idealist at heart[5])—argued that the world does not disappear even when an individual consciousness turns away from it because God continues to observe it regardless. In Berkeley's explanation, the animal dies because God continues to see the world even when the animal has buried its head in the sand. Vedic Idealism is similar to Berkeley's position, but there are some important differences. The main difference is that if God experiences the world in the same way as the other living beings, then God must also suffer and enjoy like the other living beings. When a soul experiences birth or death, God—in Berkeley's Idealism—will also be having the same experiences.

In Vedic philosophy, there is an aspect of God called *Paramātma* similar to Berkeley's God. *Paramātma* maintains the universe by constantly observing it, even when no other observer is experiencing matter. Through the *Paramātma* feature, God is omniscient. But, in this observation, God does not make choices of selection and rejection or creation and annihilation. *Paramātma* only sustains the choices that other living beings have made. If He did not maintain the universe, everything would be fleeting. If no one is looking at an object, the object would disappear. God as *Paramātma* therefore maintains the universe by observing it dispassionately.

But in Vedic philosophy there is also a time when God does not observe the world. Does the material cosmos exist in that state? The Vedas state that matter still exists but the cosmos does not. What is the difference between matter and the cosmos? Matter, in Vedic philosophy, is fundamentally undistinguished. That is, it exists, but it may not be differentiated into *objects*. When God does not observe the world, matter exists but objects don't. When matter is differentiated into objects, matter is knowable, because to know we must distinguish things from one another. If matter is not differentiated, then it is not knowable, even though it exists. In Berkeley's Idealism, there is no reality apart from phenomena, and this Idealism is opposed to Realism. In Vedic Idealism, there is a reality even when no one observes it, but it is undifferentiated. God must observe the world to differentiate it into objects. In the Vedic view, when God withdraws consciousness, matter exists but it cannot be *known* by the individual soul. God therefore does not create reality although He makes it *knowable*. Matter is real even without God's observation. God, however, converts primordial matter into observables.

At the heart of this Vedic view is the distinction between *knowability* and *knowledge*. Knowability is the properties that enable something to be known. From the standpoint of consciousness, a creation that cannot be known is not yet created, even though it may exist. Furthermore, this knowability must be converted into individual knowledge. An individual experience converts knowability into knowledge but there must be a knowable world available prior to the experience. In the Vedic view, God creates knowability and the individual living beings create knowledge. That is, God creates the ingredients that can be known, which constitute the conditions of knowability. To experience these ingredients, living beings combine and mutate them to create knowledge. These mutations require a choice, which converts the possibilities of knowing into an actual instance of knowledge. An individual consciousness does not create ingredients of knowability but he or she does create knowledge from these ingredients by choosing. Knowledge depends upon knowability and a living being's experience (knowledge) depends upon God's experience (knowability). The creation of knowability by God is the primary creation and the creation of knowledge is the secondary creation. I will describe the primary creation in this book, as the conditions of knowability. How these conditions combine to create various knowable objects is out of the scope of this work.

The Vedas describe that the creation of knowability in matter is due to God's *glance* over a primordial, undifferentiated, material reality, called His external energy or *bahiranga-śakti*. This glance imparts information from God's mind into matter and divides this primordial reality into many categories. Thus, creation begins when God "glances over" primordial matter. His glance imbues matter with knowability and makes it knowable for others. God's glance can be compared to someone shining light in a dark room to make the objects in it visible. In the case of creation, this "light" is God's consciousness which converts unknowable matter into objects.

The Vedas describe that consciousness has two aspects: *prakāśa* and *vimarśa*. *Prakāśa* is the aspect of consciousness that illuminates the universe with information and distinctions while *vimarśa* is the aspect of consciousness that observes the world. God's consciousness as *prakāśa* makes unknowable matter knowable and His consciousness as *vimarśa* observes it thereafter. This implies that matter is not knowable by itself. Rather, matter must be illuminated by consciousness before it becomes knowable. This illumination is God's glance at the beginning of creation which transforms unknowable matter into knowable entities. After knowability has been created, individual living beings can use it to generate various forms of personal or shared knowledge objects.

But what is knowability? How do we know the world? The answer that I will discuss in this book is that knowability in the material creation is the ability to draw *distinctions*.To know something is to make a distinction from other things and for something to be knowable it must facilitate a distinction. The world is built out of several distinctions. Most of the distinctions that we make in everyday life are combinations of more fundamental distinctions that God creates at the beginning of the universe. All these distinctions are embodied in the fundamental language of choices that consciousness can make. God therefore creates matter by externalizing His choices as a language called *śabda-brahmān*. The universe begins with the creation of distinctions, which are embodied in a primordial language. The language represents everything that we can choose, desire or will. The universe therefore affords the possibility for fulfilling our desires. Prior to creation, matter exists in an unknowable state, which means that distinctions have not yet been drawn. In this stage, the universe exists materially although there are no *objects*. Objectivity depends upon the ability to make distinctions because objects are distinguishable and the universe must be fundamentally distinguishable in order for objects to be created. The creativity of God is that He creates a primordial language using which matter can be divided into objects. The distinctions in language can exist both in matter and in the mind, and everything that we can experience can also be real. Note, however, that these creations are not eternal although the distinctions using which they are created are universal and eternal features of the abilities in consciousness.

If there is a fundamental distinction that God has not drawn at the beginning of the creation, other beings cannot thus use it in their personal or shared creations. The creativity of ordinary consciousness depends upon the creativity of God because the generation of distinct objects depends upon the kinds of distinctions that are available within the universe for combining or mutating. However, the Vedas state that God and other living beings are qualitatively similar in the sense that they use the same language of choices. The ways in which God divides matter into objects are potentially also the ways in which the living beings can think, perceive and enjoy.

The creation exists as long as there are observers who use distinctions to distinguish matter into objects. The creation, however, does not exist if it is not knowable. God adds objectivity or individuality to matter in order to make it knowable. The difference between God's creativity and ordinary creativity is that God generates *objectivity* and individual beings create *objects*. The Vedas thus distinguish between primary and secondary creations. Primary creations are concerned with *principles* that constitute the basis for knowability or objectivity while secondary creations are concerned with how the possible ingredients in nature combine into real objects.

This book is concerned with knowability, describing the various ways in which combinations of epistemic ingredients can be created, although I will not deliberate upon the actual combinations themselves. The key Vedic idea here is that it introduces a *definition* of the created universe: the universe is all that is knowable and *not* all that exists. Prior to creation, matter existed but was not knowable because it was not objective. The universe begins with the conversion of primordial matter into ingredients for objects. Matter is thus not *a priori* objective, as science often supposes by studying what are called fundamental objects. Rather, consciousness converts matter into objects and because consciousness is necessary for this transition, it is necessary for the universe to be knowable.

The Vedic view on creation avoids the moral dilemmas that make God accountable and responsible for everything that happens in the universe after creation. The moral dilemma arises because we presume that God controls the universe and the living being has no free will. If God creates the universe and an individual consciousness is merely an onlooker, then all actions in the universe are God's actions. How could the living being be then responsible for his or her actions? The answer to this quandary is that God controls *objectivity* but not *objects*. God defines the limits of our actions and knowledge by prescribing the distinctions in terms of which we can know and act. But God's actions do not entail a certain knowledge or action.

In short, regardless of the reliance on notions of consciousness, the crucial difference between Vedic creationism and modern science is the ideology of matter. There is no criterion in the big bang that makes matter knowable. Science *assumes* that the world is knowable and *a priori* objective such that theories about the world can be built. Science also assumes that the ultimate theory of the world would be *understood* by consciousness. These are leaps of faith, not adequately justified; they are not false, however. The Vedic theory delves into the fundamental premise of why and how matter is knowable. For nature to be understandable and knowable, it must have some property— namely, the property of being distinguishable by consciousness. Science presumes that matter is by itself knowable and objective. The Vedas rather tell us that the knowability of matter is a property of consciousness: consciousness divides matter and makes it knowable, in exactly the ways in which it can know.

Science presumes that there are certain fundamental objects that constitute the universe. The Vedic theory is that the creation of this objectivity itself is the glance of God; when God withdraws His glance, all distinctions merge into one unknowable existence leading to a collapse of objectivity. The difficulty in current science is how to justify the existence of certain fundamental objects and the scientific ideas here have parallels with Vedic theories. In science, the cosmos springs through *symmetry breaking* in which an undifferentiated reality becomes increasingly differentiated and distinct. In the Vedas too, unknowable matter is broken into objects. The question however is: What *causes* symmetry breaking? Modern science does not explain this because symmetry breaking is mathematical and not causal. Science can tell us that fundamental particles of nature are the facts of reality, which are logically related to a singular undifferentiated reality, without explaining how the differentiation is effected. In the

Vedas, this symmetry breaking is the glance of God, under which matter becomes differentiated. Present science also does not explain the *meaning* of symmetry breaking, whereas the Vedic theory does. In the Vedic view, the fundamental categories are conditions of knowability. The justification for why certain categories exist thus lies in how consciousness can know. Matter is cut up into distinctions in a way that conforms to the capabilities of consciousness to know and use objects. The atomic ingredients of nature are thus fundamental conditions of knowledge and action.

The Vedas state that consciousness precedes the manifest universe, not in the sense that consciousness creates the material "stuff" or that matter "emerges" from within consciousness, but in the sense that consciousness creates knowledge out of matter. Consciousness is the cause of the phenomenal world because phenomena[6] (in contrast to matter) come into existence only in the presence of consciousness. Phenomena emerge from matter when matter is distinguished into categories, and this emergence takes place in the presence of consciousness. This implies a distinction between consciousness and matter, and defines consciousness as the agency that converts matter into experience. Thus, consciousness isn't a passive agent that merely "looks on" while the creation exists. It is also the agent that brings about the phenomenal world of experience.

The Vedic theory holds the answer to the age-old philosophical question of "How can something come out of nothing?" If there was nothing prior to creation, then how did creation come out of nothing? The Vedic answer is that the creation did not happen out of nothing. Unknowable matter existed before creation. By glancing over it, God imbued it with knowability. Creation is the transformation of the unknowable into the knowable, not a transformation of non-existence into existence. The Vedas often use the terms "manifest" and "unmanifest" to distinguish the states of matter when it can be known versus when it cannot be known. The manifest and unmanifest states of matter are in relation to consciousness: matter is manifest or unmanifest to consciousness although in both cases it exists. The successes of modern science and the existence of mathematical laws of nature therefore do not preclude the dependence of material nature on God's consciousness. Rather, God's consciousness defines the conditions under which the laws are true, by defining the *entities* to which they apply. Present science presumes the existence of certain fundamental objects and then discovers the laws applying to them. The Vedic theory first explains why only certain kinds of objects could exist before we discover the laws. If we assume the world is objective, then it can be studied and understood per scientific laws. But if the objects are created by dividing primordial matter by choices of consciousness, then laws must pertain to the evolution of conscious experience. They apply only so long as the world is knowable or objective.

Apart from the difference that God creates knowability and individual living beings create knowledge, the development of knowability and knowledge follow very similar paths. For something to be visually observed it must be visually observable; for something to be audibly heard, it must be audible. The knowability of matter thus develops into modes of sensations, the faculty of conceptualization, the ability for propositions, and the ability to will and enjoy. In this sense, creations by God and by living beings are similar. The steps in which God creates knowability are also the steps in which a living being creates knowledge. The structure of knowledge is also the structure of knowability. An analysis of how knowledge is created can therefore be applied to the creation of knowability as well. This makes the process of creation amenable to being studied today. We can analyze the process of knowledge creation and then extend it to the creation of the conditions of knowability. In this way, by knowing how we create knowledge objects, we can understand how God creates the universe. The scale of these two creations is obviously different, but these two creations involve the use of the same *language*.

In Vedic philosophy, the creation of the cosmos follows steps similar to those used in cognitive processes of ordinary creativity. The creation that happened billions of years ago can therefore be understood by understanding what is happening in everyday creativity. We do not have to wonder what might have happened billions of years ago at the time of creation, if we can understand what is happening in everyday creativity now. The processes at the time of creation with regard to knowability are like current processes that govern the creation of knowledge through ordinary creative action.

Predicting the Past

The biggest problem for a creationist who wishes to explain things logically and scientifically is how to deduce what happened billions of years ago at the start of creation using what we can know today. Thus, we may ask, what proof exists *today* that the cosmos was created in one way or another? A big bang theorist bases his proof on the background radiation, supposedly a result of the big bang. This seems to make sense because background radiation can be observed *today*. Religionists however face a hard time justifying the creation of the universe by God, since that fact isn't available for observation. Vedic philosophy addresses this dilemma by positing that the process by which God created the universe is similar to the process in which we create ordinary artifacts. The Vedic process of creation is modeled after well-known and easily understood stages in an ordinary creator's mind. This addresses the problem concerning our inability to go back billions of years to know what exactly happened, because the processes of creativity are not unique to the origin of the universe but can be seen even in ordinary creative acts.

The process of material creation manifests God's personality into primordial matter, in an act of self-expression. As painters, musicians, or authors put aspects of their personalities into their artistic creations, the universe is created when God imparts information about His personality into matter. The Vedic theories of creation therefore cannot be understood without an explicit reference to God's consciousness. As we infer about the life and personality of an artist from an analysis of their creative works, the study of the universe can lead us to information about the creator. The study of the cosmos provides a description of the things that were latent in God, when it may not be possible to directly experience His persona. This of course does not mean that God is immanent in the world, but that the world and God are related, as a creation relates to its creator. Just as every creator leaves his imprints on his creations, and the creator's personality is evident in his distinct and inimitable style of creations, the material world is also related to God, its creator. The study of the cosmos can provide theoretical knowledge of God (what God is) before someone seeks a direct mystical experience.

We may however raise the question: Why should we model creation after a creator's act of creativity instead of more elementary facts about matter? The answer is that elementary facts about matter themselves cannot be understood without taking the observer into account. As we saw earlier, a literate observer will see a symbol as a token of meaning while the same symbol in relation to a meter or kilogram will only give physical properties. A symbolic view of nature is necessary to solve the problems of mind-body interaction, and the semantic ways in which we describe nature. These cannot be understood unless we relate matter to the observer. The Vedic descriptions are explicitly committed to the observer and they describe creation as the creativity of consciousness.

In the Vedic view, the solution to the problem of how to verify what actually happened billions of years ago lies in treating the world as knowability. The Vedic theory can be empirical because it explains creation using the same processes by which we create music, art, books, buildings, etc. Ordinary creativity follows the path of the creation of knowledge and cosmic creativity follows the path of creation of knowability. Since the structure of knowledge and knowability are similar, understanding the creation of knowledge can help us in understanding the creation of knowability. A big bang theorist cannot work with a similar hypothesis because not every phenomenon can be treated as a cosmic explosion. While the big bang posits a difference between past and present, in the Vedas they are similar as knowability and knowledge. The study of everyday creative processes can indicate the origin of the universe. The Vedas compare the creation of the cosmos to the gradual development of cognitive and conative facts in a living being, as seen in creative acts.

Overview of the Six Causes

One key distinction in the Vedas, as compared to modern science, is that the Vedas posit not one, but six kinds of causes involved in any creative act. The explanation of these six causes forms the main content of this book. The six causes are the *principles* of creation. But why are so many kinds of causes needed? They are needed to completely and exhaustively explain all aspects of an observer's *experience*. This means that the Vedas classify conscious experience as constituted of many aspects. While one kind of cause may be sufficient for a particular aspect of experience, all six are needed to cover all the aspects. In this book, these causes are named as personal, efficient, instrumental, formal, material and systemic causes. This terminology per se does not have a Vedic origin, but for the philosophically educated or even the lay person, the use of these terms simplifies the presentation of Vedic ideas and I have therefore chosen this path. The terms I have used have some similarity in meaning to the Greek notion of the Four Causes as described by Aristotle. This also helps us to more easily connect to Vedic ideas when the terminology itself may be somewhat obscure for most people.

While these causes are distinct and perform different roles in the universe, they are not independent. They act concertedly with each other and this can be understood through a simple example. Consider a potter who shapes pots out of clay, by turning clay on the potter's wheel. What are the causes responsible for creating the pot? First, there must be a potter. The presence of the potter is the personal cause of the pot; the pot comes about because there is a potter. The potter is an individual person and the existence of this person is the first cause of the pot. Second, the existence of the potter is not sufficient to create pots. The potter must act like a potter. That is why the actions for the creation of a pot are called efficient causes. Third, the potter needs implements to create pots. The potter's wheel on which the clay is turned is an instrumental cause of the pot because it plays a supporting role in the creation of the pot. Fourth, the potter must have the shape of the pot in mind to create the right kind of pot and so the formal cause determines the shape or form of the pot. Fifth, having instruments and acting with a purpose is insufficient without the matter on which these actions happen. The potter needs clay from which to create the pot, and clay is therefore the material cause of the pot. Sixth, the potter creates pots because he is rewarded and remunerated within an ecosystem of pot consumers, so the economic environment is a systemic cause of the pot. A potter is both intrinsically motivated as well as forced by external and systemic circumstances to act towards pot creation.

In science, the material cause (things that exist in the world) is supposed to be the only cause. But the explanation of conscious, goal-oriented and directed activity requires a more sophisticated and comprehensive theory. Acting without knowing where something is going may be good enough for explaining motion in matter, but it isn't sufficient to explain conscious action. So, it is incorrect to assume that conscious causality can be reduced to only one kind of cause—material or efficient. It is also wrong, on the other hand, to assume that conscious experience cannot be explained in rational terms. The Vedas provide the middle ground in which six kinds of causes are used to explain conscious experience. But while we are studying these causes, we must bear in mind that these are all part of causality in matter although aimed at explaining conscious experience, not just motion in matter. Although motion in matter is part of conscious experience, it isn't the only experience. Other kinds of experiences require us to expand our understanding of causality.

Creation and God

Since the Vedic premise is that the universe is created by God, it is rational to assume that God creates these causes. But the question arises: out of what does God create them? In other words, what is the relation between God and the six causes? The answer to this question is that the six causes are aspects of God's *nature* or personality. God therefore does not create the six causes out of another material existence that needs to be understood before the causes themselves can be understood. Rather, to understand the six causes, we need to understand different aspects of God's persona. The Vedas describe that there are three aspects of consciousness: *sat, chit* and *ānanda*. These aspects exist both in the individual living being as well as in God. When God wants to know and express His personality, these three aspects divide into knowledge and activity, creating six features. Six aspects of God can be divided into three pairs. The material cause and systemic cause are related as the external material world and the circulation of matter. The instrumental and formal causes are related as the senses and their associated sensations. The personal and efficient causes are related as individual personality and abilities that are used to realize that personality.

The quest for meaning and pleasure in consciousness is the ultimate reason for creation. The Vedas state that because God is both the ultimate meaning and the ultimate source of pleasure, these two quests can be satisfied in God. Another way to state this is to say that God as pure pleasure and knowledge expands His personality in six different ways to obtain knowledge and pleasure. Each of the six aspects of God's creation is discussed in a separate chapter.

It may seem that because the cosmos is created from God's personality, God transmogrifies into the creation and ceases to have a separate existence apart from it. Indeed, some hasty interpreters of the Vedas posit such an impersonal view of God. In their view, God during the creation is identical with the creation and regains His true identity only after the creation has been annihilated. But this view cannot be substantiated if we delve deeper into Vedic philosophy, especially when we note the Vedic statements that stipulate that God remains "transcendental" to the creation at all times. A more appropriate understanding requires us to bring into focus statements where the Vedas describe creation to be an *emanation* and not a *transformation* of God. This *emanation* isn't a material or physical ejection. It is rather the act of imbuing matter with qualities that are latent in God. God does not transform into the creation, neither does He materially create the universe out of Himself. Rather, He transforms primordial matter that exists eternally with properties latent in His personality. These properties form the basis on which we can know the world and use it. After the creation, we can know the universe in just the ways that God knows Himself (or, more correctly, wants to know Himself) prior to creation. Thus, similar to the Biblical view, God creates the universe "in His image."

Nevertheless, the notion that creation is a transformation of God is not totally incorrect because the phenomenal world exists as God's experience. In experiencing the world a person's consciousness is transformed, not materially but experientially. So, it is incorrect to assume that the creation is a *material* transformation of God. But it is correct to state that creation is a transformation of God's *experience*. The experience consists of His consciousness and its content, and while the content changes, the ability to be aware of that content does not. The transformation of His experience thus leaves Him unchanged. This simultaneous change and no-change is due to a distinction between consciousness and its content. God as consciousness is unaffected by His various experiences because consciousness does not lose its property of being conscious due to experiences. However, the content of consciousness evolves. God as consciousness therefore does not change. But God as the content of His consciousness—His experience—does evolve. Consciousness and its content cannot be separated although they are distinct. In this sense, God changes and yet remains unchanged. This implies a distinction between God's consciousness and material energy as the substrate of content. Creation combines consciousness with matter, which becomes the content of His experience during the creation.

The universe is a combination of content and consciousness to create *knowable* experience. This knowability is divided into six aspects, as six kinds of causes of creation. Because these six causes are originally present within God as aspects of his personality, the creation of knowability is in effect an act of God representing His personality in matter. God's glance over matter *communicates* information about Himself into matter, so that the living beings can later be able to experience the creation. By this messaging God objectifies Himself in matter. The Vedas thus often state that God "impregnates" matter with His "seed." This "seed" is subtle information about God that He communicates into matter to model matter after Himself.

By imparting that information, God "enters" within matter not physically but semantically. The act of "impregnating" matter by God can be compared to how a spiritual master enlightens his disciple by knowledge about God, which is sometimes also called "initiation" or *dīkṣā*[7] into spiritual life. God similarly creates the universe by initiating the material energy with His knowledge, whereupon qualities originally in God are manifest in matter. Thus there are several descriptions of "conversations" between God and His consorts in the Vedas. These conversations are acts of God impregnating His consort with information about His Self. The sexual contact between God and His consorts in these cases is simply *speech*. In other cases, as noted earlier, it may just be His *glance*. In all such cases, the original source of information about God is God Himself, and thus God is referred to as the original *guru* or spiritual master. The act of God as *guru* imparting knowledge about Himself is not different from the act of God as a lover, or sexual being, imparting His "seed" to impregnate His consort with meaning. The process of spiritual initiation is the act of knowledge transfer in which a "seed" fructifies similar to the process by which God creates the universe.

Why does God represent Himself in matter? What does God achieve by externalizing Himself into the mirror of material nature? We want to create because through this objectification and externalization of our personality we *know* ourselves. Matter is the mirror in which God sees Himself; matter helps God in self-knowledge, more specifically the knowledge of how He is *not*[8]. This self-knowledge is a source of God's pleasure. In a sense, God enjoys His self-knowledge, or He enjoys with Himself. To enjoy pleasure, we must know something and God being the source of creation needs to knows Himself. But before matter is a mirror it must acquire the properties of reflecting and being knowable. The process of creation therefore transforms matter into a mirror with God's reflection[9].

By this change, matter acquires properties similar to those in God. By the acquisition of these properties, matter becomes knowable, and we can distinguish it as different subtle and gross objects. God's reflection in matter is experienced by God as His self-knowledge. When this representation evolves, God's experience evolves although His consciousness remains unchanged. The evolution of God's self-knowledge generates pleasure in Him, the purpose for which the universe is created. Since God's pleasure comes from the energy that reflects and represents His personality, the energy is sometimes called God's consort or constant companion. The situation is analogous to a man-woman companionship in the present world but it is far more profound. God and His energy are simultaneously different and yet inseparable. While God is the content of knowledge, His energy is the potential to be that knowledge. This energy is the potential to reflect aspects of God's personality. The six causes of material creation are reflections of six aspects of God's personality into the mirror of material nature. As a reflected image is a combination of an object and a mirror, the universe is the product of actuality (God) and possibility (matter). The Vedas thus describe the universe as a product of the union of God and His consort.

God and His energy are related as an observer and a mirror. To know ourselves, we must externalize our self. God externalizes Himself as His image for the sake of His self-knowledge. Therefore, creation is the act of God becoming known to Himself as Himself. This self-expression evolves His experience although not His consciousness. In the creation, subject and object are the self-same God, but they have divided into knower and known. As representations of meanings in God, creations have attributes of God and yet they are different from Him. Without God, the images appear real but cannot be understood unless we recognize what they are images *of*. Though different from each other, images and their objects cannot be extricated. God and His creations are similarly one and different, at once.

Knowledge of the six causes is indirect knowledge of God. A reflection provides information about its object if the image has not been vitiated. However, the material nature vitiates God's image and is not a perfect source of knowledge about God. This is the root reason for separate scientific and spiritual aspects of Vedic philosophy. We cannot know the ultimate nature of God through matter, because matter vitiates God's image, although we can theoretically understand aspects of His personality through matter. Mystical aspects of Vedic philosophy require the practitioner to transcend the material world in order to know God perfectly, although the Vedas also state that by knowing God one perfectly knows matter as well.

The theory of six causes is explicated in different parts of the Vedas, which emphasize different causes at different places. Two main sources of information about material creation are the philosophies of *Sāṅkhya* and *Tantra*. These accounts of creation differ in what they emphasize and this can lead to confusion about the relative importance of the various causes and is a prominent source of ambiguity about the Vedic ideas on creation. A major goal of this book is a clear illustration of the various causes and how they operate differently from each other. A complementary goal is to show how these causes work cooperatively and constitute different aspects of experience. As a living being is part of the creation, a study of the six causes can be viewed as a generic theory of conscious experience.

Vedic philosophy is unique in the level of detail at which it describes God. As in many, but not all, religions, God is a person in Vedic thought. But the Vedas do not stop at defining God as a person beyond which His nature cannot be analyzed. They rather delve into defining the many aspects of God's personality. This definition of God's personality is relevant to the question of creation because the aspects of God's personality become aspects of creation. This *isomorphism* between God and the creation has had a two-fold implication in Vedic philosophy. First, the knowledge of God's persona can help the devout understand the nature of reality. A separate effort for understanding these two things is not needed. Second, if someone begins with the study of creation and goes to sufficient lengths to understand the nature of reality at large, he will also comprehend aspects of God's personality. The relation between God and His creation unifies the efforts of religion and science in Vedic philosophy. Traditionally, religion is the study of the nature of God and science is the study of nature. By positing an isomorphism between God's personality and His aspects in creation, these two efforts are reconciled into one unified effort. The study of nature and the study of God therefore are not two separate things in Vedic philosophy. They rather constitute a continuum on which the student may begin at any point and gradually develop their understanding of the whole.

The study of matter, God and consciousness are therefore intertwined in Vedic philosophy, and each is expected to reveal the nature of the other. While the reach of Vedic ideas is very large, this book seeks to provide a preliminary glimpse into Vedic ideas. Given that Vedic philosophy approaches reality in a way opposite to that of science, we will find that this approach is valuable where current scientific approaches have failed to satisfy, such as the study of mind, meaning, intelligence and language. I hope an unbiased reader will find Vedic philosophical ideas useful starting points for a fresh perspective on many of these currently problematic areas.

2

The Personal Cause of Creation

Some look on the soul as amazing, some describe him as
amazing, and some hear of him as amazing, while others,
even after hearing about him, cannot understand him at all.
                                                    —*Bhagavad Gita*

The Properties of Consciousness

The ultimate cause of creation in Vedic philosophy is the need in a
living being to know and express itself. To know itself, the living being
externalizes meanings in its consciousness into material objects, and
then identifies with those objects as its creations. Like an artist who
paints a picture and then views the picture as his creation, all living
beings know themselves through their actions. What existed in potential form in consciousness is manifest in the world through the creative process. Creation is therefore a transformation of the unmanifest
meanings within consciousness into manifest objective reality outside consciousness. The Vedas state that individual living beings and
God are similar in regard to their creative proclivities. The desires
and abilities to create in the individual living beings also exist in God,
although the relative magnitude of their presence differs vastly. The
scope of their creativities is therefore different, but the basic principles involved in that creativity are similar. This point is important
because it helps us understand the creation of the universe in a similar
way as we understand ordinary creative acts. Before I detail the Vedic
theory of creation, therefore, it helps to understand areas of similarity
between God and other living beings.

There are four areas of similarity between God and the living beings. These are (a) both are conscious, and their consciousness acts in similar ways through a progressive scheme of development of ideas into actions, (b) all living beings, including God, need to know themselves and search for meaning in their existence; both are eternal but nevertheless driven by this need to realize their potential, (c) all actions and exchanges devised for attaining this self-knowledge transact over a few basic types of *values* such as knowledge, beauty, power, fame, wealth and renunciation, and (d) the ways in which consciousness knows and acts are similar in God and the living beings because these experiences are described in terms of shared notions of seeing, touching, tasting, smelling, hearing, holding, walking, procreating, thinking, feeling, willing, etc.

Everything in Vedic philosophy stems from these basic areas of similarity. Matter, for instance develops from the inherent need in consciousness to see, touch, taste, smell and hear. Concepts and emotions develop to satisfy the need to think and emote. Social structures and organizations emerge to fulfill the need to exist in relationships. The universe exists to facilitate different kinds of needs for self-knowledge in different living beings. In short, everything in the creation is designed to fulfill a need in consciousness. The diversity in the universe—external and internal[10]—can be understood as stemming from the diversity in the intents and possibilities of consciousness itself. The unified theory of creation is a theory of consciousness, which is at once very simple as the awareness of the content of consciousness, and yet very complex in terms of the variety of content and the types of experiences it is capable of.

The Vedas emphasize two areas of this similarity between God and other living beings. The first is that all consciousness is individual with three features called *sat* or existence, *chit* or activity and *ānanda* or pleasure. *Sat* means that consciousness is eternal; it is never created and never destroyed. *Sat* denotes eternal existence, and this existence is individual. All living beings therefore exist as souls and God is the Supreme Soul. A living being, however, may not always be aware of its individuality. Awareness of one's individuality is yet another feature of the soul called *chit* or awareness. There is hence a subtle but crucially important difference between the soul and consciousness in

Vedic philosophy, and many times this difference is glossed over by some students of this source of knowledge.

The term *chit* literally denotes the living being as conscious. Vedas further divide the property of *chit* into three aspects called *icchā*, *jñāna* and *kriyā*. The term *icchā* denotes that a consciousness has free will. Every time we speak of free will, we must invoke the idea that the living being is an individual. Free will is therefore the symptom of individuality and the development of free will implies that the consciousness expresses individuality, not just existence. The primary action of free will is to know and express the individuality of the soul. The other two terms *jñāna* and *kriyā* thus denote knowledge and expression. The term *jñāna* refers to an individual's self-knowledge and the term *kriyā* refers to the expression of the individual's identity. Free will implies that the living being is an individual and it possesses goals and desires about knowing and expressing its self. For instance, to know itself, consciousness becomes active, and the word *chit* also denotes activity in the sense of *being* conscious. The term also means knowledge because consciousness brings awareness of reality. Finally, willing or choices are also *chit* in the sense that a conscious entity is capable of free will. This linking between individuality and free will is important because without free will one cannot know oneself as an individual, even though one may exist as an individual. When existence exhibits free will, it demonstrates itself as an individual, but it is possible to let go of free will and exist without knowing one's individuality.

The goal of self-knowledge and activity is to become happy, and consciousness becomes happy in its self-knowledge and expression. Innate to Vedic philosophy is the idea that real pleasure or happiness derives not from the possession of material objects external to consciousness but from self-knowledge and the expression of such knowledge. Self-knowledge comes through activity. Through this activity, consciousness expresses itself and through that expression it knows itself. The universe is the mirror in which consciousness sees itself. Seeing involves a self-expression through activity and self-knowledge arises through identification with that activity. As Marx said, man knows himself through his work [11].

Both God and the living beings are identical in that they exist, they have a desire to know themselves, they engage in actions to express and know themselves and rejoice in knowledge of their selves. The need to know one's self is an innate need in the living being, and most living beings are active under that need, although some living beings forego this need temporarily. They reconcile to the fact that they exist eternally and are happy in this knowledge. They don't need to know what form their existence will take, or should take, and they have no innate urges to shape or know that form of existence. Such living beings are considered merged in *Brahmān*, which is the undifferentiated aspect of God as pure existence. If a living being has no desire to know itself as different from other living beings or as an individual, it temporarily loses awareness of its differentiation from others. Such living beings thus consider themselves identical and undifferentiated from each other. That does not mean they are identical. It just means that by foregoing free will, they have lost their awareness of individuality.

In Vedic philosophy, all living beings are individual; they are thus called *chit-kaṇa* or particles of consciousness. But, part of their free will is that they can let go of that free will, and pretend that they have no choice in shaping their existence of knowing themselves as differentiated individuals. A number of interpretations of Vedic philosophy incorrectly treat this as the final goal of Vedic philosophy. They regard the innate need in the living being to know itself—the hunger by which the living being works and creates its self-images and knows itself through them—as an illusion. However, this interpretation of Vedic philosophy is somewhat recent and was brought about two millennia ago to counter the practice of blatant Vedic ritualism without a philosophical underpinning. This idea was later picked up by philosophers who wanted to give Vedic philosophy intellectual acceptance in the Western world as these interpretations are similar to Hegel's rationalistic approach to describe the nature of Being. This view of the Vedas—sometimes called *Māyavāda* because it treats the world as an illusion and cessation of all activities as the ultimate goal of religion—is not supported by most traditional schools of Vedic thought. According to the traditional schools, a living being is always an individual and always driven by a need to know and express itself as an individual. It could, indeed, temporarily forego this need and rest undifferentiated from other living beings. Eventually, however, the urge rises again and if the living being has not found the meaning and purpose of its existence, it starts the experimental search for this purpose all over again.

Creation too is the outcome of the need in God to know Himself as an individual. The urge to know the self is not a mistake, because this is the need in consciousness to be self-conscious, and it exists in God as well. The *Māyavāda* philosophy claims that creation is the product of an individual's will (who became an individual because of being covered by the illusion of individuality) and not God's will. There is thus literally no role for God as a Supreme Being in *Māyavāda*. There is also no purpose served by the study of nature, because it is ultimately an illusion and knowledge of reality tells us nothing about ourselves. The personalist school of Vedic philosophy instead regards the material world as temporary, not as an illusion. The self-knowledge gained from this world is not false, but it is always changing. It never allows a living being to truly know their eternal nature because what we know in the creation is temporary.

The personalist school of Vedic philosophy urges us to shift our methods of individual self-knowledge, rather than the quest for self-knowledge itself. The *Māyavāda* position in which we discard the attempt at individual self-knowledge is not denied, but is not regarded as a permanent state for a living being. The personalist school is therefore more encompassing than the *Māyavāda* school because it allows both possibilities although it prefers the route to permanent self-knowledge. In fact, many portions of the Vedas urge us to accept the personalist philosophy in spite of desires to give up activity and merge into *Brahmān*. The *Māyavāda* school on the other hand denies that true individual self-knowledge is even possible.

The second important aspect of consciousness is that it seeks six kinds of meanings. These are knowledge, beauty, strength, fame, wealth and renunciation. These are the six ways in which a living being desires to know and express itself. These meanings are attributes of consciousness and are therefore common to God and the living beings. The difference between God and ordinary living beings is that God possesses the fullness of all the six meanings whereas living beings can only partially possess the six meanings. God is thus all-knowing, all-powerful, all-beautiful, all-famous, possesses all wealth and yet

He is fully renounced or detached from all these attributes. The living beings on the other hand have some knowledge, beauty, strength, fame, wealth and renunciation but nothing in completeness. God and the living beings are therefore qualitatively similar but quantitatively different. The Vedas call God *vibhu* or great and the living being *aṇu* or small. These six values represent ways in which a person wants to know his self, how he acts for self-expression and how he enjoys that knowledge and expression.

The six attributes of consciousness represent types of information in the universe. The Vedic theory indicates that there are six types of information that every material object, thought, emotion, sensation or pleasure can represent. This information can be expressed as sound, touch, sight, taste and smell. It can be known as ideas, experienced as emotions or expressed as propositions. For instance, we might judge if something is beautiful and whether we like it. It also underlies the nature of our pleasures. For instance, we can hear, taste, touch and see beauty. We can feel the beauty through emotions. Amongst the six values, knowledge and renunciation are considered more important to a person's spiritual development than the others. An advanced spiritualist by dint of his spiritual advancement may also exhibit the presence of other values, namely, beauty, power, fame and wealth, although they hardly matter to the spiritualist as compared to knowledge and renunciation.

Science studies the nature of information in objects although this study is currently not a semantic study. The study of beauty or money is not even part of science, but of humanities, because we don't have theories about how these values exist natively in objects. Thus, we do not think that objects are natively beautiful or valuable. We believe that we perceive beauty and value in things and we call them beautiful and valuable. This is part of the bias in science that treats only physical properties as real. The various forms that material objects take are considered ephemeral or non-fundamental properties that *emerge* from the physical properties. On the other hand, the Vedic philosophy on the six values treats them objectively via the different forms they take. This has important implications because the study of wealth (money and economy), beauty (art, music and literature), power (organizations and politics) and fame (advertising, marketing and communication) can be formalized in scientific ways unknown so far. The Vedic view implies that there are objective criteria for beauty and economic value in nature. These scientific theories can emerge out of an understanding of forms that treats material objects as symbols with various kinds of meaning.

Kinds of Awareness

It is important to distinguish between two kinds of consciousness. First, consciousness is the awareness of an external world. Second, consciousness is the awareness of the self. The Vedas treat the second type of consciousness as more fundamental. The living being has an innate need to be self-aware and the awareness of reality is manifest as an outcome of this innate need. Self-awareness cannot be analyzed further since consciousness is *defined* by self-awareness. A consciousness that is not self-conscious is a contradiction in terms. This is different from how the problem of awareness is generally framed in cognitive terms, as a process of knowing the world. The Vedas claim that self-awareness is primary and world-awareness arises out of the *need* for self-awareness. Consciousness becomes aware of the world in order to know itself. This means that self-awareness is not automatic: we cannot know ourselves without a mediating agency[12]. The world acts as an intermediary for consciousness to know through its acts of self-expression. In this sense, the creation must be present for God to know Himself.

Self-awareness also has two varieties. The first pertains to the awareness of content: one is self-aware if he has oneself as the content of awareness. This self-awareness is like looking at oneself in the mirror, where the content of consciousness is consciousness itself. The second self-awareness is that which accompanies world-awareness: in knowing the world, we know ourselves as knowers of the world. While the first type of self-knowledge involves knowing oneself directly as the object of knowledge, the second variety accompanies all forms of experience—including when the content of knowing is not the self—but is indirect knowledge of the self. We may call these awareness *about the self* and awareness *in the self*. God's self-realization includes both kinds of self-awareness although it stems primarily from awareness *about the self.* That is, God realizes Himself by becoming the content of His consciousness and creates the universe for it. Indirect knowledge of oneself as the knower of the content results from awareness *in the self.*

For consciousness to be the content of its awareness, the content must be externalized, before being represented as content within consciousness. This creates the need in God and other living beings to externalize their personality into objects, or create things that are outside consciousness. To create self-knowledge, the self must be externalized as an object, before the self is represented as content within. Without external content, consciousness cannot know itself as the content. Without content, consciousness also cannot know itself as a knower of content. It therefore follows that for consciousness to know itself, there has to be a content of awareness. For knowledge to be about the self, the content must be related to the self, and ideally a reflection of traits with which one can identify.

Ordinary living beings also gain self-knowledge from experience, but they may not always have the power to define the world in their self-image as God can. Ordinary living beings often gain self-knowledge by morphing their self-image after objects they can easily access and experience. Thus, we often know ourselves by defining our identities in relation to the world. We define ourselves by associating with various kinds of objects, people or institutions. And we might define ourselves by modeling our lives after other great people. It follows that a world must exist before an ordinary living being may know his or her self and the living being participates in the universe that God creates in order to facilitate His self-knowledge. Because God creates the universe for His self-realization, and the living being uses the created products as sources of its self-knowledge, the living being's self-realization depends upon God's self-realization. A living being is free to create self-knowledge, but this creation depends on the presence of appropriate knowledge ingredients, which are created because of God's attempt at self-knowledge. Different creations aid the living being in thinking of his self and this is his self-actualization, although it is not independent knowledge of the self because it depends on God's self-knowledge.

God's self-awareness and the content of that awareness is the same God. God desires Himself; since God must be self-aware in a true and honest sense, the content of His awareness must be Himself. His awareness in the self is also the awareness of the self. He is *aware in Himself* and *aware about Himself* at the same time, and these two are identical. The answer to why God seeks pleasure with Himself is therefore that He seeks pleasure arising out of His true and honest self-awareness So, God's quest for pleasure with Himself is a matter of choice and not some limitation of the absence of other things to be aware of. Although the absence argument is not false, it is only a partial statement of the complete Vedic thesis.

God needs to know His Self not because He is incomplete, but because He is a conscious being and every conscious being needs to be self-aware. He creates the universe to create contexts for His self-awareness. In this sense, God's creativity is more fundamental than the creativity of other individuals. God creates the world in His self-image to use those contexts for His own self-actualization. By embedding Himself in those contexts, God aims to *be* self-conscious, both as self-awareness and the awareness of His Self. Creation is therefore not an afterthought even for God. Rather, it is an essential aspect of God's consciousness. Basically, creation exists when God is self-conscious. Of course, the material creation— as a special case of creation—doesn't always exist. The material world is created by God at the time when God becomes self-conscious, as part of the process of His becoming self-conscious. When the material creation ceases, God is said to be "sleeping" or not self-aware[13]. The sleep here is deep-sleep and not the dreaming stage where the mind can still create ideas. In the deep-sleep, there is very subtle awareness of self-existence but not of individual objects. The Vedas state that the creation automatically proceeds when God "wakes up" from deep sleep. The cyclic process of creation and annihilation in the Vedas is described as the process of God's sleeping and waking states. God's waking develops the need for His self-realization which leads to creation. When God goes to sleep, He winds up the creation. The Vedas state that the creation still exists within God in a primordial, unmanifest state, ready to spring forth when He wakes up again.

Creation from Personality

Vedic descriptions of material creation raise some important questions about variety in the universe. If consciousness is the cause of creation and all living beings use a similar process to create, then why does the universe have an enormous variety? If all living beings are identical in their basic capabilities to know, express, choose, enjoy and exist, then why do they create myriad different artifacts?

The answer to this question is that each living being has a personality that differs from the personalities of other living beings. When a living being wishes to know itself, it aims to realize this vision of its personality. Every living being in the universe is trying to know itself by making that potential into an actuality, but everyone has a different vision of his or her self. This difference across various attempts at self-realization arises due to individual *personalities* of those conscious living beings. A consciousness-based account of creation is inadequate without also acknowledging that each creator has a unique personality, which differentiates his or her acts of creation from those of others. When a creator wishes to realize his inner potential through his actions, he defines that potential in a unique way. That means that the ability to know, express, choose and enjoy are common across all living beings, but how different beings use these abilities depends on their personalities which are different.

What is personality? A personality is a picture that a person holds about himself. He identifies with that picture and considers that picture to be his innate nature. But personalities are adopted by a living being as a matter of choice: we adopt a certain type of persona by creating a vision of ourselves or what we want to *become*. This vision of ourselves exists in our consciousness as the potential of what we want to be. In a sense, the basic choice in a living being is the nature of its personality and other choices emanate or follow from this basic choice. Creative acts manifest one's potential and a living being strives to fulfill this potential through actions and expressions in the world. Both ordinary conscious beings and God are capable of creating myriad visions of themselves. Through these visions, God expands into various different forms, and the living being chooses to exist in a particular type of existence. All living beings are identical in their native abilities to know, express and choose. But they are different in their visions about themselves. Similarly, all forms of God are identical in their native abilities but they are different in the types of abilities they manifest or express.

Variety in the universe is therefore a product of a very subtle ingredient that all conscious beings adopt as their individuality. The Vedas describe this individuality as comprised of six attributes that originally constitute God's individuality. These attributes are knowledge, beauty, power, fame, wealth and renunciation. There are many further divisions of knowledge, beauty and the other attributes. Accordingly, possessors of attributes are knowledgeable or beautiful in different ways. But, in Vedic philosophy, the desire to be knowledgeable or beautiful precedes the creation of knowledge and beauty. That is, if no one ever wanted to be knowledgeable or beautiful, there would be no point in creating knowledge or beauty in the universe. We look at the world and consider certain people knowledgeable, beautiful or powerful because images about those people are compatible with our notions of beauty, knowledge or power.

There is considerable variety in how each individual envisions these six attributes of personality. We may envision knowledge as the study of economics, physics, psychology, mathematics, or philosophy. These are different kinds of knowledge, and a person might choose one amongst many possible types of knowledge as the purpose of his life. Similarly, we choose a type of beauty, power, fame or opulence as a life-purpose, and this becomes our personality. The Vedas state that God is complete in knowledge, beauty, power, fame, wealth and renunciation. This means that all the ways in which one can imagine his or self to be knowledgeable, beautiful, powerful, famous, wealthy or renounced already exist in God. God is capable of manifesting His personal vision in the universe and the creation is an expression of various aspects of God's vision of Himself.

Therefore, when a living being identifies with a certain type of personality, he is identifying with a certain aspect of God's personality. The living being is trying to realize itself as a part of God that God already knows Himself to be. All possible individual personalities are thus a part of God's personality. When God creates the universe to actualize His personality, the living being participates in that activity of creation but imagines the creation to be his effort. This imaginary idea about the creation is often called an illusion or *māya*, because although the creation is real, the idea in the living being that the creation exists for his purposes is an illusion. The creation is actually manifested by God for fulfilling His vision, and the living being is a secondary participant in the creation. The illusion is destroyed when the living being sees the creation as the play of God with His energy to fulfill His visions, and not as a vehicle or mechanism to fulfill the visions of the living being. When the illusion is destroyed, the world is no less real than when the illusion existed, however, the identification with that universe is changed. The illusion therefore lies in considering the universe a process that helps the individual being fulfill his own visions, rather than a process that is intended to enable God to fulfill all the visions of Himself.

The Vedas state that living beings are part of God's body and some impersonal interpretations take this to mean that there is only one observer in the universe. These interpreters conclude that our belief that we are individual living beings is an illusion. This view of Vedic philosophy is incorrect because of the difference between existence and personality. God and the living beings are individual existents and they have distinct free will. But the scope of the individual living being's free will is limited to everything that he can imagine himself to be. Like mentioned in a previous section, the Vedas state that the living being is *aṇu* or small while God is *vibhu* or great. God's vision of Himself is much greater than the individual living being's vision. In fact, a living being's vision is always a part of God's vision, and the living being's personality is an aspect of God's personality. We might say that God is all living beings but no living being is God. The living being and God therefore are identical not at the level of existence, but at the level of intents and visions. By aligning one's intent with a part of God's intentions, a living being becomes part of God's vision of Himself, or His personal intentions.

The Vedas use the term *svarūpa* to express the idea that all living beings have a personality. This *svarūpa* is a very subtle *form* that develops into the living being's subtle and gross bodies. Like I mentioned above, the Vedas state that a living being or soul has three aspects—*sat* or existence, *chit* or activity and *ānanda* or pleasure. The *svarūpa* is the form of *ānanda* or pleasure a living being wants to enjoy through its self-expression and knowledge. The six values thus represent types of knowledge, beauty, power, fame, wealth and renunciation that we wish to realize to become happy. These values constitute an intentional form, the source from which the free will of the soul is modified towards specific kinds of knowing and expression, and represent what we consider 'good' in our lives. At the level of activity, the same six values represent what is 'right' or 'wrong.' Thus, actions that maximize knowledge, beauty, power, fame, wealth and renunciation are 'right' while actions that minimize these values are 'wrong.' Finally, at the level of existence, the six values represent 'true' and 'false.' Some things are thus knowledge, beauty, power, fame, wealth and renunciation while other things are not. Note how the definitions of truth, right and good ultimately depend on the *svarūpa*. A person will regard something as beautiful only if their sense of beauty is similar to the kind of beauty in the external world. They will regard some actions as right if their inner sense of morality accords with the type of actions in the external world. And they will consider some experiences as pleasurable if they align with their vision of what they consider pleasure.

The subjective nature of judgments of truth, right and good should not however lead us to conclude that we are free to interpret anything as true, right or good. In Western philosophy this is called the epistemological problem of knowing truth, right and good. And most of us commonly believe that the criterion for truth, right and good is inter-subjective agreement, which can be publicly demonstrated. Inter-subjective criteria for truth, right and good are contentious because they depend on culture, society or species of life. They are known to have changed in recent times, and will likely change in future. To arrive at better and comprehensive inter-subjective criteria, we need to widen our horizons of inter-subjectivity and include ever greater number of cultures, societies and species. This makes the epistemological problem intractable given the limitations in our ability to know the universe at large. The Vedas simplify this criterion by asserting that God is the whole truth, His actions are the standard for rightness, and His pleasure is the ultimate good. This conclusion can be justified because God is the sum-total of all individual personalities, and therefore by satisfying Him, all individual personalities are satisfied. The real inter-subjective criterion is therefore God's subjective criteria. The absolute definition of what is true, right and good is not what we might inter-subjectively agree with other compatriots on but what God considers to be true, good and right. The Vedas therefore distinguish between relative (individual) and absolute (God's) truths.

Every living being starts with a self-image or personality vision of what he is. He uses senses, mind, intelligence, ego and consciousness to express this vision in matter. The worldly objects thus externalize the inner vision of knowledge, beauty, power, fame, opulence and renunciation as objective facts. The Vedas state that a living being has three kinds of 'bodies' which are called gross, subtle and causal. All these bodies represent a 'covering' of the soul. The *svarūpa* is the subtlest of these bodies and represents the basic vision or personality that the living being wants to express and know itself as. This *svarūpa* initially develops into the subtle body of activity comprising senses, mind, intelligence, ego and consciousness, and then into the gross body comprising organs and other bodily systems such as ingestion, digestion, circulation, elimination, etc.

Learned personalities have stated that the ultimate *svarūpa* of a living being must align with God's attempts to know and express. Whatever we know and express depends on God's knowledge and His expression of those things. The view that some knowledge or expression is one's own creation is therefore an illusion and once this illusion is destroyed, the living being treats acts of creation as God's knowledge and expression. This is a subtle shift in thinking because the creation is God's attempt at knowledge and expression and when the living being also thinks that creation is God's knowledge and expression, his actions are directed towards the fulfillment of God's knowledge and expression rather than his own. This shift in understanding of the nature of creation frees the living being from the illusion of material existence. It does not require a change to the living being's activities and knowledge. It only requires a shift in perspective whereby facts, actions and pleasure are viewed as God's facts, actions and pleasures rather than one's own.

Personality and Jungian Archetypes

Carl Jung used the term *archetype* to describe very subtle, and often unconscious, ideas that shape our life. Jung's thesis was that there is a set of primitive archetypes that humans carry in their unconscious which allow us to make sense of our life and the lives of others. Examples of such archetypes include ideas such as 'The Mother' who sacrifices her happiness to ensure the happiness of her children, 'The Martyr' who dies upholding a higher cause, 'The Warrior' who is fearless and crusades against injustices in the world, and others. Modern society too creates new archetypes. For instance, the idea of the'American Dream' where a person builds a successful life through dint of their hard work and merit is a recent archetype. The Vedic idea of *svarūpa* is similar to the Jungian idea of *archetypes*. Essentially, we carry some notions about what we are and want to be, and we shape our lives and actions after those elementary archetypes.

The Vedic idea of *svarūpa* is predominantly seen in spiritual and mystical aspects of Vedic philosophy. Here, a living being enters into relationships with God based on different relationship-types such as a friend, parent, servant or lover. Being a friend, lover, parent or servant is therefore considered the *svarūpa* of the living being. These different forms of living beings have different ideas about the meaning of 'happiness' or 'pleasure.' These different notions of happiness develop into their senses, mind, intelligence, ego and consciousness, and then into their body of organs and systems. The genesis or basis of this development is their choice about what kind of happiness they wish to enjoy, which shapes their vision of themselves and that vision in turn defines their actions and bodies.

In the material creation, this *svarūpa* is manifest as different species of life that have different ideas about happiness, minds, intelligences, senses and physical bodies. Different species of life are obviously different in their gross and subtle bodies, but the root of this difference is their different views of happiness or pleasure. Some living beings eat fresh green plants, others like to hunt and kill their prospective food, while yet others thrive on dead bodies. For some living beings, life is in the air, for others in water, or on land, and the Vedas describe that living beings are found even inside fire. Each form of existence requires a different kind of body, sense, mind and intelligence, and these life forms afford different kinds of pleasures. These bodies are developed based upon different *svarūpa*.

Impersonalists claim that to free oneself from the cycle of birth and death, one must drop all kinds of forms. That would include the subtle *svarūpa* or archetype that we model our lives after. But note that this archetype is a choice, or the *chit* aspect of the soul. The *chit* also comprises *jñāna* and *kriya*. So dropping all kinds of forms implies dropping one's free will and thereby the need to know and express oneself as a particular type of individual. The impersonalist believes that all living beings are identical, and they have been artificially distinguished based on their choices. By dropping their free will, they can be free of material minds and bodies. The personalist interpretation of Vedic philosophy disagrees with the idea that freedom from forms is needed to attain freedom from the material body and mind, although it does not disagree with the fact that a living being can temporarily suspend its free will. To have free will is to have the option of denying that free will. But the dissatisfaction with a body or mind is because no living being can be permanently happy with just one form. Living beings desire to change forms because all forms of life provide some happiness and some distress.

The Vedas describe that one can attain higher forms of life through various penances, but in due course of time these forms are automatically destroyed and the living being falls into lower forms. The cycle of birth and death exists because the passing of time destroys all forms. We know this fact in modern science as the increase in entropy that destroys all forms and order in the world. Of course, in modern science, entropy in nature always increases, because there is no source that can create information. But, in Vedic philosophy, mind and intelligence can also create information under the influence of Time. The Vedas state that Time has three aspects that create, maintain and destroy order. Once order is destroyed, it must be recreated by the mind. In the best case, thus, forms of living beings will be created and destroyed under the influence of Time.

A pertinent philosophical question therefore is: Is there another type of form that isn't created or destroyed by Time? The Vedas state that there is a spiritual existence called *apara prakṛti* where forms are never created or destroyed. The *svarūpa* of the living being is never annihilated in this realm, even though these living beings experience the passing of Time. This idea can be understood through the relation between information and Time. Information is created and destroyed because it represents distinction between things. Something is X because it is not Y, and being something specific implies not being other things that are distinct from it. Individuality is therefore constructed out of oppositions between things. This opposition is seen as strife and struggle between opposites in the material creation, which destroys and creates order. Hegel called this a struggle between Being and Nothingness, which combat to create a new Synthesis. Information in the spiritual creation is however not defined through oppositions. God is the synthesis of all oppositions and these oppositions exist in harmony because living beings align with God. Unlike matter, where oppositions lead to strife, the spiritual creation sees the differences harmonized.

This harmony is a consequence of the fact that all living beings see their forms as part of God's form and while God is the composite of many elementary forms, these forms are reconciled in God. Freedom from birth and death therefore, in the personalist view, is attained by reconciling forms with the Absolute Form. The import of the personalist view is that both material and spiritual forms are real, although spiritual forms are eternal while material forms are temporary. Neither material nor spiritual form is an illusion. In fact, material forms can lead us to an understanding of the spiritual form, rather than lead to the discarding of any form whatsoever.

Values and Reality

The values of knowledge, beauty, power, wealth, fame and renunciation represent possibilities of form in nature. Living beings adopt these forms of creation as their personality, and the subtle and gross bodies are developed from this personality. Unlike the spiritual creation where diverse personalities exist in harmony as aspects of God, in the material creation, under the influence of Time, these forms struggle to dominate each other. Thus, a person who has knowledge may lack power and fame, a person who is very famous and powerful may lack beauty and a very beautiful person may not have knowledge and renunciation. Living beings are caught in a struggle amongst values and cannot have perfect knowledge, beauty, renunciation, power, fame and wealth at once. There is always someone who has something that a person doesn't have. Living beings struggle to attain the state of perfection by realizing themselves as the completeness of all forms, but they cannot.

The deeper point we can understand from Vedic philosophy is that in the material creation, knowledge, beauty, fame, wealth, power and renunciation are opposed and they cannot exist in equilibrium simultaneously. Thus no person can have all these attributes at once in fullness. The Vedas state that the creation consists of three modes of nature—goodness, passion and ignorance—which exist in equilibrium prior to creation. In this stage, they are balanced and consistent. The creation disturbs this equilibrium or consistency to create various things which are in mutual conflict with one another. The disturbance causes one of the modes to dominate or subjugate the other modes. Nature is a constant struggle between the modes and this struggle is visible as the dynamic evolution of nature.

Another point that we can understand from Vedic philosophy is that knowledge and beauty or fame and wealth are not merely human constructs that we have recently invented as part of a civilized society. These values precede the creation of subtle and gross bodies, and are embedded in these bodies as the personality of the living being that develops. The evolution of the universe under the influence of Time and individual mind and intelligence is the evolution of these six values. Modern science models changes to the world as changes to matter. This change is further modeled as the motion of particles in space. The fundamental categories of reality in the Vedic view however are not particles, or space or motion of particles in space. The fundamental categories are the six values. The evolution of the universe is the evolution of knowledge, beauty, wealth, fame, power and renunciation. This in turn implies that gross matter must be described in terms of semantic categories like knowledge and beauty, and not as material particles in motion.

The truth of such a science is whether some material object

represents correct knowledge, whether it is beautiful, whether it is valuable, whether it makes us renounced or powerful, etc. This might seem like a very human way of describing things, but in Vedic philosophy these categories are not unique to humans. Rather they exist in all forms of life, as their very subtle personalities. Since all living beings are in the pursuit of enhancing their knowledge, beauty, power, fame, wealth and renunciation, matter can be described in relation to this pursuit rather than independent of it. The Vedic description of reality therefore brings a very basic contrast to the study of nature in the sense that nature is described in terms of its relevance to living beings rather than by precluding the living being from the study of nature. Atheists sometime ask whether the existence of God or consciousness makes any difference to the study of matter. They ask: Is the existence of God or consciousness of any empirical relevance to science? If not, then we can keep doing science just the way we have been doing it thus far. If religion makes no difference to science, then it should not interfere with the practice of science. The Vedic rebuttal to this view is that religious theories make a fundamental difference to the study of matter in that matter must be described in terms of its relevance to life. The laws of nature are the laws governing the evolution of knowledge, beauty, power, fame, wealth and renunciation and not laws of motion.

Modern scientific concepts like energy, charge, mass, momentum, quarks, etc., are mutations of more basic values that were created because living beings wanted to know and express themselves as those values. These values exist because their presence is the basis of conscious transactions. The Vedic view is also scientific although it involves a different conceptual foundation than modern science. Unlike modern science that begins with the study of gross matter and its transformation, Vedic science begins with the idea that the soul needs to find meaning and pleasure in life. In modern science, mind, intelligence and consciousness must be modeled in terms of the motion of particles, governed by mathematical laws. In the Vedic view, gross matter is governed by the laws of transformation of semantic categories like knowledge and beauty. The question we need to ask ourselves is: Which of these approaches holds a greater promise in the longer run? Will we successfully explain sensation, experience, emotion and personality in terms of mathematical laws, or will we explain gross material reality successfully in terms of semantic categories like knowledge, power and beauty?

Of course, this question is yet to be answered, but I hope I have succeeded in showing the reader that there is an alternative world-view that can be made scientifically rigorous and which better relates to us as conscious beings. This worldview reconciles our practices of science and religion. Such reconciliation cannot be attained between religious ideas and modern science simply because modern science is conceptually inadequate even to explain the mind, let alone our unconscious or consciousness. Mystical experiences which form the core of religious thought and which are becoming extremely rare today do not stand a chance of being understood through such a science. On the other hand, both mystical experiences and material phenomena can be studied by adopting the Vedic view. Therefore, I consider the Vedic view more sophisticated.

Conscious and Unconscious

Archetypes of the unconscious pose an important problem for a consciousness based account of nature. If our conscious thinking and actions are governed by the unconscious archetypes, does it not mean that consciousness is secondary to the unconscious? Indeed, the study of the unconscious in psychology leads us to this broad conclusion. In this view our conscious experience is just the tip of the iceberg while the majority of the iceberg remains submerged under water as our unconscious. Experiments in neuropsychology have confirmed this idea experimentally. These experiments show that electrical activity in the brain is seen a few milliseconds earlier than conscious reports of decision making by subjects whose brain was being observed. Some philosophers[14] now conclude that consciousness is an afterthought of an actual material cause in the brain. In other words, consciousness does not make decisions; these are made in matter, but we believe that consciousness chooses.

To understand the Vedic response to this quandary, we need to note that there are four stages of consciousness, called waking, dreaming, deep-sleep and transcendent. What we call consciousness, and which is measured by experiments that compare brain activity and reports of volition, corresponds to the waking stage. Deeper than the waking stage is the dreaming stage where the bodily organs are inactive but the subtle body of senses, mind, intelligence and ego is active. This subtle body controls the gross body in the waking stage, but the subtle body is not independent. As psychologists like Jung and Freud have argued, the dreaming stage is controlled by the unconscious. Actions of the subtle body—which correspond to reports of conscious decisions—are manifestations of causality in the unconscious. The unconscious is also not independent, because archetypes in the unconscious are choices of a transcendent state of the soul. The soul chooses the archetypes, and the unconscious mutates these archetypes under the influence of Time. This mutation manifests itself as dreams and thoughts in the subtle body. Finally, the actions of the subtle body change the gross body.

In Vedic philosophy, causality is ultimately in the transcendent state that chooses archetypes, which form our vision of the self. But in the material creation, the deep-sleep state controls actions of the subtle and gross bodies. Therefore, what we call consciousness represents only the waking and dreaming states, which are produced as an effect of the unconscious. There are also experiences beyond the waking and dreaming states, represented by the unconscious and transcendent states. It is thus correct to presume that our waking and dreaming states are products of the unconscious, but it is incorrect to presume that free will is an illusion. Waking and dreaming are caused by the unconscious which is caused by a transcendent choice. The biggest paradox of consciousness, from a waking perspective, is that we don't know the nature of transcendent consciousness. Mystical practices are designed to assist the experience of the transcendent state. Theories of awareness based on generalizations of waking and dreaming states are inadequate because experience depends on unconscious and transcendent states as well.

In fact, if subtle forms of matter cause the gross forms, modern theories of science that were constructed by studying waking phenomena are not correct descriptions of causality. Theories about the waking phenomena are derived by generalizing the waking experience into concepts. But these waking concepts are not causes; they are the effects of the subtle body which is experienced during the dreaming stage. A deeper science may therefore postulate subtle causes by generalizing the mental phenomena of the subtle body. But even this science would not be perfect, because the mental phenomena too are effects of the unconscious. The causality in the material world is that which we never experience currently and which lies dormant in us as the unconscious or the deep-sleep state. The Vedas state that when a living being advances in spiritual development, he can see the actions of the unconscious. This stage is therefore sometimes called the *paśyanti* or the 'seeing' stage where the living being can 'see' the real causality underlying all actions.

This leads to the conclusion that knowing the real causality in nature means raising our level of consciousness to observe what happens during deep-sleep. But the Vedas also state that various stages of material reality are manifest in gross matter. Thus, for instance, material objects too can represent information about other objects just as minds represent facts about the world. Likewise, matter can also represent information about the observer's personality. For instance, we recognize signatures of people's personality in their writing, creations and actions; we 'see' something that tells us this phenomena must be the act of that person, so the personality is embedded even in gross matter. This fact is confirmed by the observation of brain waves which are classified into alpha, beta, gamma and delta based on different stages of consciousness. This implies that even when we are in dreaming or deep-sleep, brain studies can give us *knowledge* of that state, although not its *experience.* We can conclude that the unconscious causality in matter is visible in gross matter, although to generalize it into a theory we need to invoke *concepts* that are derived from the analysis of the unconscious. Progress in material science therefore depends upon our ability to study ever deeper aspects of our consciousness—waking, dreaming and deep-sleep—and use it to formulate empirical theories of matter. An ultimate theory of reality is that in which we look at a phenomenon and say that a *type* of personality caused it.

Modern science studies gross matter and classifies material objects into types, which are governed by mathematical laws. This science is inadequate because behind types of objects are types of minds and a theory of mind is needed to explain behavior of gross matter. Even the theory of the mind will be inadequate because behind the mind is a type of personality. Science can thus progress from studying types of objects to types of minds to types of personalities, and all these sciences will classify phenomena and then use different types of laws to explain the behaviors of those classes.

Ultimately, we need to transcend science because science can only take us up to the point of studying *types* of personalities or the ingredients that make up a personal self-image. A type of personality indicates an individual soul, just as a type of mind denotes a personality, and a type of body denotes a type of mind. The body is therefore a symbol of the mind, the mind is a symbol of the personality and the personality is a symbol of the soul. Science can study symbols and articulate them in a symbolic language. The soul however is not a symbol of anything. The soul is the real thing-in-itself, and this thing-in-itself is first described as a personality, then as a mind, and finally as a body. But these different types of coverings of the soul give us *knowledge* but not *experience* of the soul. We can know about the soul through the study of matter, but we cannot *be* that soul by analyzing matter. Matter is ultimately a symbol of the soul, reflecting its properties in matter, and to be that soul, we have to go beyond matter. The meaning behind a particular symbol of the soul can only be grasped by that individual soul. Science therefore ends when language and symbolism arrive at their logical limits.

Personality and Realism

The Vedic view about the tiered levels of consciousness addresses the age-old problem of realism in science. The problem of realism arose because of possibilities of error, hallucination, mistakes or deceit in our processes of knowledge acquisition. If, for instance, we are dreaming we have the experience but that is not reality. The experience exists but we cannot relate that experience to an external reality. Recent discoveries have however shown that while experiences of the dream do not correspond to facts in the world, there are facts in the brain that correlate with the experience. The state of the brain is therefore like a book on traveling. The dreamer derives the experience of travel by reading the book, which is different from the real traveler who gets the experience by traveling. But, in both cases, there is some reality that corresponds to the experience. In the case of the dreamer, the reality is similar to the book, while in the case of the traveler the reality is the material world he sees.

Both physical states in the brain and events outside the body are material in the same way. During dreaming, the brain state is not related to the world state, but during waking, the two states are related. In other words, the brain state is a representation of reality during waking and it is a creation during dreaming. Regardless of how the brain state is produced, in both cases the experience corresponds to the brain state, not to the state in the world. Furthermore, in Vedic philosophy, the brain state can also be created by the mental state. The dreaming state is one where the brain state is created by the creativity of mind and senses, while the waking state is one where the brain state is created through interaction with the external world. There is hence a two-way causal connection between mind and matter. When matter doesn't exist, it can be created by the mind. When matter exists, it can change the states of the mind.

In modern science, experiences are produced from matter, although matter cannot be directly known. In the Vedic view, the gross material world is created by actions of the mind, which is created by a personality and the choices of the soul. Each of these realities are directly accessible to us, but experiencing them requires a development of consciousness through, waking, dreaming, deep-sleep and transcendent stages. We may not have direct access to the external world and we may know it through sensation and conception[15] but we have direct access to the subtle reality that underlies the gross world. Therefore, the reality underlying phenomena can be known by advancing our capabilities of consciousness to experience subtle phenomena. The pursuit of knowledge is not complete until one knows all the tiers of reality. Knowledge culminates in the awareness of the self. This self, must however be known in its full capacity for existence, free will, pleasure and the use of the free will to know and act.

3

The Efficient Cause of Creation

Watch your thoughts; they become words. Watch your words; they become actions. Watch your actions; they become habit. Watch your habits; they become character. Watch your character; it becomes your destiny.

— *Lao Tzu*

Acts of Creativity

In Vedic thought, as in many other religious traditions, God is the efficient cause of creation because His *actions* create the universe. God's actions, however, don't require hands and legs. In the Vedic view, God creates by *willing* the creation and His *will* is the foremost efficient cause of the universe. This will is free in the sense that it is not caused by factors external to God's existence. But one may ask, "Why does God will the creation?" or "What purposes in God are achieved by this creation?" In other words, it is proper to claim that God wanted to create, but we must also presume that God is a rational being and He must have had a *purpose* in mind before He willed the creation. It makes sense to talk about a will that is free when the possessor of that will can utilize it for some ulterior purposes. Without a purpose, willing is equivalent to the actions of an irrational person. So when we say that the creation of the universe was not preceded by other causes external to God, are we allowing for reasons *internal* to God that must be considered underlying the will? Unless we also understand the purpose behind the creation, the claim that God's free will created the universe is only marginally better than the claim that the universe was created as a matter of random chance events. In fact the positivist[16] could even argue that the hypothesis of free will without additional supporting reasons is indistinguishable from random chance events and may be cast off.

Fortunately, the Vedas explain the reasons for creation. For ease of our understanding, these reasons in God are not very different from the reasons for which ordinary people are generally creative. So before I discuss the manner in which God creates the universe, it helps to examine the psychology of creativity in people.

What motivates a creator—be it a musician, artist, actor, scientist or others who create implements, cars, furniture, computer programs or philosophy textbooks? Livelihood is one answer but it isn't the only answer. Most people in this world work for livelihood needs (food, shelter, security for self and families, etc.), and ostensibly these are the primary driving forces in worldly actions. But it is also well-known that people wish to create and be creative even when they don't have to worry about livelihood needs. So the need for creativity goes beyond the need for livelihood. Some of the most creative people in the world either did not have to worry about livelihood needs or often disregarded the livelihood needs in favor of creative needs. So in terms of needs, every primate has needs for food and shelter, but when these needs are satisfied we may still be left with needs to create and continue working in the world. It is this need, as distinguished from basic needs, that underlies creative actions. Psychologist Abraham Maslow who highlighted a hierarchy of needs called this the need for self-actualization. In Maslow's theory, self-actualization is deeper than the needs for survival, security, love and esteem. While this aligns with the view that there are creative needs still residual when basic needs have been satisfied, it has been difficult to define what self-actualization is. It is relatively easy to decipher what a person is restless for when he needs food, security, love or esteem. It is much harder to define what people are restless for when they need self-actualization. Indeed, Maslow himself did not define self-actualization much better than the need to "realize one's potential"[17]. I will attempt an answer to this question here.

As described in the previous chapter, every person holds an image of himself, which he attempts to express in the world. Through this expression the person realizes this image. When a person engages in labor, his self-image presents him as a laborer. When he engages in intellectual activities, he may regard himself as a very intelligent person. Similarly, people know themselves through the kind of food they eat, the clothes they wear, the work they do, the place they live in and so forth. All these activities can be carried out as part of sustaining a livelihood, but eventually they are responsible for shaping our view of the self. The fact is that we know and actualize ourselves even through ordinary activities, including those that we do to earn a living. Indeed, it was one of the original ideas of Marx's theory of labor that individuals have a native urge to create because they know themselves through their creations. If the process of production is in accordance to an individual's native needs to self-actualize, the labor is satisfying. If the labor is forced by socio-economic forces then it results in "alienation" whereby although laborers create products, they are unable to identify with them. The need to identify with our created products is an inalienable feature of life because consciousness needs to know itself through its activities. We know ourselves through the products we create. Different people choose different activities because they need to know themselves differently. Our vision for ourselves can drive us towards a certain kind of profession against other kinds of professions. Or urge us to change from one situation to another because it has become incompatible with our vision of ourselves. The project to realize and maintain an internal self-image can therefore be called the project of self-actualization. Indeed, Maslow construes self-actualization as something like painting as a hobby in one's personal time, because by doing it a person realizes his or her "potential."

The Vedas explain that there are six constituents of a self-image. Actually, the Vedas deal with God's self-image, but the same ideas can be applied to any self-image. These constituents are the six *values* that make something valuable: knowledge, beauty, power, fame, wealth and renunciation. Each of these values indicates the search of meaning in life, because we want to be valuable. So we want to be knowledgeable, powerful, beautiful, famous, rich and (when none of these is operational) renounced. While the majority of the world is pursuing the first five, there are several individuals who want to be renounced from the world. Knowing oneself as one of the six attributes or values is the realization of a self-image. Everyone carries a self-image that conveys "I am rich" or "I am beautiful" or "I am powerful" or "I am knowledgeable" or "I am renounced" or "I am famous." The pursuit of these values underlies the drive for self-actualization. The importance of Vedic thinking is that it goes beyond considering wealth as the only value. It recognizes that not everyone works for money. Some people work so they can be powerful, knowledgeable or famous, sometimes at the cost of being rich. If a theory of pursuable values is to be built, it needs to broaden its scope of considered values beyond wealth. Of course, values are not just about self-actualization. One may want to be powerful or rich, not because of an internal need to know the self, but because it provides livelihood or security. But when we speak of self-actualization we must divide this quest into the quest for the six values

God is complete in all the six values. He has full beauty, full knowledge, full power, full wealth, full fame, and finally He is also fully renounced from all of these values. So for God to know Himself is to know the fullness of the six values. Living beings too desire to know their self as one or more of these values. Students and academics want to be knowledgeable; politicians want to be powerful; businessmen want to be rich; most women and men want to be beautiful or attractive; movie stars want to be famous and the mendicants want to be renounced. Every individual seeks one or more of the six values. The need to know oneself as one of these values impels people to work in the world when their basic needs of food, shelter and love have been satisfied. So these six values should be viewed as the self-image that drives the actions of conscious beings.

Five Stages of Creation

The Vedas describe a five-fold process by which a self-image is externalized as a person's individual reality. These five-fold causes are the efficient causes of bringing forth action. In Vedic thought, creation is a process that manifests in five stages called *thinking, feeling, willing, knowing* and *acting*. Prior to creation, God exists as the fullness of the six values. At this time, He holds a self-image which hasn't yet been externalized. The attempt to externalize the self-image begins with the creation of thoughts. Thoughts mature into feelings, which lead to will or determination. Will matures into a plan of fulfilling the will, and then the plan is acted upon. This five stage process from thought to action represents the efficient causes.

The first thing to arise from a self-image is *thought* about what a person wants to be. Before God creates the world, He engages in the thinking process of what He wants to be. Someone may think about being a rich person as part of a self-image. This is the stage of contemplation and is a necessary precondition to the further development of creations. Western philosophers often compare thoughts to propositions about the world. However, the thoughts here are not propositions about the world but propositions about the self. These thoughts also don't correspond to any external state of affairs since the self-image is yet to be actualized and it is the realized self-image that becomes the affairs in the world. So, these thoughts are about what a creative individual can be. Since these thoughts are not about the world, they are also not true or false; they are what we consider good or bad. These thoughts are innovative ideas about how God should realize Himself as some combination of the six values, held internally as a self-image. The living being too has similar thoughts of self-actualization to attain a combination of six values.

But how do we create varieties of schemes? To illustrate this, consider an example. Suppose someone wants to become a rich person. There are many kinds of rich people. Which kind of rich person does one become? Does one become rich like a modern corporate czar or like an ancient Maharaja? To say that one intends to be rich isn't sufficient; one must also define what kind of richness one intends. The answer to "What kind of rich?" is: it depends upon what kind of richness one is *aware* of. Thoughts about richness depend on experiences or notions of richness one already has. If one has never seen or heard of a Maharaja, one will never think of being a Maharaja. On the other hand, if one has heard of a rich Maharaja and a famous movie star, one can think of being someone who is as rich and famous as the Maharaja and the movie star combined. The Vedas explain this by the notion of *chitta*: every action leaves behind an impression and the repository of all impressions from the past is called *chitta*. When thoughts arise, they do so due to impressions stored in the *chitta*. Thoughts are created from past impressions with the aim to realize the self-image. So, if someone wants to be rich, then the impressions of richness from the *chitta* are combined to create a suitable thought. The need for richness results in the thoughts of a Maharaja or a corporate czar. The created thoughts must be consistent with a particular image. If one knows only about rich Maharajas, he or she cannot imagine being a corporate czar.

Because thoughts are still possibilities, the universe does not emerge out of thoughts, as God does not will or desire them right away. Willing is necessary for the creation of the universe, but God—just like us—does not will the thoughts immediately. Before thoughts can be willed, they must be *felt*. Feelings are basically our likes and dislikes. A thought shall progress (or continue) being a thought only if we like it. If we dislike a thought we generally stop thinking about it. Before a thought becomes a will, it must be *felt*.

Consider what goes on in our minds when we think of our favorite food: provided someone is hungry, he will most likely develop a *desire* for that food. This desire is still a feeling; it is not a will yet. That is, we have desired the food, but not decided that we want it immediately. It is also possible that we dislike the thought. The development of desires is a step forward in the maturation of the thought process. In our lives, we come across hundreds of thoughts that never mature into desires and hence actions. Memories of past events may continuously flash as thoughts, although they may not develop into desires. I might suddenly remember an encounter with a friend that happened many years back, or the taste of food consumed last night. But they don't always develop into desires. There are also many thoughts that do develop into desires. We may think of a favorite food and then desire it; we may also develop aversion for the memory of a bad experience. The development of thoughts into a feeling is necessary in God's mind for creation to proceed.

The development of thought into desire is mediated by a *taste* for things. We develop feelings of liking or hatred for a thing depending upon good or bad past experiences associated with identical or similar things. Feelings are therefore based upon the *tastes* we have developed over one or many past experiences. When we encounter something for the first time, the typical reaction is neutral. If the reaction isn't neutral, positive or negative, the feeling may be based upon a past experience in which we developed a like or dislike towards a certain color, form, or other aspect of the object. It isn't necessary that we habitually recall all our past experiences before determining a feeling toward something. In fact, most feelings are generated quite automatically, so much so that we may consider our preferences or likes and dislikes to be our very intrinsic nature.

The Vedas however urge that this so-called nature is acquired over time and can be changed; it should not therefore be considered our true nature. A collection of all of our preferences or tastes is called *prakṛti* in the Vedas. *Prakṛti* is sometimes also translated as *nature*, and we should understand it as a person's predispositions, tastes, temperament, tendencies or likes and dislikes about things. A person who likes to eat sweet things is to be considered having a *prakṛti* different from the person who prefers spicy food. *Prakṛti* is an important supporting cause in the development of feelings from thoughts. At the time of the creation, the collection of all individual tendencies—the cosmic *prakṛti*—develops God's thoughts into feelings. This cosmic *prakṛti* is often just referred to as *prakṛti* although we should distinguish between the individual and the cosmic *prakṛti*. The cosmic *prakṛti* determines in God which schemes of self-actualization are going to proceed to the next stage of manifestation. In a sense, *prakṛti* develops God's thoughts into His feelings or desires. The Vedas describe that God actually never desires the material creation, in a positive sense. Rather, the material *prakṛti* is everything that God doesn't want. In a sense, *prakṛti* is God's revulsions, and it "stands behind" God, as the kinds of things towards which God has turned His back. I will discuss the details of this negative relation[18] between God and *prakṛti* again later on.

After a thought has matured into a positive desire or feeling, it must further develop into a will. Not every desire may develop into a will. If, for example, I think about my favorite food and that thought develops into a desire for that food, I might still stop those desires if I have been advised medically to refrain from eating such food. In such cases, thought development is terminated after the desire stage. On the other hand, if we are capable of eating the foodstuff, and there is desire to eat it, then thought and desire would mature into the will: "I will eat that food." Will is different from desire in the sense that the former is a determination to do something while the latter is merely a want. The determination to do something comes after the desire to do it; this is willing following feeling. Note that feeling here is different from other kinds of psychological "feelings" such as pleasures, emotions and sensations. The Vedas clearly distinguish between these varieties, and I will discuss these distinctions later. Here, feeling specifically denotes a desire or aversion, as mediated by the *tastes* in a person based on their *prakṛti*.

The development of a decision from a feeling is mediated by *intelligence*, and it is easy to understand this. Intelligence helps us decide whether or not to proceed with a desire based upon known facts or knowledge (such as whether or not to eat a certain foodstuff depending on whether we are medically forbidden to eat it). Intelligence controls or tempers desires arising in the mind. It allows certain desires to proceed and bars others from progressing into further action. Intelligence is a type of knowledge—more appropriately the memory of desires that are forbidden or allowed—and the Vedas acknowledge that this knowledge may be remembered or forgotten. When the knowledge is remembered, it is applied; if forgotten, it is not applied (the case of *knowingly* eating forbidden food is the case of forgetting at the right moment the implications of eating such things). In the context of creation, this intelligence is called *mahattattva*, which is the cosmic wisdom—or the set of all possible *normative facts*. For example: "eating sweet things for diabetics could be fatal" or "early to bed and early to rise, makes a man healthy and wise." The Vedas describe that cosmic intelligence or *mahattattva* arises from *prakṛti* and aids in the development of will. Just as individual intelligence helps progress an individual's desire into a will, the *mahattattva* plays a supporting role in developing God's desires into His determination. The crucial idea here is that knowledge about what the creation is precedes the creation itself.

Mahattattva is the collection of all normative injunctions that determine whether or not something must be done. In ordinary life, these normative injunctions include social customs, legal laws, cultural rules and regulations that we must follow. In the case of creation, *mahattattva* is the rules by which God designs the universe. *Mahattattva* is therefore the principles of the design of the universe[19]. Just as design precedes the creation of an actual object, *mahattattva* precedes the creation of the universe. If rules forbid the desires, then the thoughts that had been desired will not be willed. If on the other hand, rules allow desires, then desires proceed to the stage of God's determination to enact a feeling. Cosmic intelligence then determines in God the knowledge of moral principles under whose influence He carries out creation. What should and should not be done is sometimes called *dharma* or *ṛta*. This *dharma* is not religion or duties in the ordinary sense but normative principles by which God determines what should and should not be done in the creation. God uses *dharma* as a guide to create the universe.

After a decision has been reached on a particular desire, and the desire has become a will, the person willing must know how to execute the desire. In the foodstuff analogy, in order to fulfill the desire to eat, one must know how to cook the food or where to obtain a ready-made preparation they wish to eat. It might involve coaxing someone to cook the foodstuff for them, or perhaps going to a restaurant where they can eat food cooked by experienced chefs. In the case of self-actualization, the person must know how to achieve what they want to be. For instance, in the case of someone desiring to be a painter, one must know how to paint. This knowledge may not necessarily be with the person who wills a thought. In such a case, the method of fulfilling the desire must also include a plan on how to acquire the necessary talent by which the desire can be fulfilled. For example, if someone does not know how to paint, then they must know how to learn painting—e.g., through experienced painters. If they don't know which teachers to approach, they must know how to ask others who can point them to the experienced. In all the above cases, there is an element of procedural knowledge involved before the will can be actualized.

Philosophers sometimes contrast procedural knowledge with normative knowledge. Intelligence or *mahattattva* is normative knowledge and procedural knowledge is the maturation or development of normative knowledge (in terms of development of a creation you first know whether or not something should be done before you acquire knowledge on how to do it). Each individual arrives at a relevant procedure on how to achieve the goals depending upon the current set of capabilities or skills. If the individual knows painting, the self-actualization to be a painter just needs the effort of starting to paint. If the individual does not know painting, the action plan must first include the procedures by which the individual will first learn painting. An individual's currently known procedures are called *ahamkāra*[20] (the ego) in Vedic philosophy. Cosmic *ahaṃkāra* is that which develops God's will into knowledge of procedures about how to create. This knowledge is the collection of all doables, or methods of doing something; it is action in potential form that exists as possible procedures. The next level of the efficient cause—acting—is the maturation of possible procedures, which converts potential actions into actual actions. It is noteworthy that in this stage of thought development the person is not really acting, but developing a plan of action. Hence this stage is called *knowing* (how to act, before starting to act). The cosmic *ahaṃkāra* plays a supporting role in the cosmic creation by moving consciousness from the determination stage to the knowing stage. Arriving at a suitable procedure to realize a will needs the support of knowledge of various procedures that can be used. If some skills are missing, the game plan must include the procedures to acquire these skills.

Once a person knows how to do something, he must actually do it to achieve the desired results. For example, knowing how to get the desired foodstuff is not sufficient. One must go to the right place, get the food and then eat it to fulfill the desire of eating. In order to do something, one needs to be *skilled* at it. For example, even if a person knows how to do something, if he does not have the skills to do it, the acting will not manifest. The skills to do something must be in conformance with knowing how to do something; that is, the skill of acting must align with the knowledge so that it actualizes the knowing. In terms of fulfilling the desire, it is the last pre-condition before something can be actualized. Different types of thoughts, desires, judgments and procedures are not manifest externally; they are confined within the individual. If a skill is present, then the manifestation can begin. In terms of the creation of the universe by God, the actual manifestation of the grand plan generated at the knowing stage now needs the support of His skills to enact it. With the necessary skills, plans begin to manifest into actions. Therefore, knowing is theoretical know-how whereas acting needs practical skills that transform the plan into action. An additional supporting cause of skills is therefore needed before a plan can be executed.

This supporting cause is called God's *śakti* which literally means the power to act in a certain way. God and His *śakti* are said to be simultaneously one and different. *Śakti* acts under the will and plan created in prior stages, and in that sense *śakti* is different from the thinking, feeling, willing and knowing stages of God's psyche. But the *śakti* cannot act on its own unless the plan and will already exist. In that sense, *śakti* and God are identical. God has innumerable powers which translate different types of plans into reality. Indeed, even the thinking, feeling, willing and knowing stages of God's psyche are different forms of power. The creation of the universe, however, requires the specific *śakti* that actually converts God's plan into reality. This *śakti* is therefore the executor of God's intentions.

Ordinary living beings may have the power to think, feel, will and plan but they may not have the power to execute these plans. Thus, their mental capabilities may go beyond their ability to achieve. The power to execute a plan is therefore different from the plan, and all these powers, in the case of ordinary living beings, are subject to the *karma* from prior actions. *Karma* denotes the hidden stockpile of powers that a living being can use and this stockpile is allotted to a living being under the control of Time. Thus, at certain times, a person may become very powerful to influence his circumstances and at other times powerless to defend himself. However, God isn't constrained by *karma* and His powers are never increased nor depleted. Even when a living being acts in a certain way, the actions are actually performed by God's *śakti* on the basis of God's approval, the conditions of Time and the living being's *karma*. God thus helps a living being fulfill its desires based on its past *karma*.

The skills needed in action are slightly different from the knowledge of how to act. The knowledge is theoretical but the skill is practical. For example, one may theoretically know how to swim, but may not be able to swim because he or she lacks in the skills of swimming. Or a computer analyst may know the algorithm to solve a problem, but without the skills of a programming language he will not be able to actually create a program to solve the problem. Here, knowing the algorithm is knowledge of procedure, but knowing how to program in some particular computer language is a skill. Western psychology does not adequately distinguish between knowledge and skills, and both are called procedural knowledge as long as they are related to actions. In the Vedic view, however, there is a difference in the stage in which we are creating plans of actions and when we are acting. The plans of action require a theoretical understanding of what needs to be done, while the acting requires the skills to execute that understanding. Books on law, surgery, experimental physics, military operations are all procedural (and not declarative) knowledge, although reading these books does not necessarily make someone skilled in these actions. Similarly, one can read books on how to get rich, but cannot get rich simply by reading books. The difference between knowing how to do something and actually doing it is skills. Skills come to a person because of his *karma* and so it seems that successful people are successful because they are skilled. But it is also seen that many people skilled in thinking, feeling, willing and knowing are still not successful because they are unable to transform their ideas into reality. This is often called a person's luck. Whether people are skilled and whether they get lucky both depend on *karma* and there is no dichotomy between skills and luck in this theory. One may fail in life because one is unskilled or may fail even if he is very skilled. On the other hand, one may be successful with and without skills. *Karma* therefore ensures a person's success either by making them skilled or even without it.

Efficient Causes and the Unconscious

The five efficient causes, namely, *pradhāna, prakṛti, mahattattva, ahaṃkāra, śakti* together with *karma* form our unconscious, which is also called the causal body. The conscious body of waking and dreaming states is manifest based upon the unconscious body of efficient causes. Thus, *pradhāna* is the repository of thoughts, *prakṛti* is the tendencies for likes and dislikes, *mahattattva* is our unconscious leanings for right and wrong, *ahaṃkāra* is the unconscious intuitive ability to find solutions to problems, *śakti* is the unconscious power to execute solutions to problems, and *karma* is unconscious reactions to past actions that shape our life. Even small children manifest specialized thinking patterns, likes and dislikes, moral understanding, intelligence and uncanny abilities. Psychologists often attribute innate traits to the individual's genetic makeup, although experience tells us that many of these traits are absent in their parents. Evolutionary biologists attribute the explanatory gap in genetic makeup to random genetic mutations, but this view fails to *justify* why a person is born with riches and intelligence while another person is born into poverty and suffering. The Vedic explanation is that the innate tendencies that shape a person's life are the products of past impressions and actions. Thus the subtle and gross bodies, and their activities, are based upon the unconscious body.

The five types of efficient causes exist outside the material creation even when the universe has been annihilated. This is a very significant idea because it implies that the real causality underlying changes in the universe is outside the universe. Modern science assumes that material causality is within the universe and this leads to the problem of how to explain the origin of the universe, or the origin of causality itself. In Vedic philosophy, the real cause of the universe is a subtle realm of impressions that exists outside the universe, and persists even when the universe is destroyed. Thus, the seed for our thoughts, desires, morality, intelligence and activity is not destroyed with the destruction of the universe. These seeds persist between creations and lead to new kinds of subtle and gross bodies of waking and dreaming experience when the universe is recreated. The five efficient causes are thus part of the unconscious.

When the universe is annihilated, the living beings are said to be in 'deep-sleep', and they do not have a dreaming or waking experience. The unconscious is therefore not active by itself, although it is the root of all activity in the universe. The unconscious acts under the control of Time, which manifests thoughts, desires, wills, plans and actions. Time acts in the manifested universe and therefore the causal body of the efficient causes lies inert during the deep-sleep state. The soul is subtler than the deep-sleep state of consciousness, and the soul waits for an opportunity to have thoughts, desires, wills, plans and actions, when the living being is in deep-sleep state. The subtle body of (dreaming and waking) consciousness, ego, intelligence, mind and senses is created as a result of the unconscious.

The unconscious helps consciousness in its self-realization, by creating thoughts, desires, wills, plans and actions that are aimed to fulfill the self-image. Our vision about ourselves therefore combines with the repository of thoughts, desires, wills, plans and actions from the past, and under the influence of Time, creates activities of self-knowledge and self-expression. These activities are manifest in the waking and dreaming states and we tend to think that we are creating them through our effort. But the fact is that they are automatically created based on our unconscious and the effect of Time. Thus, new thoughts and desires are created spontaneously and we rebound from situation to situation, creating new experiences and performing new actions. These new experiences and actions leave behind them an impression, which is stored in the unconscious. Thus the unconscious memory of thoughts, desires, wills, plans and actions creates new activities which in turn create new memories. The living being is in a constant cycle of actions and reactions. The living being's past shapes their present and the present in turn shapes their future. Since all the causality is unconscious, we are not aware of what drives and motivates us, or makes us suffer silently.

Spiritual practices are meant to 'cleanse' the unconscious and they contend with innumerable past experiences dormant in the unconscious. A spiritual practitioner who has tried to control his mind and its innate tendencies quickly finds out that thoughts and desires arising in the mind are not under his volitional control. Rather, thoughts and desires arise automatically and we have to exert to stop their continuance. The spiritual practitioner therefore struggles with his mind and its purification can take a very long time.

The Cycle of Efficient Causes

The five efficient causes create a cycle. Thoughts, feelings, wills, plans and actions are manifested in the subtle and gross body and they leave behind impressions. These impressions in turn lead to new thoughts. A person is constantly in the cycle of manifesting the unconscious into the conscious, which then again becomes our unconscious. This cycle is shown in Figure-1. Both virtuous and evil actions are self-reinforcing. An evil thought leads to evil action, which leaves behind an evil impression. This evil impression then leads to another evil thought at a later time. When a desire is fulfilled, new desires are automatically created from past impressions. Virtuous actions lead to virtuous thoughts and evil actions lead to evil thoughts. The individual stays in a cycle because of the cyclical nature of the efficient causes. The *chitta* is the supporting cause for the creation of thoughts and aids in the first stage of creation, namely thinking. Thinking further develops into feeling, then into willing, then knowing and finally acting due to other supporting causes.

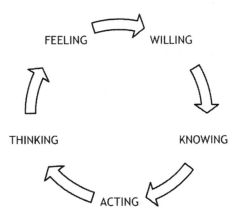

Figure-1 The Cycle of Efficient Causes

The cyclical nature of efficient causes creates a moral dilemma. If a person performs evil actions once, will he or she then be forever conditioned to think evil thoughts and perform further evil actions in a repeating cycle? How does a person resurrect oneself out of a vicious cycle? The Vedic answer to this dilemma is that although efficient causes are cyclical, consciousness is free to accept or reject these thoughts and actions. With free will we can select or reject the thoughts automatically created by the *chitta*. Dissociation from thoughts involves observing them dispassionately, analyzing their effects, before deciding to accept or reject thoughts, and this is a scheme for *mind control* described in the Vedas. Mind control works not by creating virtuous thoughts but by allowing virtuous thoughts to proceed while nipping the unwanted ones in the bud. Both permissible and unwanted thoughts are however generated automatically by the *chitta*. Free will does not control which thoughts are generated by the *chitta* although it controls which generated thoughts will be felt, then willed, known and finally acted upon.

In the Vedas, God's creativity is explained on principles similar to how one would explain ordinary creativity. The Vedas break down the creation into discrete steps of progressive manifestation, which can be understood both at the level of individual or cosmic creation. The difference between God's creativity and ordinary creativity is one of degree and not of kind (there is however the qualitative difference between the knowability and knowledge being created). An important fact to note at this juncture is that the stages of thinking, feeling, willing, knowing and acting described above are actually causes in the unconscious, although we associate thinking, feeling, willing, knowing and acting with a waking or dreaming stage. This is similar to how we might construe a 'particle' in physics as something that we see (e.g., a billiard ball) even though the particle is a cause in physics; in the experiment we only get to see its effect and not the particle itself. Similarly, the efficient causes—which constitute the causality behind the scenes—are similar to scientific concepts rather than the conscious activities we construe by the same names. Nevertheless, since subtle and gross bodies are manifested based on the unconscious causal body, these activities are seen in the conscious experience as well. Like the concept of a particle in physics is understood by abstracting and generalizing the experience of a billiard ball, notions of thinking, feeling, willing, knowing and acting are also abstracted from conscious experience, but they refer to underlying causes rather than the experience itself.

Indeed, the five efficient causes act not just in relation to our mind or waking consciousness, but in relation to all aspects of our subtle and gross bodies. For instance, we can see the efficient causes acting through the senses. A 'thought' in the senses is the preliminary desire to perceive certain types of objects. The 'feeling' in the senses is the like or dislike for certain types of sensations. The 'willing' in the senses is the determination or unstoppable urge to proceed with a certain type of sense activity. The 'knowing' in the senses is manifested in emergency situations when we react impulsively, such as to obstruct an attacker, or during activities such as swimming, cycling or typing that have become habits and require no conscious intervention from the mind or intelligence. The 'acting' in the senses is the prowess or the power in the senses to execute plans and specialized sensory skill is visible in artistic or talented people.

Psychologists have studied the automatic actions of the senses. For example, our instinctive attraction towards certain sense objects, our innate likes and dislikes for certain sights, sounds or tastes, the native ability in the senses to act autonomously without mental thought, all point towards the fact that our senses also have a 'mind' of their own. Biologists who have analyzed this ability in the body to act intelligently and autonomously conclude that mind and intelligence are not localized functions of the brain but spread throughout the body. Like our analytical mind thinks concepts, uses grammar and logic, and we are unaware of their cause, our senses too have reasoning abilities although we are not aware of them. From the Vedic descriptions, however, we can understand that these abilities in the senses are originally caused by the actions of the unconscious. The causes of thinking, feeling, willing, knowing and acting act through the senses just as they act through mind, intelligence, ego and consciousness. This generality across many facets of experience can be very useful in formulating new kinds of scientific theories about experience based on the efficient causes.

The fact that our senses have reasoning abilities implies that even descriptions of the process of sensation require us to invoke the full repertoire of conscious abilities. While the senses are not themselves conscious, the properties of consciousness are 'reflected' in the senses, just as they are visible in the mind or intelligence. The five efficient causes act 'through' senses, mind, intelligence, ego and consciousness, and waking or dreaming experiences can be used to surmise the existence of the unconscious and its various facets. These causes are actors behind the actions of the senses, although they are not always manifest to others or even to us. The analysis of waking and dreaming experiences can point us to the existence of such causes, through abstraction and generalization.

The Instruments of Efficient Action

Each stage in the creation is supported by subtle material elements: thinking by *chitta* (the repository of past experiences that gives rise to thoughts); feeling by *prakṛti* (a person's nature, likes and dislikes, that determines the development of desires or aversions towards a thought); willing by *mahattattva* (unconscious notions of morality or rightness that we consider *dharma*); knowing by *ahaṃkāra* (individual ego that creates plans for acting); and acting by *śakti* and *karma* (abilities that make a living being capable of actions). These unconscious abilities, carried by living beings in different degrees, play an important role in affecting a living being's conscious actions.

Each stage of unconscious development from thinking through feeling, willing, knowing and acting is carried out by a different unconscious ability. But why do we need additional capabilities when we have already postulated the existence of consciousness? Can consciousness not directly perform these transformations? The Vedic answer to this problem is that consciousness can directly act although its native abilities are covered and conditioned by the unconscious abilities. Under the influence of these abilities, consciousness believes that it is limited by certain capabilities, and this belief is an illusion that covers the native abilities of consciousness. Consciousness is the individual corresponding to the potter and his pot-making abilities correspond to the prowess in the unconscious that helps him convert his choices into thinking, feeling, willing, knowing and acting. These activities are not natively produced by consciousness, although consciousness permits their continuance by accepting the activities through its choices. Consciousness therefore relies on other instruments to execute its choices in the material creation.

The causal body underlying gross and subtle bodies is a vehicle that consciousness uses to travel in the world and it constitutes the *abilities* that are at the disposal of consciousness. If a vehicle can run on the road, then its passengers can travel on the road. If the vehicle can float on water or fly in the air, then the passengers of such vehicles can also move in water and air. Just as passengers in a car or airplane don't need to change themselves in order to travel on ground, water or air, consciousness need not change itself to experience different things. Consciousness only needs to change the vehicle in which it is riding. In Vedic philosophy, the abilities available to a living being are acquired as a consequence of past experiences and activities. Changes to abilities cause changes to the bodily vehicle suited to new abilities. The new body depends on past actions and a person carries his abilities along to a new body. Consciousness can control the abilities in the senses to perform different actions. Consciousness thus enjoys the experiences created by the bodily vehicle. All bodily actions are attributed to consciousness only because they are performed based upon intents in consciousness, although they are actually performed by the unconscious instruments.

The Nature of Chitta

The first efficient cause is *chitta*. Although the term *chitta* is often used to indicate everything subjective, I will use it to indicate the memory of all past experiences. This memory pertains to various kinds of schemes in which the living being has known itself in the past. Past experiences are recorded in *chitta* and stay there as a memory. Western psychologists often use the term "unconscious" to denote hidden memories that play an active role in determining our thoughts and actions. The *chitta* is roughly the "unconscious" of Western psychology[21] although the Vedic unconscious is broader than just the memory of past experiences. The memory of past experiences acts as a source of ideas on possible ways in which consciousness can self-actualize. If a person wants to be rich, the schemes of richness must come from the *chitta*. A person can be rich like a Maharaja or like a corporate czar, and his or her choice will depend upon the ways known to the *chitta*. Similarly, if one wants to be beautiful, *chitta* can generate ideas on how to be beautiful. Consciousness selects one of the many schemes generated by *chitta*. If a scheme does not exist in the *chitta*, consciousness cannot choose it.

New thoughts lead to new desires and hence new actions, which again create memories. So, unconscious memories are important because these give rise to thoughts. The Yoga philosophy compares *chitta* to waves in an ocean. Like rising and ebbing waves, we *remember* and *forget* unconscious memories, which appear as random thoughts. What masquerades as creative thinking is in fact a product of impressions created in the past. All so-called new ideas are suitable combinations of earlier impressions. If these memories are absent, then *chitta* cannot generate thoughts and then feelings, willing, knowing and acting will also not take place. In effect, there is no "free" creation; all creativity results from past experiences. There is, however, freedom in how impressions are combined. For example, the idea of a "golden mountain" is a product of memories of "gold" and "mountain" from prior experiences. The *chitta* may combine the impressions in new ways leading to new thoughts but the semantic roots of these thoughts are fixed in past experiences.

This idea has important implications for how we acquire new knowledge, a debate that vacillates between the relative importance of nature and nurture. All knowledge is gained by relating what we know to what we don't know. *Chitta* as the unconscious repository of memories consists of the things that we know, although we may not be conscious of them. Worldly sensations activate unconscious memories and make them conscious. We are thus reminded of what we knew but were not aware of. This remembering is the "a-ha" experience of learning when we grasp "new" concepts. Depending upon what is already present in the *chitta*, new learning can be very quick or extremely tedious. If someone is grasping new ideas quickly, we must understand that his *chitta* has acquired the relevant concepts already in the past. On the other hand, a slow learner takes time because his existing conceptual framework isn't accustomed to the new ideas being encountered. Then, it takes time to establish the relation between what he knows and what he doesn't. *Chitta* is the innate *nature* that conditions us to think in certain ways. Experiences encountered during learning are *nurture*, which trigger the *nature* and make it conscious. Both nature and nurture condition knowledge acquisition in complementary ways. Nurture provokes the unconscious ideas into consciousness and nature selects which nurture will stoke it. The Vedas state that consciousness carries the *chitta* acquired in past lives and it is thus possible that some individuals have stark inborn thought patterns right from birth.

When we look at things or events in the world, some experiences trigger new thoughts in us. This triggering is almost deterministic in the sense that a thought can be recalled by bringing the earlier objects into focus again. This fact is used by psychologists to explore the unconscious by asking people questions about the first thing or idea that comes to their mind when they see or hear something. Similarly, people who cannot recall their past consciously are subjected to objects or events that may evoke in them memories of the past. In the Vedic view, the recollection of all these experiences comes from the repository of memories in the *chitta* where they are stored as impressions of past experiences. These memories are not random but are organized in a systematic fashion such that one kind of thought can lead to recall of other kinds of related experiences. By subjecting a person to different experiences, resonances between what is being seen and what is stored in the memory unconsciously can be created causing the unconscious memory of events to be excited into a conscious experience of recall from the past.

The nature of memory recall attests to the existence of *chitta*: a memory recall sometimes produces not the actual facts but a caricature that is semantically identical to the actual facts. For example, when we recall conversations had with another person in the past, we may not recall the exact sentences uttered during the conversation. We do, however, recall the meaning-form left behind in the *chitta* from which we generally *construct* the sentence. So what we recollect isn't always the uttered sentence but the meaning. This deeper meaning lies in an unconscious state in the *chitta* and is used to construct a recall. This also means that an experience will help us recollect things that may be semantically similar although not factually identical to the past. We might also mix up two or more different events and construct a recall in a manner that seems perfectly meaningful although it never happened. Such combinations are again the outcome of combining impressions latent in the *chitta*.

The Nature of Prakṛti

The next efficient cause is *prakṛti*. Out of the experiences that we can remember, some experiences develop into our preferences as *taste*. *Prakṛti* thus develops *within* the *chitta*, since *tastes* are part of all that we remember. Likes and dislikes in a person are a matter of getting accustomed to things. People can get addicted to things that they did not at all like earlier. So, taste is a kind of memory although it isn't a very conscious type of memory. We automatically like or dislike things without conscious effort, although we may have acquired these tastes through practice or repeated experiences in the past. *Prakṛti* is unconscious because it becomes a person's nature to like or dislike certain things. Individuals conditioned by certain types of *prakṛti* don't have to think about whether they like something or not; the likes and dislikes are effected in them automatically. In fact, our likes and dislikes are often so unconscious to us that we may find it hard to understand why other people think or behave differently, and this is the cause of discord and conflict in the world because different people just cannot understand each other.

Likes or dislikes assist in the development of *feelings* from thoughts. These feelings include desires or revulsions towards something. This desire is different from the free will of consciousness, which pertains to a pure intent in the living being to know itself. This intent is conditioned by *chitta* as a specific kind of scheme to know the self, and desire pertains to that thought. Likes and dislikes are also sometimes called *nature*, because they are triggered automatically and unconsciously. We have inherent dislikes for certain kinds of food, weather or people which are not conscious. *Prakṛti* represents these tastes in us that lead to likes and dislikes.

The Nature of Mahattattva

From tastes arises the ability to judge—which is the ability to decide whether something is right or wrong, and whether a desire must be pursued because it is good and right and true. Only a subset of things that can be liked should be allowed to proceed, and therefore, the instrument of judging comes after the instrument of liking. Note that this is only true for unconscious actions, as the unconscious feelings or likes and dislikes happen before a judgment. In the unconscious, thoughts are automatically liked or disliked by *prakṛti* and conscious intervention doesn't control them. Similarly, the judgment too takes place automatically. The instrument of judging is however called *mahattattva* and sometimes called intelligence.

During the time of cosmic creation, the cosmic intelligence is created, which is the sum total of all individual intelligences. The individual and cosmic intelligence are different in their degree of influence, although not the *kind* of influence they have. Both evaluate and judge desires and determine whether a desire is allowed to proceed towards action. For example, based upon preferences from the past, someone may desire sweet food as they have developed a liking for sweet things. After the desire has developed, however, the person may realize that he has been, owing to diabetes, forbidden to eat sweet things. At this point, the person decides not to pursue his desire. The person who refrains from eating sweet things may have a strong liking for sweet edibles and desires are not hindered. However, desires are evaluated before being allowed to proceed to the planning stage. The decision to proceed on a desire is the intelligence that guides and controls the desires, a form of memory about allowed or forbidden actions. The example above is somewhat mundane, and *mahattattva* should not be equated with day-to-day prohibitions but with unconscious notions about right and wrong.

Mahattattva includes knowledge of unconscious normative injunctions such as "it is bad to lie" or "it is bad to hurt other people." Normative injunctions are not merely universal; we also carry personal values about right and wrong and use them in judgments. Another name for *mahattattva* in the Vedas is *ṛta* which is the collection of actions that should and should not be done. In modern terms this is called *dharma* but this does not comprise spiritual duties. It rather consists of moral rights and wrongs that have to do with living in the material world, rather than with spiritual advancement. The moral good and spiritual advancement are not opposed although they are distinct. *Ṛta* or *dharma* simply mean that our desires must be subordinated to higher moral principles, such as avoiding lying, not hurting other people, being charitable and kind, respecting elders, etc. The *Manu-Samhita*, which is considered a supplementary Vedic literature, outlines the principles of *dharma*, normative procedures and practices that are needed to lead a morally correct and just life within this universe. These moral principles can in some cases be obviated by spiritual injunctions, and they could be adjusted by the expert spiritualist for a particular time, but for the most part, abiding by these injunctions is considered necessary.

The difference between *prakṛti* that creates desires and *mahattattva* that creates wills can be illustrated by a similarity these two ideas have with ideas in Sigmund Freud's psychoanalysis. In Freud's terminology, *prakṛti* is the Id and the *mahattattva* is the Super-Ego. The Id creates desires and the Super-Ego decides on them. The tastes of *prakṛti* are unconscious relative to the *mahattattva* that determines the will. In Freud's psychology, the Id is unconscious whereas the Super-Ego is conscious. It is here that, according to the Vedas, Freud is wrong because morality is not always conscious. There is a debate on this topic within evolutionary theories of morality that posit that being good is simply good for survival. The evolutionary theory posits that these principles about being good have been imbibed in a living being through evolution and we have become hardwired to think in moral terms. This is then extended by psychologists to suggest that this hardwiring is present in us as the unconscious. The Vedic view supports unconscious notions about *dharma* but does not support the evolutionary thesis about it. This is because moral injunctions are different for different classes of people and for people in different stages and circumstances of life. So, we are not born hardwired with a shared sense of morality, but different individuals have different notions about morality and accordingly they should be placed in different situations in life. Also, in Vedic philosophy, the principles of *dharma* are meant for spiritual upliftment and not merely for a safe and secure continuation of life.

The Super-Ego also includes cultural or social restrictions, as they embody the notion of a moral society. A significant aspect of Vedic philosophy is that we are born with a native sense of morality that may or may not be compatible with the morality of the society in which we are born. Over long periods of time, notions about morality may be imbibed and when practiced repeatedly, their application becomes unconscious for us. That is, we behave morally and ethically not because we always judge a desire against those injunctions consciously but because we have been doing so over a long period of time such that ethical behavior comes to us automatically and unconsciously. It must however be noted that the memories of *mahattattva* are more conscious than memories of *prakṛti*. This means that we can control our desires by the application of moral principles by a conscious intervention although the prevention of thoughts in *chitta* or of desires from *prakṛti* is harder. We are almost completely unaware of how thoughts arise, we are more aware of how desires or likes and dislikes arise and we are even more aware of how and why we apply moral principles. They are all unconscious for the most part, but these levels of unconscious can be graded by their relative degree of closeness to full awareness.

The interaction of desires and intelligence can create interesting scenarios where a desire is modified in a way as to not violate moral injunctions. If we have to do forbidden things, then we must find ways to do them in ways that are allowed. For example, if someone is forbidden to eat sugar, she might invent a process by which she makes sweet things not made out of sugar. This could mean using saccharine or other sugar-like products, without the ill-effects of sugar. People do financial planning to avoid taxes, legally. We follow traffic rules to reach our destination without bumping into others. In other words, fulfillment of a desire needs to avoid things that are forbidden and that requires modification of the desire in ways to avoid what is forbidden. The action of *mahattattva* can therefore put a thought development back into the desire stage.

Once a judgment is passed, the desire becomes a will. This will is a determination to execute a desire based on a moral conviction, and it has the force or backing of an innate unconscious power of *dharma*. We have experience of people who act on the conviction that what they are doing is for the common and greater good, and therefore their actions are right. These actions are performed more forcefully than those that are just desires but may not have the conviction of the moral right. Of course, misplaced notions of morality can cause immoral acts to be performed vigorously, but the point is that this sense of morality makes the actor of these actions feel righteous. The greater collective good caused by the moral act, the more force it carries. Conversely, a person who acts selfishly on desires but may be causing others or himself harm through those actions constantly feels guilty. He lacks the conviction in his actions because the act isn't morally justified and the acts are therefore not performed forcefully. Many New Age healers urge people to rid themselves of their sense of morality, which they believe 'inhibits' us from acting forcefully to fulfill our desires. They see the conflict between the Id and the Super-Ego and they tell us to get rid of the Super-Ego so the Id can act freely. They also recognize that the Super-Ego is our sense of morality that we are born with and which we were taught during childhood, but they believe that the Super-Ego is an impediment to the fulfillment of desires. However, ultimately no society can function without a moral fabric, and while our notions of right and wrong may change with time and circumstances it is naïve to think that we can get rid of them altogether.

The Nature of Ahamkāra

Once a desire has developed into a determination the unconscious develops a plan to execute it. The Vedic category here—called the *ahaṃkāra*—comprises the memory of various types of actions that can be performed to fulfill a desire. The term *ahaṃkāra* is sometimes translated as the ego, and this conjures up ideas about personality. This is misleading because the *ahaṃkāra* is an individual procedure (*aham* = individual, *kāra* = action). Process philosophers will recognize this quickly as a new kind of category in which the world consists not of things but of *trajectories*. In classical physics, for instance, every independent object has a unique trajectory. The object may be uniquely identified as a particle or as a trajectory because in classical physics two objects can never have the same state and hence trajectories cannot intersect. The notion of *ahaṃkāra* is similar to that of process or trajectory that connects the present state to the desired goal through a sequence of steps. It comprises the unconscious memory of things that we know how to do, but these actions don't have to be performed consciously.

Planning to achieve goals requires intimate knowledge of what will or will not work in the real world. Theoretical planning must take into account the *laws* of nature and the levers to be pulled to move things forward. As *mahattattva* is normative knowledge, *ahaṃkāra* is theoretical knowledge of the laws by which nature operates. The Vedic view implies that we intuitively have some understanding of the laws of nature, although this understanding (like the understanding of normative laws) may not be perfect. It doesn't matter at this point whether we perfectly know the laws of nature, but only that we believe that we know how the universe works. Philosophers of science tell us that every scientific theory is the outcome of some kind of worldview that the creator of a theory tries to externalize through a theory. Most of us believe in the orderly nature of the world, but we may differ in our beliefs of the kind of order it represents. *Ahaṃkāra* is our unconscious personal theory and philosophy about nature, or our view of how things are interconnected and causally affected by our actions. This theory doesn't have to be correct or perfect; it only has to exist for every individual because without it we can desire or will, but we can't plan.

The Vedic view implies that we are all philosophers of nature at some unconscious level because we all form theories about nature. Every living being has a theory about reality that he or she uses to plan. This theory may include general principles or specific facts and procedures that make the person successful. Some of this knowledge is obviously learnt and gradually becomes unconscious through practice, but there is also an innate view of the world that we are born with. Children for instance, innately know how to grab attention and get what they want, although no one has taught them so. Most animals innately know the difference between solids and liquids and that they can swim through a liquid but they cannot walk through a solid. Our environment also shapes our worldviews and many things such as 'hard work fetches good results', or 'honesty is the best policy' are innate theories about the world that we learnt and imbibed during our childhood by experience. The opposite experiences could lead to a different set of personal theories.

The Vedas describe this *ahaṃkāra* at the cosmic level as *Hiraṇyagarbha* or the 'Golden Egg', which is a primordial stage of the creation, when the universe isn't fully manifest. This nomenclature appears mythological but it is in fact very instructive and illustrative. What the Vedas describe is the fact that the living beings have a set of ideas about what they want to do, they like doing these things according to their innate nature, they have consulted their sense of morality and obtained the go-ahead, and they have also prepared plans of how they are going to go about realizing these desires in practice. They haven't, however, started acting on these plans yet. The living being is prepared to act on his desires although activity is not manifest yet. This situation is likened to a ripe (golden) egg (inactive, but about to manifest). The living being is ready to start executing his plans, and the universe will manifest as soon as plans are brought to fruition with activity. The Golden Egg therefore represents the state of the universe when all the living beings are conjuring up ideas and preparing to be born into nature as activity.

The Nature of Śakti

Plans become activity by the application of skills and the next capability that the living beings must have is called *śakti*. *Śakti* is also unconscious and it represents the skills by which a living being can convert a plan into an action. To generate a plan one needs the ability of knowledge to create plans. To enact the plan one needs *skills*. *Śakti* is the skills by which one can achieve results. Results are achieved when capabilities are applied to procedures, thus a person with good plans but without necessary skills will fail, whereas a person with plans and skills will succeed. *Śakti* is given to a person based on *karma* which is the results of past actions, in order to fulfill desired goals. Thus, a person with good *karma* can succeed because he has got the skills to succeed, although he is free in whether or not he chooses to apply the skills. Popular accounts of *karma* sometimes misleadingly equate this with "destiny." It is supposed that we are predestined to enjoy or suffer, regardless of our actions, as this pleasure or suffering is fated. This construal of *karma* misleads us into thinking that we will attain good or bad results without (or regardless of) actions, implying that our choices in actions are inconsequential. What is correct, instead, is that (a) one gets results by correctly employing the skills acquired from past good actions, so the skilled person is successful while the unskilled person is not, and (b) the skills must be used in the right manner to retain and enhance them in the future. *Karma* is the practical ability to act effectively and can be used or misused; proper use enhances the instrument and improper use depreciates it. The ability exists unconsciously and is applied automatically without any conscious effort.

Philosophers sometimes distinguish between two types of knowing—the knowledge of facts or *know-that* and knowledge of procedures called *know-how*. Much of the know-how knowledge is unconscious. This includes for instance how we brush our teeth, or drive a car, or ride a bicycle or swim in a pool. At some point in experience, some of these things may have been learnt consciously, but as this conscious activity becomes a habit, it becomes unconscious and can be performed automatically. Infants know how to suck a mother's breast, and many animals know how to swim right from birth. There are several capabilities that we are born with and by using these capabilities we can enact our plans for action.

There is need for a clear distinction between theoretical knowledge to swim (which may be acquired by reading a swimming manual) and the practical skill to swim that comes from experience. In everyday life, procedures come to us in cookbooks, instruction manuals, and even scientific papers that tell us how to carry out experiments. There is ample literature that tells us "how to do things." This literature does not give us skills, although reading it does give us knowledge of procedures. When we are creating a plan of action, we don't employ skills of doing actions. In fact, a person who creates a plan need not be skilled in the activities he plans (a common malady in dysfunctional organizations where people who make plans are not skilled to execute them, resulting in plans failing during execution). He only needs to have theoretical knowledge of how something is done—akin to what is given in books. Planning in *ahaṃkāra*, however, consists of detailed procedures that are knowledge of what needs to be done, rather than theoretical procedures that need to be adjusted by people who will really do things. But this is still inadequate without the practical power to execute procedures.

The Vedas describe that a form of God called *Garbhodakaśāyi Viṣṇu* who has all living beings inside his body 'breaks' the Golden Egg and enters it. This breaking of the egg corresponds to the universe, which was so far in a planning stage, now entering the execution stage. The universe progresses from an inactive embryo stage to a manifest stage. The *Garbhodakaśāyi Viṣṇu* enters the universe together with living beings and their unconscious abilities—*chitta, prakṛti, mahattattva, ahaṃkāra, śakti* and *karma*. With the influence of Time, *karma* begins to fructify and gives the living being various kinds of bodies. The living beings use these bodies to fulfill plans, learn from that fulfillment or failure, and develop further plans.

The Causal Body

The five efficient causes and their instruments constitute what is called the *kāraṇa śarīra* or causal body. It is a body, and therefore external to the soul. And yet it is the most rudimentary and subtle covering of the soul and impels the soul to create other experiences. The causal body can be equated with the unconscious of the Western psychology. The unconscious creates the conscious experiences and therefore its effects are conscious. However, the cause itself remains unconscious. That is, the living being may not consciously control the instruments that cause the activities. The living being however can become aware of the existence of the unconscious realm simply by inference and by applying the idea that if conscious activities are being created internally and we are unable to know their exact cause then there must be something unconscious by which they are being created. The reverse position—where conscious activities are created without a conscious effort on the part of consciousness and there is no other agency that causes these activities—would lead to an explanatory gap. The Vedas describe that there are causes, of which we may be unaware and of which we cannot become aware in the normal course of life, but which are of utmost importance in how they contribute to conscious experience.

A spiritually advanced person becomes aware of his unconscious when he realizes his difference from matter and is able to distinguish between the material conditioning and his true spiritual nature without this conditioning. Such a spiritually advanced person understands that he is eternal existence, free will, the desire to know and express the self, and he has the ability and need for pleasure. These native tendencies—a spiritualist realizes—are not products of matter, although these native tendencies are conditioned or modified by matter. Under this conditioning, the soul develops different kinds of subtle and gross bodies, which create various experiences.

Note that the five instruments of the efficient cause are material but they create an impression in consciousness. Vedic philosophy tells us that creation begins not with material objects, but with a subtle conditioning over consciousness that creates a specific type of embodied individual. This individual does not yet have a material body or mind, but the soul considers itself an individual with specific ideas, feelings, judgments, plans and abilities. The living being becomes embodied in matter in a subtle covering of restrictions.

The Role of Other Causes

Of course, the efficient causes are not the only causes of creation but they are responsible for bringing the soul into the universe whereupon other causes can be relevant. Until a living being enters the universe, other causes (described in later chapters) cannot act. A living being uses material creation to know itself in a certain way and derives pleasure from this realization. To perform these things, the living being needs the support of other causes, in addition to the efficient causes. Efficient causes act in the universe, but they are responsible for bringing a living being that is initially situated outside the universe, into the material universe. Implicitly, this means that a living being outside the universe is not pure consciousness. In fact this living being carries subtle material capabilities that enable it to think, feel, will, plan and act. In the Vedas, the universe isn't always manifested; rather the universe appears and disappears. When the universe is not manifested, the living beings 'sleep' along with their capabilities. The living being is actually never asleep, although its capabilities stop churning. The living being depends on its capabilities to conjure up ideas, desires, plans and actions and when these capabilities become inactive (due to the ceasing of the influence of Time on the capabilities) the living being also becomes inactive.

When the universe is manifested again, under the influence of Time the living being begins to see new ideas, desires, plans and actions, and it is motivated to enter the active phase again. The soul thus takes a leap into the universe, attracted by the prospect of experimenting with its creations. This prospect is alluring but under the control of Time, and even though a living being believes that he is the origin of these ideas and plans, they are actually created by the efficient causes, under the influence of Time. Time selects different ideas, desires and plans, and the living beings are allured by it.

This view of the Vedic creation appears depressing and it needs to be further illuminated by the spiritual aspects of Vedic philosophy. While it is true that Time deludes a living being into the material universe and causes it to enjoy and suffer, the action of Time isn't on a living being itself but on the subtle causes of *chitta, prakṛti, mahat-tattva, ahaṃkāra, śakti* and *karma.* Time doesn't force a living being to enter the universe, although it presents allurements to tempt him into the universe. The temptation could be interpreted as the 'original sin' in the Biblical sense due to which Adam and Eve enter the forest of the material world to eat the 'forbidden fruit' of pleasure and are entangled and condemned to live there forever. Yet it must be noted that a living being is tempted to act in this way because of its aversion towards God. The temptations created by Time are alluring only because of an aversion that a living being has towards God. If this aversion were destroyed by spiritual advancement, the temptations created by Time would not seem inviting and the living being could exit the material creation. The binding to the universe therefore exists only because of a living being's attractions, which are fanned and brought to fruition by the actions of Time.

The Vedas accept Western psychological notions about the unconscious and relate them to creation. Freud and Jung, who popularized the study into the unconscious, highlighted aspects about our subjective existence which are deeper than the conscious cognitive functions such as recognizing objects, using language to express and communicate, etc., and yet seem to have an important bearing on the conscious functions. In the Vedic view, the difference between the conscious and the unconscious is not absolute. There is rather a gradual progression from the completely unconscious *chitta* to the relatively more conscious *prakṛti, mahattattva, ahaṃkāra* and *śakti*. As reality is manifested from the unconscious to the conscious in a living being, similarly the universe is manifested gradually through stages of increasing manifestation from unconscious to conscious.

4

The Instrumental Cause of Creation

*Equipped with his five senses, man explores the universe
around him and calls the adventure Science.*
                                                  —*Edwin Powell Hubble*

What Is an Instrument?

An example of an instrumental cause is the potter's wheel used to create pots. The potter molds clay into a pot using the potter's wheel. In creation, instrumental causes do not play an active role; they aren't material or personal causes of the creation. The instrumental causes play a supporting role as implements similar to the potter's wheel used for creating a pot. The Vedas similarly state that the subtle body, like a potter's wheel, is inactive, but it is a necessary implement for carrying out actions. Everyday material instruments are made out of matter, the same matter that any object is made of. Indeed, depending upon the kind of use we put an object to, we could name it as some kind of instrument. In this view, instruments don't seem to have a fundamental role in the description of nature. They are merely complex configurations of matter and ultimately reducible to matter. So is the Vedic view about instruments similarly another type of configuration in matter, reducible to matter?

The Vedas hold that the instruments of consciousness are also material, but they belong to a different *category* of matter than material objects. Conscious instruments are devices that enable consciousness to interact with matter. This intermediate level of material reality converts information in matter into different kinds of sensations, thoughts, propositions, intentions and pleasures. The soul under-stands *forms* of knowledge and *forms* of action, which are created by the senses of knowledge and action. *Forms* of knowledge include sen-sations like seeing, touching, hearing, tasting and smelling, which are the ways in which the soul knows. *Forms* of action on the other hand are holding, walking, sex, excretion and speech; these are the ways in which the soul can act. The external material world is transformed into sensations of sight, touch, taste, smell, sound or speech, excre-tion, holding, walking and sex by which we experience matter as sen-sations. So in order to know the world or modify it, we must translate what we can know and do into the ways in which the world exists by itself and the ways it can undergo change. The senses are instruments that carry out this translation.

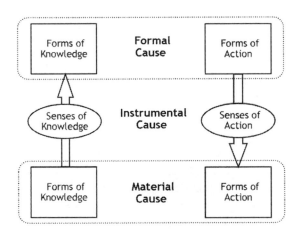

Figure-2 Senses Relate the Material and the Formal Cause

Consider the case when a scientist has to measure a property like momentum or energy. The instruments that measure this property cannot directly tell us that they measured momentum or energy. Instead they indicate their detections through pointer movements or detector clicks, in ways that *we* can understand the reality. Thus, momentum and energy must be translated to pointer movements and detector clicks if we have to know about the world, which is something the measuring device does. Post measurement, we *inter-pret* pointer movements or detector clicks as a value of energy or momentum. Similarly, we change the world by pushing buttons or pressing levers. Some button pushes translate into "start the electricity flow" while others into "stop the electricity flow." Some lever presses translate into "start the engine" and others into "stop the engine." In all such cases, instruments act as mediators between what conscious beings can know and do and what the world is. This view of measurement in science creates the problem that matter is physical properties (which are defined in relation to other objects) which we perceive as sensations (which are defined in relation to our senses). The scientific view implies that the world is not red, sweet or rough because these are merely appearances of reality. Therefore, when we see red or smell sweet, we cannot say the world is red or sweet. We must rather say that matter appears to us as red or sweet, which is a form of misapprehension created by matter.

In short, in modern science, senses are not a source of true knowledge of reality, because we can never apply sensations back to reality. The Vedic view counters this idea by describing reality differently. Matter, in Vedic philosophy, is a representation of the observer's experiences, and everything in experience can potentially be objectified in matter. Matter and experience are therefore not identical, although they are related as a symbol and its meaning. A consequence of this view is that while we cannot assert that reality is exactly as we experience it, we can use the same *words* to describe both reality and its experience. Thus, when we experience redness, the world is also red—not as sensation but as a symbol of redness. The senses of knowledge are subtle instruments that convert objective information into sensations. The senses of action are subtle instruments that convert sensations into objective information. The words that describe our sensations can also describe reality, but the meanings of these words are different. In the external world, the word is a symbol of knowledge or action. In the senses, the same word is sensations. Senses therefore connect sensations with external objects. By definition, the senses must always be associated with an observer, because they convert between things that consciousness knows or does and external material objects.

The manner in which we experience sensations is a considerable area of research and debate in science today. There are at least three ways in which we can think of sensations. In the first view, we could suppose that sensations are objective entities that exist in our mind, and they are 'measured' by the senses quite like scientific instruments measure physical properties. Unlike scientific instruments that directly interact with the external world, the senses interact with the mental representation of this world, which exists objectively as sensations. Here, sensations are mental representations of the external world and they must be created in the mind before the senses can experience them. This view creates the problem of how matter creates sensations through material interactions.

In the second view, the senses can be thought of as *operators* that extract properties from matter and represent them as sensations to the mind. In this view, sensations are byproducts of the interaction between the external world and the senses, and we could call sensation a relation between the senses and the external world of objects. Here, sensations are produced by the sense-world interaction but they exist as separate kinds of objects in the mind. This view too does not fully explain how senses interact with matter.

In the third view, the senses do not measure sensations, but *become* sensations when they come in contact with objective information about the world. Think of clay and a clay pot. When clay is molded into the form of a pot, it becomes a clay pot. There are two things in the clay pot—the property of being clay and the shape of a pot. In a similar way, we can think of sensations as comprising two things: the qualitative feel of being a touch, sight, sound, taste or smell, and a specific form or information that makes that quality a specific type of touch, sight, sound, taste or smell. For the sense to become a sensation, information about the world must be present. These views of sensation are represented pictorially in Figure-3.

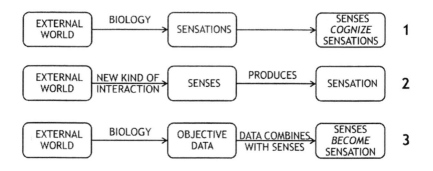

Figure-3 Three Views about Sensation

In the first view, a sensation is objectively complete in itself and it exists in the mind just like an object in space. The senses may or may not know this sensation, but the sensation exists objectively in the mind. In the second view, a sensation is produced by the interaction between matter and the senses, through a new kind of yet unknown interaction. In the third view, the senses themselves become sensations and we can't distinguish between sensation and the senses when a sensation occurs. A sensation is comprised of a specific quality and data that makes it into a sensation. The sensation doesn't exist unless information combines with the senses.

The first view is downright reductionist. It treats sensations as products of biology and chemistry and the senses are also ultimately treated in terms of gross matter. This is where most of the mainstream scientific view lies today. Scientists postulate that matter encodes sensations, which are then experienced by consciousness. What we call 'sense' in this case is identical to consciousness.

The second view originated in medieval times, and says that sensations are produced by the interaction of senses with the world. That is, there is something more to our existence than the material body. We might call this a living force, which is responsible for the creation of a subjective view of the world. The senses in a sense 'reach out' into the world and 'grab' the essential properties of matter and then represent it as sensation. Sensation, in this view, is a relational property of the interaction between the world and the senses. This view is inconsistent with what we know from biology and neuroscience where the world is first represented as information in the brain. For instance, it is known that the eye detects the color of light and converts it into an information representation of the color using three primary colors Red, Green and Blue. This representation is then transported to the brain with each of the primary colors being carried in its separate communication 'channel.' Before the sensation occurs, there is a brain representation of that sensation. We must now incorporate the idea that sensation depends on an information representation of the physical world.

The third view is consistent with the existence of such an informational representation. Sensations, in this view, are created when the senses combine with the brain representation. The senses thus don't interact with the external world. They rather interact with information about the world in the brain. The senses don't perceive the data. They rather become the sensation by combining with the data. The Vedic view of sensation resembles this viewpoint.

In the Vedic view, the external world exists as information (I will detail this view of matter in the next chapter). When the brain interacts with the world, it creates a representation of the world. Both the external world and the brain representation are of similar *types* although the brain representation is obviously more *condensed.* Externally, information is an objective symbol of sensation and internally it is a condensed representation of that symbol. The information about the external world is called *tanmātra* which literally means "form-only." The *tanmātra* represents a condensed form of the external world and it combines with the senses to create sensations. Of course, in the Vedic view, senses don't necessarily have to depend on the external world to have sensations. The senses can also create the *tanmātra* which is the process by which dreams and hallucinations are created. Even the external objects are created by the senses by creating the *tanmātra* which is then encoded as objects. In the Vedic description of creation, therefore, the *tanmātra* are created from the senses, which are then encoded into objects.

The senses are therefore different from information about objects, and this information can be encoded in matter. However, when information combines with the senses, it is experienced as sensations. In other words, senses do not *sense* the sensation. The senses *become* the sensation when combined with information about reality in a way similar to how clay becomes a pot when combined with form. That means that information about reality must be first extracted and represented before it can be sensed. This informational representation, we already know from modern science, is created by organs—which are different from the senses that perceive the representation. However, this information is abstract; for example, we can represent a color using the relative degrees of red, blue and green in a shade of color. Biologically we know that the eye has rods and cones to cognize color. This cognition takes different light frequencies and classifies them as red, green and blue. The physical property of light is thus converted first into information and represented as {R, G, B} in the brain. The informational representation of the light's color is different both from the physical properties of light (such as frequency) and from sensation. For instance, the representation does not give the subjective 'feel' about the sensation. However, the information can be processed by the senses. The senses in Vedic philosophy are subtle instruments that absorb information to create the subjective 'feel' of the sensation. The information, however, can be extracted by organs, such as the eye, tongue, skin, ear and nose. These organs extract information but they do not create the sensation. The senses—which produce the sensation—are therefore different from the sense organs.

Ten Vedic Senses

Today, the process of observation is treated as something that converts reality into sensation, although the forms of knowledge and the form of reality are different. In empiricist language, this is the difference between primary properties in matter and secondary properties in the senses. The modern view helps us understand how matter can exist independent of the observer, but it does not explain how the observer knows that matter, because the transformation of matter into sensation remains a very hard, unsolved problem. It also forces us into the view that senses are not sources of *knowledge* of reality because reality is fundamentally different from how we perceive it. In Vedic philosophy, the *indriya* are the senses of knowledge because they give us knowledge of reality. What the senses experience is therefore not an illusion because the world has a form similar to how we perceive it. The language by which we describe sensations can therefore also be applied back to reality. If senses correctly gather information about the world, the perceived image aligns with reality. If, however, the data about reality is distorted, the perception and reality are different. While the organs should generate the sensations according to reality, these organs are subject to defects of perception and can distort the reality in representation.

The Vedic senses are, however, not the *tabula rasa* of Lockean empiricism for two reasons. First, the senses are not blank slates because they have been conditioned by past sensations. This makes the senses 'desire' certain types of sensations and this desire impels living beings towards objects of the senses. Second, the senses don't just experience sensations; they can also create sensations. During dreaming, for instance, the senses produce sensations and then observe them. During hallucination too, the senses create sensations. The senses are therefore a different kind of matter because they can both produce information and consume it. While the transformation of matter and energy involves laws of conservation, information can be created and destroyed. The senses create and consume information. They may also distort the information based on past experiences. The Vedas therefore state that the senses need to be 'purified' of the past conditioning to see nature just as it is. That is, the senses are not *tabula rasa* but they need to be purified to become such.

The Vedas state that when a person dies, he leaves behind his gross body and carries with him the senses into a new body. The evidence of this carrying forward is in the innate tendencies that living beings have right from birth. Today we suppose that these tendencies are genetic, but nothing in biology explains the experience of sensation, conceptual understanding or the feeling of doing. In the Vedas, the senses are a different class of matter from the body because they persist even when the living being leaves his gross body and we consider the body to be dead. When the gross body is dead, the subtle body of senses is carried with consciousness, and these senses then give rise to the abilities in the next body. The senses in the living being act as the abilities of knowing and action.

There are ten such senses in Vedic philosophy: five senses of knowledge and five senses of action. The five senses of knowledge are called ear (*śrotra*), skin (*tvacha*), eyes (*chakṣu*), nose (*ghrāṇa*) and tongue (*jivha*). The five senses of action are called speech (*vāc*), hands (*hasta*), legs (*pada*), anus (*guda*) and genitals (*śiśna*). Higher than these ten senses are the senses of mind (*manas*), intelligence (*buddhi*) and ego (*ahaṃkāra*). Beyond these subtle senses is consciousness (*chitta*) which is also a type of sense that creates and consumes pleasures[22]. Matter in Vedic philosophy is only a possibility. It is put into a definite state by the actions of senses, mind, intelligence, ego and consciousness. The fact that mind, intelligence, ego and consciousness are senses implies that there are other kinds of sensations beyond the sensations of sound, sight, taste or smell.

The senses of mind, intelligence, ego and consciousness perform several mental functions such as comprehending and creating ideas, comprehending and creating relationships or comprehending and creating pleasure. The ten senses of knowledge and action with mind, intelligence, ego and consciousness constitute the instruments of conscious experience. They are different from the efficient causes which act unconsciously. The efficient causes are subtler than the conscious senses and they act through the senses thereby creating conscious experiences. Many things unconscious in efficient causes become conscious in instrumental causes. For instance, we are conscious about many likes and dislikes, moral preferences, abilities to create plans and powers to execute these plans. But, equally, many things in the unconscious remain unknown to us. Many times these unconscious memories are suddenly manifested, which may surprise us and others. In comparison, everything that happens in the senses, mind, intelligence and ego can be traced back to prior conscious experiences (which may have been originally created as an effect of the efficient causes). Essentially, the efficient causes are a much larger repository of impressions, only a subset of which is manifested in the senses. This relation between the conscious and unconscious realms makes Vedic philosophy very contemporary, useful to further study, and easy to relate to for a modern educated person who is aware of these ideas from psychology.

The Nature of the Mind

Let's commence the discussion of the conscious realm with a description of the mind. As we discussed earlier, the efficient causes reflect in the senses, and therefore their activities of thinking, feeling, willing, knowing and acting are visible in the mind. The only difference is that these actions become conscious in the mind, whereas as efficient causes they were unconscious. We might also call the thinking, feeling, willing, knowing and acting in the mind as an *effect* whose *cause* is the efficient cause by the same name. The mind understands concepts, whose meanings are given in relation to other concepts. This is an important difference between sensations and concepts; a single sensation can be sensed while a single concept cannot be understood. The understanding of concepts involves other concepts, which are understood collectively. The same words may, however, be used to describe both sensations and concepts. The word 'yellow' can mean a universal property when denoting a sensation and a relational attribute when denoting a concept. Even things that don't produce the sensation of yellow can relationally represent the meaning of yellow. Thus, there can be a symbol of 'yellow' which does not have the property of yellowness.

The mind perceives the meanings of sensations by seeing the contextual relations between sensations. For instance, a piece of wood becomes the leg of a chair within a context. The red light denotes a stop sign at a street intersection, and the gift of a red rose from a man to a woman symbolizes an expression of love. The meanings of leg, stop and love are not in the sensations themselves, but they are symbolized by the sensations in a specific context. In a different context, the same sensations could denote a different meaning. The mind is capable of perceiving interrelations between multiple sensations. These sensations may have been obtained by different senses—e.g., color from the eyes and taste from the tongue. By correlating and analyzing sensations from multiple senses, the mind derives meanings from them. While the senses of sight, sound, taste, touch and smell can perceive individual sensations, the cognition of meaning requires at least two sensations.

Since all meanings arise within a context, which divides a system from its environment, the genesis of meanings lies in the mind's ability to create collections. Parts within the collection are accorded a different meaning, just as a person in a team is given a specific type of duty. Just as a team, organization or society organizes itself into logically distinct but related functions, the mind perceives the world in terms of logically distinct but ultimately unified parts that combine to form a whole. Matter by itself is not aggregated or divided into parts. Space itself does not have boundaries that partition matter into a system and its environment. This division is carried out by the mind. Through division, the mind divides our perceptual field into systems, which are then partitioned into logically distinct concepts. The mind is also capable of dividing the perceptual field of changes into the perception of different kinds of activities. An activity in time—like a system in space—is a logical and temporal combination of elementary actions. While the senses of action and knowledge perceive and execute an elementary sensation or action, the mind constructs macroscopic collections by aggregating sensations, before attaching meanings to these sensations within those collections. While the senses perceive sensual atoms, the mind gives these sensations meanings. Thus, some color becomes a sign of danger, while some motion becomes the activity of writing. The mind is said to coordinate the actions of the senses, and it performs its function by attaching meanings to elementary sensations and actions.

An important preliminary step in cognizing objects is cognizing object *boundaries* that separate things from one another. Everyday perception divides sensations into objects by drawing boundaries around things. These boundaries have a form, such as the shape of objects like tables and chairs, or the form of living beings like humans and birds. Boundaries however are not limited to objects and they include more abstract constructs like teams, organizations, society, countries and planets. The significance of this idea is that the boundary serves as a *context* for the interpretation of meanings. People in a team are divided into distinct roles, society is divided into organizations, countries are divided into societies and planets are divided into countries. These divisions are not just physically smaller parts; they also play semantically distinct roles in the whole. In Vedic philosophy, the universe as a whole is bounded, and the boundary makes the parts in the universe semantically distinct. The universe as a whole is treated as a living body that consists of logically distinct functions. The mind sees meanings because it divides the field of sensations into system boundaries. Without this, it would be impossible to apply roles and functions to the parts.

Western philosophers in the 20th century believed that all concepts are reducible to sensations. This scheme did not work effectively because it ignored the fundamental difference between sensations and concepts, namely that concepts acquire meanings in relation to other concepts, unlike sensations that exist in an object even when no other object exists. Concepts, however, are not just in the mind. They can also be applied to objects, because objects also have contextual properties. In Vedic philosophy, the mind is not just an instrument of creating concepts; it is also a type of sense. The mind is capable of sensing concepts, just as the senses are capable of sensing taste, color, smell, sound and touch. Thus, concepts such as 'yellow' or 'red' are not merely mental constructs; they are also real.

Once the mind has constructed or perceived a concept, it can like or dislike it based on its past conditioning of concepts. In the mind, these feelings are experienced as attraction or revulsion. We intuitively like some ideas or are repelled by other ideas. The Vedas describe that there are six basic kinds of feelings in the mind—desire, anger, pride, greed, confusion and envy. Confusion is a feeling when we are not able to comprehend a concept and this leads us to feel confusion. When scientists face facts that aren't yet explained by theories, they feel confusion. Confusion is an emotional state and the mind cannot deal with confusion for long. The scientific mind is thus also mediated by emotions, although we don't realize it.

The mind, like the senses, is accustomed to certain types of ideas, and has tendencies to like and dislike particular ideas. This is called feeling in the mind whereby the mind accepts and rejects ideas based on its past conditioning. Obviously, if we desire something we want to take it. If we feel anger, we want to hurt or change what is causing anger in us. When the desire develops further, it becomes a will or determination, and we might call it a belief. These beliefs may not be rational or true, because rationality and truth require connecting the belief to the world of actual objects. The mind has beliefs which need to be validated by the intelligence and the ego.

Different kinds of feelings lead to different kinds of actions. The stage of willing is the goal or intent developed from emotion. The emotional state is not permanent as it leads to a determination that we must get out of thinking and emoting and act upon that knowledge or emotion. This is a transition from the cognition of ideas and feelings to the beginning of action. This means that we are *motivated* to act based on feelings, and action is mediated by our motivational state. People may not act upon an idea—even if they understand the idea—if that idea does not also stir emotions in them. Powerful speakers therefore don't just convey ideas; rather, through speech, they also pass on some of their emotion to their listeners. They engage their listeners by forcing them into an emotional state and the listener's mind must determine what to do to get out of that state. The will to act is not activated unless there is an emotion attached to the thoughts. The next activity in the mind, therefore, relates to what we would do with the feeling of emotion.

The thinking and feeling stages represent cognitive and emotional understanding of reality, whereas knowing and acting represent plans and execution. Between the feeling and knowing lies willing that represents our choices. Choice, or will, is the boundary between knowledge and action. Note that willing begins after thinking and feeling, and this means that we cannot formulate a theory of willing unless we have a theory of thinking and feeling. Scientific theories need to explain how action is mediated by meaning. In current science, matter acts automatically, governed by laws of force. However, in semantic theories there must be an explicit role for willing that converts meanings into actions. The relation between meaning and action is seen in everyday objects. If something is a knife then it can be used to *cut*, if something is a gun then it can be used to *shoot*, if something is a car, it can be used to *transport*. In these cases, meaning leads to action, but only if we choose to *use* the object according to that meaning. The conversion of meaning into action is therefore not automatic but mediated by the mind's will.

We can use knowledge of behaviors to fulfill goals, and this cognition of the behavior of things is called *knowing* in the mind, but knowing is different from thinking. *Thinking* pertains to concepts of sensation while *knowing* pertains to concepts of action. We may also call this *knowing* procedural knowledge or knowledge of laws or programs that govern the behavior of things. It is a theoretical understanding of reality, the kind that scientists aspire for through scientific theories. Through this knowledge we can then build technology. The knowing pertains to a theoretical knowledge of reality which can be used to build specific applications for everyday use. The development of such applications depends on the feeling and willing states. Whether we use knowledge of reality to use that reality depends whether we are motivated and determined to do it.

Once a plan has been identified, action can begin. The mind at this stage mediates the creation of action. It creates concepts of action and passes them to the senses of action as instructions. The senses of action create the sensation of activity: e.g., we sense that we are running, or holding, or talking while the organs of action convert information underlying change into change in the external world. Through the involvement of organs and senses, the world is changed, and we get the feeling that we altered the world. Note that a machine that changes the world doesn't necessarily realize that it is acting. That is, there is no *sensation* corresponding to its actions. The senses of action create the sensation of acting within us.

The Nature of Intelligence

The Vedic notion of intelligence is different from notions about intelligence in Western psychology and philosophy. In the West, intelligence includes the ability to cognize concepts, but in the Vedic view this is done by the mind. So what does intelligence do? Intelligence in Vedic philosophy is said to be the sense that combines the concepts in the mind into propositions. The mind is a creative generator of concepts and actions, but intelligence controls the mind's creativity by structuring and ordering it into propositions. The mind divides the sensual world into boundaries, and parts within the boundary are distinguished logically. These logically distinct parts are combined by intelligence into propositions by *ordering* them. For instance, intelligence will produce sentences by ordering words.

Intelligence also judges propositions by checking their syntax and logical correctness. This judgment is different from assessments of truth of statements that refer to other facts, which is called 'speaking the truth' in ordinary parlance. Speaking the truth is a moral judgment and not a logical one. Morality resides in *mahattattva* while logical judgments are performed by intelligence. In a sense, therefore, intelligence is the instrument of logical truth which checks if a proposition formed using some elementary concepts is syntactically correct and conforms to conditions of logical structure—e.g., contains some subject-object distinction, uses part of speech like nouns, verbs and adjectives in the right manner. Looked at in this way, one aspect of intelligence is linguistic grammar.

To judge the correctness of a proposition, the intelligence analyzes and compares a proposition with prior knowledge of linguistic rules and conventions. A syntactically and logically well-formed proposition is semantically consistent, although it may be inconsistent with the facts (in which case we are logically lying). To assess the consistency of propositions, we might also compare some propositions with others that are already formed within the same conceptual domain and are believed to be both logically and referentially true. These prior formed propositions are known as beliefs and they are stored as *smṛiti* or memory. When intelligence encounters new propositions that are different from already held beliefs, the propositions are rejected. Memory includes knowledge of grammar, logic and those propositions that are already known to be true. The statement 'colorless, green ideas fly furiously' is not meaningful and intelligence will detect the lack of meaning. Thus, even when the constituents of a proposition are individually meaningful, the proposition as a whole may not be. One important sign of intelligence is, therefore, that a person behaves in a way that is consistent with established norms of well-formed propositions.

Intelligent people are able to learn new things and change their belief systems. When new facts that contradict existing beliefs are encountered, the new facts are generally discarded in favor of existing beliefs. However, as the new beliefs accumulate, the newer system of thought becomes internally consistent, but inconsistent with the older belief system. Over time, we find that the newer belief system is so strong that the older system is now discarded as it is found inconsistent with the newer system. In modern times, for instance, scientific thought has replaced the older religious philosophies.

Intelligence begins in doubt, and a new proposition is treated skeptically, especially if it contradicts established notions. Doubting is thus considered a sign of intelligence and is called *saṁśayaḥ*. To quell doubts, we recall facts from memory that we consider to be true. Memory is the second feature of intelligence called *smṛiti*. Based on the memory of prior known facts which are believed to be true, intelligence arrives at correct judgments, called *niścayaḥ*. If some important facts have not been accounted for while assessing the truth of a proposition, a wrong judgment is created, which is called *viparyāsaḥ*. Finally, during sleep, the discrimination between true and false is inactive and the mind and senses act without control. They may produce propositions that are not well-formed. This is akin to dreaming where the mind and senses are active, but the intelligence is not. This stage is thus called *svāpaḥ* as during sleep intelligence is suspended or weakened. A person who is thinking and acting without judging is asleep. Many brilliant ideas were perceived as dreams and their application was done after waking up.

Intelligence also judges if actions are well-formed, in the sense that they will produce something logically coherent. This aspect of intelligence includes compliance to standard rules and procedures that make a set of meaningful concepts into meaningful propositions. The Vedas describe that there are two kinds of senses—the senses of knowledge and action. The mind deals in two kinds of concepts—sensation-concepts and action-concepts. The intelligence combines the two types of concepts into two types of propositions.

Like meanings in the mind depend on contexts, judgments too are contextual. For instance, the rules of grammar and syntax in English are different from those in German. The rules of appropriate social etiquette are different in different societies. A judgment of correctness employs context-sensitive knowledge and a proposition can be judged as being correct in one context and incorrect in another. Psychologists have thus postulated many kinds of intelligences such as musical, linguistic, social, emotional, logical, kinesthetic, etc. From a Vedic view, there are not separate types of intelligences but rather different domains of semantically well-formed propositions. There are obviously places where domains overlap and there it becomes imperative to align their propositions. For instance, it is musically incoherent to sing a song with sad words in an up-tempo and musically happy composition. Intelligence would comprehend disconnects between words and the musical tones. But, in so far as the domains do not frequently overlap in the everyday world, it is not wrong to think of them as separate proposition domains.

Figure-4 Figure-Ground Perception and the Intellect

Intelligence combines sensations to form objects and this is visible in figure-ground perception problems where sensations need to be combined to produce objects. In a bi-stable picture—such as that of Rubin's vase—the same picture can be interpreted as a light-colored vase or as two dark faces on either side of the vase. We either see a light vase or two dark faces, but never both at the same time. The sensations are identical in both cases, although their cognition is radically different. The cognition depends on how the intellect combines sensations into distinct objects. In one case, we draw a solid boundary around the vase, and in the other, a solid boundary around the two faces. The intellect draws boundaries around sensations and divides percepts into distinct *objects*. The intellect also *orders* the objects, putting one in the foreground and the other in the background. Once the sensations have been divided into objects, we have identified which sensations belong to an object and which sensations must be left out from that object cognition. The memory of prior cognitions now helps recognize sensations as object-types.

The intellect has adaptive capabilities and it helps us cognize objects when we may not have actually encountered an exact object in the past. For instance, we might see a new kind of apple, which looks different from any apple that we have seen before. We still cognize it as an apple because the combination of the sensations has many similarities to the prior cognition of apple. Note how the mind sees red, round and sweet while the intellect perceives an apple. If the apple is green, then the mind will see green, round and sweet while the intellect shall still cognize an apple. The mind and intellect therefore work hand-in-hand acting in complementary ways.

The Nature of the Ego

Higher than intelligence is the sense of ego. The term ego in everyday usage is equated with pride, which isn't a sense but a kind of emotion. Pride arises in the mind as an emotion. The Vedic sense of ego, instead, is a function of the conscious psyche that creates a sense of identity and relates a living being to other living beings and things in the world. The Vedas define two aspects of ego—*aham* or the sense of individuality and *mameti* or things that are related to the individual. Philosophers often talk about *intentionality* in the sense of ownership of experience—this term was first introduced by Franz Brentano— and this is created by ego. When we experience some sensation we know that it is *our* sensation but it is *about* some reality. These attributions are not automatically given by the sensation itself but are added by the psyche at a later point in the development of the experience. Ego is the sense that generates the feeling that 'I am experiencing that thing.' In other words, while the senses, the mind and the intelligence develop the content of experience, ego creates a relation-distinction between self and the world. This self is not truly conscious. It is rather the sense in which we have manufactured our identity out of many known facts such as 'My name is such-and-such', 'I was born in so-and-so country', 'I am employed in this-or-that job', 'I belong to this race', etc. This ego is a conscious set of facts about the self, and not the unconscious covering of consciousness that forces it to think itself as conditioned to be a limited being in terms of space, time, knowledge, abilities and preferences.

The ego can include subtle ideas like 'I am beautiful or ugly', 'I am intelligent or dumb', 'I am rich or poor', 'I am loved or disliked', etc. Coupled to this ego is everything that we regard as 'mine.' We have a sense of ownership or proprietorship over our bodies and properties—both physical and intellectual. We also have a sense of belonging to organizations, societies, races or countries. The ego contains impressions about what I am, the entities that are mine because they belong to me, and the entities to which I belong. The ego adds a personal touch to everything that we are involved with because it divides the world into what is related to me and what is not related to me. We can thus talk about my truth, my action and my pleasure. The ego conditions the intelligence to reason about everything that it regards as 'I and mine' and to neglect or deprioritize things that are outside its limited notions of 'I and mine.' Thus a dear one's suffering may cause us to suffer and their happiness may make us happy. A loss to a friend seems like our loss and the profit of a friend seems like our profit. The ego creates a narrow (I) and an extended (mine) sense of identity and any perceived damage to the narrow or extended identity causes us to suffer while any perceived success to the narrow or extended identity makes us happy.

The sense of ego underlies the notions about property—both physical and intellectual. Ownership of property forms the basis for all legal and economic theories. This sense of ownership is not a physical connection between things. For example, if I purchase a house, I'm not physically connected to the house. Or, if I create a new idea, the idea isn't always connected to my mind. And yet, we establish a connection between ideas, things and people, which become the definition of what makes somebody a unique individual. Our sense of individuality is a memory of who we are. If a person forgets who he or she is, they will have sensations like others, they could think of ideas and experience feelings like others, they could even judge true and right like others, but they will not be able to use their senses, mind and intellect for selfish purposes. The senses, the mind and the intellect give sensations, ideas, emotion and propositions. But none of it is 'mine' until I make it so through the ego.

In Vedic philosophy, intents towards an object are physical and exist in that object. So, for example, when we observe a painting, we call it *Picasso's work* that belongs to the *Paris Museum*. Or when we listen to a symphony we call it *Beethoven's composition* played by the *New York Philharmonic*. Or when we see the *Taj Mahal* we consider it *Shah Jahan's construction* for his wife *Noor Jahan*. During this cognition, past intents about the object must interact with our intents towards them. A creator has a stake in the object that he or she created. Those who observe the creation develop intentional relations with the creator through their creation, and may find themselves admirers of Picasso or Beethoven or Shah Jahan even though they never met them. Intents help us relate objects as Beethoven's composition or Picasso's painting or Shah Jahan's construction. Interaction between the intents puts us in contact with the creators or owners of a work, although the creators are not physically present. The knowledge that some object was created by Picasso, Beethoven or Shah Jahan is public although it isn't physical. The intents are perceived by the sense ego and stored in the go as intents.

The Nature of the Senses

The most well-known aspect of the psyche is sensations, or the experience of color, taste, touch, smell or sound. But there is a considerable debate about how sensations come about. In modern science, material objects don't carry sensations and science doesn't attribute smell, taste, touch and color to objects directly. Science describes the world in terms of *primary properties* such as length, mass, time, momentum, mass, charge, etc. which can be measured in relation to other objects, but not in relation to senses. Measuring instruments register pointer movements or detector clicks that are cognized by senses and presented to us as sensations. We then *interpret* these sensations as the measurement of physical properties. This fact underscores an important difference between physical properties and sensations. The pointer movement is sensation and mass or momentum is properties.

The pointer movement is a translated effect of interaction between physical properties and those properties cannot be regarded as a pointer's properties. That implies a difference between the sensation of pointer movement and the physical properties that are being measured by the pointer movement.

An important problem in the current scientific view of perception is how physical properties lead to sensations. Everyone recognizes that sensations—or *qualia* as they are often called—have a luminescent and affable quality which is absent from the physical world. How can the physical world produce sensations, when matter has no qualities? The perception of color in the eyes is, for instance, mediated by color detecting cones that register different ranges of light frequencies. Three different types of cones register the colors red, green and blue and signal this detection to the brain through electrical impulses. The brain obtains an objective and informational representation of the color but this is distinct from the sensation itself. How does this informational representation lead to the experience of sensation? A commonsense view about perception is that we perceive the color of light directly in hind parts of the brain. This is incorrect, because light itself doesn't go to the hind part of the brain. What travels there are electrical impulses carrying an informational representation of light, although not light itself. This representation always decodes light into three components—red, blue and green—which is similar to how we *digitize* color.

In computers, color is represented electrically as digital signals. A color hue can be denoted by a triplet {R, G, B}. If we read the {R, G, B} color code we would get information about color but not the sensation of color. Color digitization creates a representation of color, which makes it possible to store knowledge of color without the color. Through digitization the brain can hold information about the world, even though the brain is much smaller than the world. Sensation is based on digitized information and not on reality itself. This is because reality cannot enter our brains directly. Human organs are designed to digitize reality and transfer it to the brain where it is stored. Before we can understand sensation, we must know how nature digitizes reality because sensation is based upon a representation of reality but not on reality itself. Senses combine with digitized information and this combination is sensation. Gross matter too combines with information and becomes physical objects. The digitized information thus lies midway between physical objects and internal sensations, and the nature of this information plays a crucial role in the perception of sensations and creation of objects.

Physical objects are created by combining information with matter and sensations are created by combining information with senses. I will describe subsequently that, in the Vedic view, matter is *a priori* formless space-time instead of objects. An object (and its distinction with other objects) is created when space-time combines with information. The distinctness comes from information, and by combining with space-time, information creates objects out of matter. Space-time can therefore be characterized as a void of a specific type of information. In a similar way, senses too are characterized as the void of the same information. Just as space-time combines with information to create an object, the senses too combine with information to create a sensation. The senses are therefore just like space-time although they create sensations instead of objects. Information that lies midway between sensation and objects is digitized information and it interacts with both senses and space-time. This Vedic idea can be used for further developments in science, particularly in the development of the notion of space-time as a carrier of information. Space-time lies between objects and senses, and it encodes information that creates objects as well as sensations.

One important difference between Vedic and modern notions about information pertains to semantics. Physical information is non-semantic. This distinction can be illustrated through an example. Modern science describes sound in terms of frequency and amplitude but in music, we see these sounds as *notes* of music. The same frequency can denote different notes depending on the relation with other frequencies. In other words, the physical property is measured in relation to a *standard* scale of frequencies, while the semantic property is given in relation to any *arbitrary* set of frequencies. Notes are defined via logical distinctions between tones. As a note, a sound has additional properties than as a frequency. To perceive sounds as notes, senses have to account for the context of various notes. The perception of notes requires development of the senses, whereby they can correctly 'interpret' the sounds as notes.

A Theory of Errors

The Vedic theory of cognition is related to its theory of mistakes, errors and illusions. Just as there are various methods of acquiring knowledge via the senses, errors in this acquisition process can also lead to mistaken conceptions about the world. Corresponding to the four levels at which the psyche operates, namely, senses, mind, intelligence and ego, there are four kinds of errors in knowledge. These errors are respectively attributed to imperfect senses, committing mistakes, coming under illusion and the cheating propensity. The errors of imperfect senses are due to senses perceiving something different from what it actually is. For example, different moving observers cannot agree upon the length of an object. We commit mistakes when we associate a sensation with a wrong concept in the mind. For example, we might see a rope but perceive it as a snake. The errors from illusion happen when we judge wrongly the relation between concepts. For example we may think that sweet things are good for health, although they are not good for diabetics. Finally, the cheating propensity means that we create relations between the self and the world in ways that we should not. I may thus regard something to be mine, even though I don't own it.

Obviously, there is no single method to overcome all errors. Vedic philosophy recommends *pratyakṣa*, or observation, and *anumāna*, or reasoning, as two methods that we are familiar with from Western epistemology. The Vedas also profess a method called *śabda,* which is direct observation of forms in matter. This method is unique because it bypasses the organs involved in representing reality within matter. It avoids the need for senses to generate sensations from representations and it avoids errors arising from misrepresentation. Of course, direct perception itself is inadequate if the senses themselves are conditioned by prior experiences in a way that distorts perception. Listening from authority is therefore also considered as a form of knowledge. Of course, if the senses are conditioned, even listening to authority does not guarantee perfect knowledge. The only way to acquire perfect knowledge now is purification of the senses by which they can avoid erroneous knowledge through prior conditioning. The *śabda* method is considered superior and different from experience and reason because we can know things as they exist, without passing them first through organs or reasoning. The development of *śabda* epistemology represents a crucial step forward in the evolution of science where we can know the real nature of things by developing our perceptual faculties.

Much of Vedic philosophy is devoted to finding what is simultaneously true, right and good. The Vedas state that ultimately only God is always true, right and good. A living being must dovetail his life in relation to God, because it makes his knowledge true, his actions right and his experience pleasurable. Much of Vedic literature is therefore devoted to instructions on how a living being can lead a true, right and good life by following prescribed duties. But the Vedas eventually conclude that the goal of human life is to develop one's relationship with God. The conflicts between truth, right and good in the everyday world—which makes the world seem untrue, unjust and unhappy—can be resolved by relating our existence, actions and pleasure to God. The senses, mind, intelligence, ego and consciousness are ultimately meant for the upliftment of the soul.

5

The Formal Cause of Creation

The mind, the senses and the vital force, or living entity,
have forms, although they are not visible to the naked eye.
Form rests in subtle existence in the sky, and internally it is
perceived as the veins within the body and the circulation
of the vital air. Externally there are invisible forms of sense
objects. The production of the invisible sense objects is the
external activity of the ethereal element, and the circulation
of vital air and blood is its internal activity. That subtle forms
exist in the ether has been proven by modern science by
transmission of television, by which forms or photographs of
one place are transmitted to another place by the action of
the ethereal element.
        —A.C. Bhaktivedanta Swami Prabhupāda

Greek Ideas on Form

The notion of a formal cause has a history in Plato's distinction between substance and form. Plato believed that all objects are material, although matter is not the only constituent of these objects, because matter is amorphous and objects have "form." Matter must therefore be combined with "form" to convert it into objects. An ordinary object—such as a clay pot—is comprised of both substance and form; the latter can be loosely equated with the *shape* of the pot. But where do forms reside? Are they coexistent within objects? Or they live somewhere else? The problem that Plato faced is formidable and can be stated as follows. Assume that forms exist in this world. Why do we then call broken pots so? Or imperfect circles as round? Unable to satisfactorily answer these questions, Plato claimed that forms live in a separate world comprised of pure forms. There are ideal pots, pans, houses, cars, and ideal things that we see in the present world. The present world is an imitation of the perfect world of forms. We call imperfect pots and circles by those names because we see a similarity between the perfect and the imperfect worlds. Plato's solution however creates problems about how forms are known. If forms exist in another world, how do we see or hear that world? Plato believed that the world of forms is intuitively known. We apply pure forms to the present world because we know them *a priori* from the pure world. The other-worldliness of forms is problematic, because it does not explain how we come to know them. Aristotle, who succeeded Plato, sought to replace the other-worldliness with the present world. He suggested that forms are immanent in objects themselves. This of course begs the original question of why we call an imperfect circle by that name, but it avoids the other-worldliness. Neither Plato nor Aristotle delved into explaining what they really meant by form. Indeed, this idea has been variously interpreted to mean ideas, besides the uncomplicated notion of *shape* that the distinction with substance leads to.

The notion of form used in Greek times did not distinguish between forms of the world and *forms* of our understanding. *Forms* of understanding are *properties* in terms of which we know the world; for example, color, taste and touch are properties in terms of which we sense reality. The form of the world is not as obvious, and depends on your favorite view of reality. Some believe that nature is comprised of objects; others claim that nature is processes of change, and yet others argue that the world is just sensations. Accordingly, the relation between forms of the world and forms of understanding is explained differently. In science, perception and reality are distinct as primary and secondary properties, but how primary properties become secondary properties isn't very clear. In Kant's philosophy, some forms of understanding—e.g., space, time and causality—are applied back to the external world. And, in naïve realism, the world is just as we perceive it to be. The relation between reality and its perception has become a type of mind-body problem in current science, given that the manner in which science describes matter is significantly different than how we perceive it.

In science, matter is mass, charge, motion, energy, etc. which we perceive as color, taste and touch, etc. The conversion of primary properties in science to secondary properties in the observer is today an unsolved problem. When a meter detects an atomic particle, the perception is that of pointer movement, but the reality is that of a charged particle. So, we cannot apply pointer movements back to reality, although we can interpret them as symbols of something in reality. That something depends on a theory of nature, because in another context, the pointer may indicate a different property.

The Vedic Notion of Form

In Vedic philosophy, the forms of understanding and the forms of reality are related through information that resides in the ether. Material objects are created when ether combines with information and sensations are created when information combines with the senses. Information exists both in the senses and in the ether and can be described by symbols of language. This means that sensations and reality can be described by the same words, although the words don't mean the same thing. To understand this better, consider the equation $A + B = C$. This equation has several possible meanings, depending on the context. Each such context constitutes a *model* in which the equation is true. All these models are isomorphic because the same logical equation holds true in each case, but they are not identical. In the case of information, similarly, symbols can denote material objects and sensations as two different models of the same symbol. In each model, the symbol describes either an object or a sensation, and therefore they have different meanings. And yet, sensations and objects are being described by the same words.

The ability to use the same word to describe different meanings is well-known in ordinary language. The word 'red' can denote an objective fact, a sensation, a concept, a noun, a desire and a pleasure. These interpretations of the word 'red' are all valid, but they are not identical. The ability to use the same word to denote different things is also known in philosophical paradoxes such as the Barber's Paradox where the word 'barber' denotes both an individual person and a class of people who shave others. In everyday usage, the intended meaning of the word is known contextually. This ability does not exist in mathematics, where a number can denote an individual object as well as a class of objects and the inability to distinguish between two different meanings of a number leads to paradoxes when a statement made about an individual is interpreted to be a statement about classes or vice versa[23]. However, if numbers were distinguished from their interpretations (as different models of a symbol system) these paradoxes would not arise.

The Vedic notion of form is based on a language that has several interpretations. The language is called *śabda-brahmān* and its interpretations are called *artha-brahmān*. Interpretations include the elements earth, water, fire, air, ether, senses, mind, intelligence, ego, consciousness, *pradhāna, prakṛti, mahattattva, ahaṃkāra* and *śakti*. A symbol in earth, water, fire, air and ether creates different physical properties (the different ways in which a meaning can be objectivized). The same symbol represents a sensation in the senses, a thought in the mind, a proposition in the intelligence, intent in the ego, and a pleasure in the consciousness. The symbol becomes a personality in *pradhāna, prakṛti, mahattattva, ahaṃkāra* and *śakti*. The philosophical import of this idea is that matter, sensations, concepts, propositions, intents, pleasures and personalities can be described using the same words not because they are identical meanings but because they are different models of a symbol-set. To understand the variety in the universe, one needs to know logically distinct symbols and the various possible meanings of each symbol.

In Vedic philosophy, the world is known not through interaction between senses and the world but by the senses interacting with information. This information represents the form of objects and it becomes the form of our sensation when it combines with the senses. When the senses modify the world, the modification is first represented as instructions for modification in the ether, which are then translated by organs—such as hands, legs, tongue, etc.—into actions in the world. The information is also perceived by the senses of action to create the sensation that we are active. The interaction between the world and our senses is therefore mediated by information that exists in the ether. The ether lies between the mind and the body of Western philosophy and represents an intermediate realm that is objective and yet also semantic. When, therefore, we speak of form, it can mean either the forms of understanding or the forms of the world, and there is a specific sense in which they are the same—they are both based on a common realm of information.

This aligns with the Greek notion of form that exists inside material objects. It also aligns with modern notions of form that are studied in mathematics and physics, where the relations between objects in the world are formulated as logical laws. In science, however, information is not real, and this is an area in which further development is needed in order to solve the mind-body and a host of other semantic problems. Information in Vedic philosophy exists not within matter but in space and time. A new theory of space and time is needed in order to understand the manner in which senses interact with the world by interacting with information in space.

Form and Empiricism

This chapter focuses on the *forms* of understanding, which are different ways in which the observer experiences the world. In Vedic philosophy, the observer knows reality as sensations, concepts, propositions, intents and morals. A naïve reading of these types of knowing leads to the belief that they must involve different words, and hence descriptions of nature. Since different types of descriptions must use different words, they must all be mutually incompatible. This is the basis of the mind-body problem where mind and body are seen as different since they use different words. The mind, for instance, speaks about color, taste, smell, while the body has properties of length, mass, speed, etc. The mind and the body, in this view, can never be reconciled because they are *linguistically* incompatible. Vedic philosophy has some revolutionary insights into this problem, as different types of perception can be described using the same words, although they mean different things. The mind and the body are therefore different meanings, but not different words.

We have seen how a word can describe objects, sensations and concepts, and each time it means something different. The rose is red, it is perceived as red, and it is conceived as red. This fact gives us an insight into higher forms of perception as well. A desire about rose, for example, is also red, as is the happiness from the rose. This is a profound idea about the nature of perception. For example, when we desire a rose, there are not two separate things—a rose and a desire—because their separation will create a mind-body problem of how mental desires and physical roses combine. There is just one thing—the desire—that exists in the *form* of a rose. Similarly, when we judge that a rose is red, there are not two separate things—a red rose and a judgment. There is just a judgment that exists in the form of a red rose. It follows that the word 'red rose' does not just denote an object. It can also denote a sensation, a concept, a proposition, a desire and a pleasure. The same language can be used for a variety of perceptions, but in each case the word means something different. The happiness of rose cannot be reduced to the intention of rose, intents cannot be reduced to judgments, judgments cannot be reduced to concepts and concepts cannot be reduced to sensations. There are several kinds of meanings, but only one language. Words in that language have many meanings, creating sensations, concepts, judgments, intents and pleasures.

The Vedas speak of the sensations such as taste, touch, smell, etc., and this can be misleading because it creates the impression that the senses detect these sensations as bodily organs detect external world objects. For senses to detect sensations, new causal processes would be needed. It also creates the problem that if sensations are detected from matter, then they must be properties of objects, although we know from everyday experience that this isn't the case, since the world of objects doesn't itself have taste, touch, smell, etc., as these are created at the point of sensation. The correct approach to understand the Vedic view is to treat the Vedic description about the creation of sensations as a creation of information.

The Vedic term for this idea is *tanmātra* which literally means 'form only' as I already mentioned in the previous chapter. The term *tanmātra* represents the idea of a *form* that is devoid of matter. When the Vedas speak of the creation of *tanmātra* such as taste, touch, smell, etc., the description doesn't pertain to sensations. It rather pertains to the information which underlies both the sensations and the material objects. Using information, we can say that the form of the sensation is the same as the form of the world, although this form doesn't indicate sensation or matter, but rather information. The creation of *tanmātra* is the creation of forms embedded in the world as objects and into our senses as sensations. The world and its sensations are isomorphic but not identical. By sensing the world as sensations the observer doesn't become the world although he obtains the information that prior existed in matter. The words used to describe sensations can also be used to describe material objects, and while these descriptions have identical information (or knowledge), they will represent different realities.

Different experiences created by language correspond to different forms that language can take. Language can be objectified as symbols, and this creates material objects. Language can also exist as sensations, concepts, propositions, intents and pleasures, which are different kinds of experiences. The varieties of experiences and various types of objects are all forms of language, and they can be described by the same words. The combination of language and space-time creates objects. The combination of language and senses creates sensations. And, the combination of language and mind creates concepts. Furthermore, when language combines with intelligence, propositions are created. By combining with ego, language creates intentions. And by combining with consciousness language creates morality, happiness, goodness and pleasure. In summary, while the Vedic language about *tanmātra* is identical to our language about sensations, it does not represent sensations but forms. The names of the *tanmātra* may seem to describe sensations, but these actually represent various kinds of information, which combine with senses and matter to create sensations and objects.

Science studies the physical properties of objects. But thus far scientists have kept away from explaining how we know the world in everyday experience. Science has been content with one kind of properties—called the primary properties (objective, measurable properties like momentum, mass, energy, charge, etc.)—as the only valid set of properties. Everything else, color or taste or smell included, it is believed, must be reduced to the primary properties, although such a reduction is in most cases yet to be carried out. Science straight-forwardly assumes that any experience for which there is no primary property does not require an explanation. This is the bias of assuming that because primary properties can be directly applied to the world, these are the only valid properties in terms of which to know, and all other *forms* of understanding are irrelevant to knowledge of the world. This seems justified, although as any scientist will say, the primary properties of science are *not* the *forms* of our understanding. Consciousness does not understand or experience momentum, mass, energy, charge, etc. Measurements do not say if a detector click or pointer movement is mass or energy. *We* interpret pointers and detectors as detections of physical property. Thus, Berkeley said that all so-called primary properties are derived from secondary properties (color, smell, taste, sound, touch). Actually, only secondary properties are known; but *we* interpret secondary properties to be revelations of primary properties. But for that science assumes that primary properties exist in objects even prior to measurements. This construal is now known to be false, because different observers moving relative to each other will measure different values of length and temporal duration. It is impossible to assert that measurements discover an observer independent reality. To bring realism into science there should be a difference between phenomenal properties and noumenal reality although they are different embodiments of the same information. A measurement, if correctly carried out, represents the world to us as information.

The difference between the scientific and the Vedic approach is that in science some properties are *real* but in the Vedas all properties are potentially real; all properties present to us the form of the world. There are some properties, however, that are *fundamental* because other properties can be built by combining them. In science only fundamental properties are real, while other properties are unreal. In the Vedic view, all properties are real although some properties are more fundamental than others. The Vedic descriptions pertain to fundamental properties, which combine to create other properties. While it is customary in science to derive properties from an analysis of the objects in the world, it is customary in Vedic philosophy to arrive at fundamental properties through an analysis of experience. The quest for properties in experience brings into focus all elements of experience that can and should be explained. This quest must include not just primary properties but other properties currently outside science. The Vedas base fundamental properties on the wide applicability of these properties, quite similar to the idea of objective properties in modern science.

A property defines the form of experience because we experience the world in terms of the property. In effect, I see the world as blue because I see it through blue goggles. Changing the goggles would change the perception. When we choose different properties to explain reality, the measurement context defined by the new properties will create different experiences. How do we then fix the properties in terms of which we will know the world? The Vedic answer is that the properties in terms of which we *should* experience are already fixed by the manner in which consciousness *can* experience the world. The possibility of measuring other kinds of properties and seeing the world in terms of those properties is only a theoretical possibility because knowing the reality in other ways requires different kinds of senses, and abilities to experience in those ways, which don't exist. The abilities of consciousness fix the properties of the world in experience. This seems very Kantian, but there are differences. Kant posited that we know the world in standard ways due to categories in terms of which we *conceptualize*. But the Vedic limitation is both sensual and conceptual. So we must sense the world in terms of sight, sound, taste, touch and smell, because these are the ways in which consciousness can sense. These also become the ways in which we formulate concepts about world.

Properties are important because they allow us to distinguish objects. Science aims for a complete set of properties, because that set will tell us about all ways in which things can be differentiated. So a complete set of properties is the collection of all possible ways in which objects can be identified. Ideally, a complete theory of nature should use all properties given in the complete set. Most current theories are however far from close to this kind of perfection. Classical mechanics, for instance, does not use *temperature*. Thermodynamics similarly does not use *charge*. Biology does not use *mass* and *velocity*. This means that none of these is a final theory. They work well in some cases but will not work in others. A universal theory must employ all possible properties from the complete set because it is expected to explain all possible experiences, which include all kinds of sensations. Physical properties are the entities in terms of which the world must be explained. So an exhaustive list of physical properties is an essential precondition to a universal theory, as these properties must be accommodated in the said theory.

But how do we find the complete set of properties? Given that a universal theory would explain any kind of experience, one possible approach is the exploration of conscious experience itself. If there is a physical property that can be used to distinguish one thing from another, then it must be incorporated into the complete set. But this would lead to a very large number of properties, as we use many different notions to distinguish things. Thus, while we are searching for properties, we must also aim to minimize the property set. Notably, also, since we are looking for the essence of experience generically, and not of any individual experience, these elements must transcend individual conscious experience. That is, the search for properties must look for the basic ingredients of conscious experience that appear across different kinds of experiences. It is easy to see that this method of finding a complete set of properties is not a very practical one. We are limited to a human viewpoint in experience and there can be difficulties about which human way of distinguishing is more fundamental. Instead of proposing a generic method of discovering properties, thus, I will simply rely on the Vedic revelations. In the Vedic view, a complete set of properties means the fundamental *modes* in which we can sense, conceptualize and act.

Sensation and Forms

The Vedas describe two kinds of sensations—knowledge and action—which are perceived by two kinds of senses, namely the senses of knowledge and action, respectively. The properties of knowledge are revealed by the senses of knowledge (eyes, nose, ear, skin, tongue). The properties of action are similarly those used by the senses of action to manipulate the world. Knowledge properties are ways in which we know the world; action properties are ways in which we manipulate the world. For example, we know the world by hearing, seeing, tasting, smelling and touching while we manipulate the world by holding, walking, speaking, sex and excretion.

Two important things need to be noted here. First, action also involves sensation. While acting we don't just conceptually know that we are acting, but we actually *sense* it. Second, just as we associate concepts with sensations of knowledge, we can associate concepts with the senses of action as well. The concept 'yellow' is applied to classify yellow sensations and the concept of 'holding' can be applied to distinguish sensations of holding. Here, I will focus on forms of knowing, and leave forms of acting to a later effort. The ideas developed here can be applied for forms of action as well.

The sensations of knowledge come to us through five senses—hearing, touching, seeing, tasting and smelling—and this distinction is the first way in which the division of concepts is fixed. In the Vedas, the five senses of knowledge are organized hierarchically. This organization gradually manifests information in Ether as sound, touch, sight, taste and smell. That is, all the information about sensation exists in Ether, but it is manifested into objects gradually. Ether itself manifests only the sound portion of the information as objects. Air manifests information about sound and touch. Fire manifests information about sound, touch and sight. Water manifests information about sound, touch sight and taste. Finally, Earth manifests all the information that was originally present in the Ether.

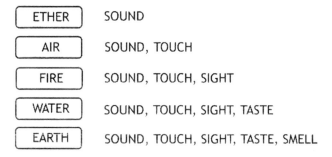

ETHER	SOUND
AIR	SOUND, TOUCH
FIRE	SOUND, TOUCH, SIGHT
WATER	SOUND, TOUCH, SIGHT, TASTE
EARTH	SOUND, TOUCH, SIGHT, TASTE, SMELL

Figure-5 The Hierarchy of Sensations

Sound is the first sensation. From sound, we derive five properties—tone, form, pitch, distance and direction. The information
in sound is expressed as tone, form and pitch, and words in language are combinations of tone, form and pitch. The Ether creates
a physical object of this information called sound. Words are sound
objects which embody information into the physical properties of
pitch, tone and form. When the same information combines with
the senses, it creates the sensations of pitch, tone and form. In effect,
information in matter is expressed as physical properties, detected
as physical properties by organs and then stored in the senses
as sensations.

MODES OF SENSATION					
HEARING	TONE	PITCH	VERSE	DIRECTION	DISTANCE
TOUCHING	HARDNESS	HEAVINESS	ROUGHNESS	DIRECTION	DISTANCE
SEEING	COLOR	BRIGHTNESS	SHAPE	DIRECTION	DISTANCE
TASTING	FLAVOR	INTENSITY	FLUIDITY	DIRECTION	DISTANCE
SMELLING	ODOR	INTENSITY	AROMA	DIRECTION	DISTANCE

Figure-6 Modes of Sensations

The second property of touch gives us sensations of hardness,
heaviness and roughness. Things that can be touched can also be
heard, because the information that expresses touch is a development of sound. The object of the touch information is therefore called
Air because we can both hear and touch air, although this label could
potentially be misleading as it is not the air we breathe. The third
property of sight gives us sensations of color, brightness and shape.
Brightness or intensity can also stand for the perception of heat.
Things that can be seen can also be touched and heard, because the
information that expresses sight is a development of sound and air.
The object of visual information is called Fire because fire represents
both heat and light, which is responsible for objects becoming visible
as form and color. The fourth property of taste gives us sensations of
fluidity, flavor and intensity of taste. Things that can be tasted can also
be seen, touched and heard because the information that expresses

taste is a development of sound, touch and sight. The object that expresses taste is called Water because water plays an important role in the detection of taste. The fifth property of smell gives us sensations of odor, intensity of smell and perception of odors combining to create aroma. Things that can be smelt can also be heard, touched, seen and tasted. The object that expresses smell is called Earth because ordinary earth can be perceived by any of the senses as sound, touch, sight, taste and smell.

While the names of these objects have everyday meanings, these meanings do not depict how these words should be actually understood. These words denote scientific concepts expressed in ordinary language. For example, the word wave or field in classical physics has a different meaning than in everyday parlance. In everyday usage, the notion of a field evokes images of cows grazing on grassland and the word wave gives the impression of oceans rising and falling. If we were to think of fields and waves in these metaphors, we would get a crude picture and semblance of what is being indicated but we would be far from grasping the true meaning of what these words mean in physics. Similarly, Earth, Water, Fire, Air, and Ether have different meanings than everyday things. They are objectifications of sensations. If we see an object as red, there must be something in the object that makes it seem red to us. That property in the object is Fire. Fire is a type of property, of course, differentiated by information into many colors, shapes, shades, etc. Similarly, if I find that something tastes sweet, there must be something in that object that makes it seem sweet to me. That property in the object is Water. Water is again a class of properties, which will be differentiated by information into several types of flavors.

Concepts and Forms

Higher than sensations are concepts, perceived by the mind. Everything that can be known through a sensation can also be known as a concept. For instance, the sensation of 'yellow' can be known as both a sensation and concept and the word 'yellow' can denote either. In what way are concepts then different from sensations? If you see yellow, then the sensation and concept are both yellow, and they seem identical. The cognition of yellow may use the mind, but it does not actually need the mind. But if you read a book, while you see shapes and colors, you actually derive meanings that are different from those shapes and colors. Now, sensations and concepts are different, and a mind is necessary to even cognize the meanings in a book. Concepts and sensations use the same words, but concepts are different from sensations because a concept can be denoted or represented by a sensation that is quite different from the way the concept may have been originally formed. Take for example two colors, red and pink; these two can be both sensations and concepts. Furthermore, take two genders, male and female. Again, these two can also be sensations and concepts. Finally, use red to represent male and pink to represent female. Red and male are both concepts and sensations. But using the sensation red to denote the concept male requires the mind, because the senses (seeing, tasting, touching, smelling and hearing) cannot grasp maleness from redness.

Generally, all concepts are formed by generalizing sensations. Once the concept has been formed, however, the rigid association to sensations can be dropped. For example, we can look at square and circular objects and form concepts of square and circle. Once the concepts have been formed, these concepts can be applied even to objects that are not perfectly square or circular. In addition, the idea of square and circular may also be conveyed through means other than showing circular and square objects, in a way similar to how the concept of male and female can be conveyed through colors. At this point, the concept has been generalized to an extent where only a distinction between tokens is needed to see them as symbols of the concept. The ability to convey a concept using physical properties not equal to properties from which the concept was originally created forms the basis of all knowledge representation. If concepts were always applied to objects with corresponding sensations (e.g., the concept of a circle to perfectly round objects) we would always need a circle to convey the idea of a circle. No one could *think* about the circle, because to think a circle, the brain would have to become circular. Knowledge representation requires the ability to convey one concept using quite different physical properties.

In ordinary language, various concepts are conveyed using letter shapes.

The mapping between a sensation and a concept is created by the mind which sees some physical property as a *token* of another meaning. Unlike the senses which see sensations in the world, the mind interprets the world as symbols of meaning. To achieve this, the mind 'reads' the world in terms of a language of signs. This language of signs is context-sensitive. For example, the word 'momentum' and 'cycle' have different meanings in physics and in business. The same token— in this case words that have physical properties—are associated with different meanings. The association is not arbitrary, but it is also not fixed. It is rather a property of the *context* of interpretation which the mind provides by fixing the *domain* of the symbols. There are distinct domains of science like physics, chemistry, biology, medicine, etc. Each of these domains is divided into many sub-domains. A domain is completely specified if a given set of tokens can be unambiguously given a meaning within that domain.

In mathematics, symbols may be given a meaning by associating them with a particular domain of interpretation, also called the *model*. Generally, every symbol system allows many interpretations, in which the same token has a different meaning. To fix the model of the symbol system, a particular type of interpretation must be chosen. The mind picks the vocabulary that interprets the tokens into their meanings. The physical properties of tokens may not be related to the meanings of those tokens within the model. But, generally, the mind sees these relations, which the senses do not. The mind sees that red denotes passion, green denotes prosperity, blue denotes eternity, yellow denotes intellect, and so on. This insight is based on the fact that redness and passion have a similar form. The mind sees these similarities which the senses do not. The mind is therefore able to use physical properties to represent meanings.

Meaning and reality can, therefore, be created from the same physical material, although the mind perceives this matter context-sensitively while the senses see the same matter independent of contexts. However, the senses can only perceive a single sensation while the mind must perceive a collection of sensations because meanings only arise within a collection of sensible objects.

Propositions and Forms

The mind, however, does not combine elementary concepts to form propositions. For example, 'all men are mortal' is a proposition, comprised of the elementary concepts 'men' and 'mortal.' The mind understands 'men' and 'mortal' while intelligence understands the proposition. The mind, therefore, does not know the truth of propositions, which the intelligence judges by comparing propositions to reality or beliefs (these beliefs are called axioms in a formal language). In the symbolic view of reality, both propositions and reality are symbols. A proposition that combines elementary concepts is not pre-determined by those concepts. Indeed, the same concepts can be used to create different propositions. For instance, the words in a vocabulary can give rise to many different sentences. The meaning in the sentence, and indeed the meaning of each symbol in the sentence, depends on the *order* in which the symbols are combined.

Meanings are formed in collections of objects, which are logically consistent within the collection but may not necessarily be consistent with other collections. Intelligence compares concept collections to check if different concept collections are consistent. Since both the mind and reality consist of such collections, the consistency check between these collections can include a check whether our mental theories align with the nature of reality. The check can include whether two scientific theories are mutually consistent. They can also involve the question of compatibility between two different individuals, organizations or societies, as different symbol systems. In playing this role, intelligence does not necessarily merge two distinct domains of thinking into one. For example, the check whether our physical theories are consistent with the nature of physical reality may not dissolve the difference between the theory and reality. Similarly, the check whether a physical theory is consistent with a biological theory may not collapse the separation between physics and biology. The consistency check is only whether these two domains can co-exist simultaneously in harmony or not.

An individual domain of concepts is created by the mind. Our everyday experience contains several such independent domains. Intelligence combines these concepts to create propositions and measures the differences between the domains and harmonizes them. Intelligence is the sense in which different information domains exist in the same world and must therefore be consistent. By making them consistent, or showing that they are inconsistent, intelligence relates the world of ideas across different domains. Intelligence generates theorems out of the axioms in a theory, and then checks whether different axiom systems are consistent or discordant. If the two axiom systems are theory and reality, then intelligence assess the truth of a theory against the nature of reality. If the axiom systems are just two theories, intelligence sees if these theories are consistent. The intelligence produces propositions that are true only within the context of an axiom system. It also checks whether the axioms themselves are true, given other axiom systems.

When a sentence has multiple meanings, the intelligence can interpret the sentence as distinct propositions. It will then relate which of these propositions may be true[24]. If a single proposition is altered, then other propositions may no longer be consistent with it. By deriving the truth of a statement, intelligence judges if the observer can believe in the statement. Of course, intelligence does not derive every possible proposition from first principles. There is a ready cache of beliefs from which other propositions can be constructed. This cache of beliefs is called *smṛti* or memory which is one of the functions of intelligence. If the beliefs are true and the logical derivation is complete, the intelligence arrives at correct conclusions, called *nischaya*. If the beliefs are false, or the logical derivation is incorrect or incomplete, intelligence can also create false conclusions called *viparyaya*. When propositions are being created but they are not being judged to be true or false, the intelligence is said to be asleep, and this is also called *svapah*. The symptom of waking up is that intelligence doubts the truth of propositions, and this feature of intelligence is called doubt or *samsaya*.

Intelligence also relates actions to their context, and judges whether some action is syntactically and semantically well-formed. Judgments about actions depend on the rules and procedure that apply to the context, time and place. For instance, the notes of music and the order of musical notes changes with time, place and situation. What is considered a grammatically well-formed proposition in one context may not be well-formed in another, because the meanings associated with words in that context determine what is well-formed. For instance, most countries stipulate different tax filing procedures for different income groups. Using a procedure incompatible with your level of income makes your filing ill-formed[25].

Intentions and Forms

The intelligence is capable of creating and validating propositions but it does not know which type of proposition to create or validate. The intelligence is a semantic computer that is consistent and complete but does not have a goal. The ego provides that goal by supplying intentions to intelligence. Intentionality has two forms. First, intentionality denotes aboutness. In this role, the ego connects a proposition to an object and concepts thereby become *names*. For instance, the proposition "The sun rises in the East" has some meaning and it may also be proven true based on semantic and logical facts. But for this proposition to be *empirically* true, it must refer to some facts in the world. The ego establishes the connection between a proposition and its referenced objects. It converts a proposition of concepts into an empirical proposition. Second, intentionality denotes goals or purposes. By giving goals to intelligence, the ego focusses the semantic computation towards a solution to a specific problem. An observer's intelligence is therefore not engaged in finding a solution to problems for the sake of solving them. The ego mediates and decides which problems are relevant and useful to the observer. The first role of ego connects a proposition to the external world while the second one connects a proposition to the proposition's owner.

The ego creates and perceives relations of ownership or proprietorship. Through these relations, the ego attributes changes to the world as changes to itself, because the ego *identifies* with the objects it considers itself related to. For instance, we call something *Picasso's painting* or *Mozart's symphony*. Similarly, in society, there are notions about ownership of property, even intellectual property, which form the basis of our legal systems. These intentional relations between objects and their owners, creators or controllers are a property of the ego which results in impressions of "I" and "mine."

The ego is the basis of the survival instinct in living beings, because ego has the property of self-preservation. Gross matter, the senses, the mind or the intelligence don't have the self-preservation tendency, but the ego does. Evolutionists posit that the fittest being survives but they can't explain why a living being wishes to survive. Evolution cannot explain at which point in the development of complexity the sense of identity and survival emerges. In Vedic philosophy, the sense of identity and the need for survival is not an emergent property, but a fundamental property that is manifested when the ego is present. When a living being dies, the entire subtle body comprising the senses, mind, intelligence and ego leaves the body and the body no longer has the need to survive. The ego therefore plays a crucial role in the creation of the need for self-preservation.

This need for self-preservation exists not just in individuals but also in organizations, and an organization is the extension of the personal and individual egos by which people become related to each other and become organized so as to compensate for shortcomings in the organization as a whole. The ego of the organization is an emergent property, but it emerges from the individual egos of its members, stakeholders or other well-wishers. As organizations become large, there are more egos involved and the organization becomes more and more resilient to change for its self-preservation.

6

The Material Cause of Creation

Descartes...never attained to a full understanding of his own words (quantum in se est), and so fell back on his original confusion of matter with space—space being, according to him, the only form of substance, and all existing things but affections of space.

— James Clerk Maxwell

Scientific Realism

Material causes appear to be the easiest to comprehend, but they have proven to be the trickiest. By definition, a material cause is the substance out of which things are made. If a potter is shaping a pot, clay and water are materials that constitute the pot. The difficulty, however, lies in how to distinguish clay as a substance from the properties that define something to be clay. The properties of clay lead to sensations by which we detect the presence of clay and they include distinguishing features such as density, stickiness and malleability by which we can tell clay apart from other sorts of soil, for example. Clay is however also the substance that "holds" or "carries" these properties. It is the agency, so to speak, that stands *behind* the façade of phenomenal properties—like a puppeteer's hand responsible for the puppet's actions but remaining invisible during the puppet show. This notion about the material cause leads to an interesting question: If matter stands behind the façade of appearances, then how do we know its existence? If we have never seen it standing behind, how can we even know that it indeed exists?

In the scientific view, we know the world through sensations, and matter is the reality that causes sensations. This reality, however, cannot be sensed. This leads to the problem that if we cannot sense reality, how do we know that there is a reality? What is matter over and above the properties by which we sense it? Immanuel Kant termed this as the contrast between phenomena and noumena. The noumenon is the reality that stands behind the phenomena. Given that we only have direct access to phenomena, it seems superfluous to suppose that there is indeed a noumenon apart from sensual properties. This is the trouble with the material cause: it is hard to define what we mean by a material cause in a way that the definition would be useful in the search of these entities. But, if there is no reality beyond phenomena, then the world is a phantasmagoria. We are imagining the world, and we could not talk about the nature of reality. In fact, we could not even communicate with others, because even the idea that we perceive others would be a hallucination.

Science handles this problem in a peculiar manner. Given that it cannot postulate a material substance, science postulates *object-concepts*. Object-concepts include things such as particles, waves, quanta, fermions, bosons, quarks, etc. Then science conjures properties—such as position, momentum, energy, charge, etc.—and it attributes them to the object-concepts. Object-concepts are not matter, but science believes that these are notions *about* matter. This is an important point that is often misunderstood and requires some careful consideration. In everyday thinking, we conjure a two-stage process by which objects are created. In the first stage we have matter but no objects. In the second stage, objects are created out of matter by giving matter some form. Science foregoes the two-step everyday approach given the difficulties in postulating matter and supposes that the world is directly fundamental objects. That is, just as we think of the world as consisting of tables and chairs, science postulates the existence of some fundamental kinds of objects, akin to tables and chairs but much more fundamental. Typically, we would think of objects as in turn comprised of matter, but science does not do that. Rather it assumes that because object-concepts are themselves very fundamental objects, there is no need to in turn look for a material substance out of which they are comprised. The substance hypothesis postulates the existence of "stuff" out of which objects are created in assorted ways. Science substitutes the substance → objects thesis directly with objects by supposing that there are indeed fundamental objects although no substances. The underlying assumption is that matter is already individuated at fundamental levels. So if we visualize these fundamental object-concepts, we don't need the hypothesis of a material substance[26].

But how do we know that the world is indeed comprised of these fundamental objects? The answer is that we never actually know, because we never directly grasp the concepts, given that our knowledge only uses sensations. When a theory is empirically successful, we *presume* that the world is actually built up of these object-concepts. The reality of an object-concept is therefore indirectly entailed by the success of the physical theory that employs it. It is effectively saying that if I can make correct predictions using a particle based theory then I am justified to believe that particles are indeed real. Of course, concepts play an important role in aiding the *human understanding* of science. Human understanding is important for popularizing science, for drawing pictures of motion and depicting causal interactions that explain how things are connected causally in the world. So while object-concepts add little value to the stated scientific goals of "making predictions" (object-concepts are not directly involved in any of the predictive mathematics itself), these concepts nevertheless help us *understand* a scientific theory. Object-concepts also aid intuitions about further developments to a theory by cross-pollinating ideas with other theories. For example, particles and waves are analogous to solid balls and water waves, and theories that employ these concepts can be understood by relating these concepts to everyday intuitions about solid balls and water waves. Similarly, theories that employ object-concepts that cannot be related to everyday intuitions (such as quanta) seem fraught with problems of interpretation despite empirical successes.

The scientific approach makes ordinary concepts epiphenomenal. Since the world is already individuated as fundamental object-concepts, those are all that exist or can exist. Ordinary non-fundamental object-concepts like tables and chairs are built out of fundamental objects, but they have no role in science. In fact everyday concepts aren't considered real because there is nothing corresponding to them in the world. Everyday concepts exist only in our minds. This view of science has had widespread detrimental effect on the role of concepts within science, philosophy and linguistics. Scientific reductionism reduces everything—including ourselves—to fundamental object-concepts, and minds with meaning, in this view, emerge from a fundamental realm of objects. The fundamental realm itself is devoid of meaning. For instance, this realm does not have *representational* properties. Fundamental objects describe themselves, but they cannot describe other objects. If everything in the world describes itself and nothing else then there is no meaning in the universe. Our perception of meaning must be an illusion or a crafty construction out of things that are otherwise meaningless.

Yet another problem in current science is related to two observers seeing the same reality differently. If we know the world through sensations and two observers have different sensations, how can we assert that they are seeing the 'same' reality? If two people disagree on the color of the sky, before they can have a meaningful conversation they have to agree that they are at least talking about the same sky! In everyday language we individuate reality separately from sensations (the basis of this individuation is not clear, but the difference between appearance and reality does exist). Through this individuation we know that we are talking about the same object before we express our disagreement with others' views about that object. That individuation is missing in science because object-concepts don't express the individual object, but the type of object. Physical properties do not individuate the object because they are always changing. Thus, we have physical properties that are always changing and object-concepts that are the same across many objects. There is no way of individuating the objects, by which we can say that if an object moved from point A to B, then it is the *same* object that moved. This leads to the problem that if two people disagree on observed properties, there is no way to distinguish the cause of their disagreement. Are they disagreeing because they are observing the same reality differently? Or are they are disagreeing because they are observing different realities?

Science works because we *assume* that when two people are looking in the same direction they must be seeing the same thing. But if observers were light years apart they could not easily know if they are observing the same thing or different things. Their disagreements about the nature of observation could not be resolved because they could not refer to the object they are seeing independently of the sensations by which they detect its presence. This problem is caused by the fact that sensations and concepts are not enough to *identify* objects. Sensations are not enough because an object presumably produces many sensations, and we don't know how to connect these together into an object[27]. Concepts are insufficient because many individual objects are described by the same concept; indeed, science aims to reduce everything to one concept.

Two observers must know that they are seeing the same object before they can talk about it. For instance, if we say that 'Object X has the momentum Y,' we need to know what X is. X is a way of distinguishing the object without knowing its properties (e.g., momentum). That doesn't exist in science today, because we can only speak about properties, but not the identity of objects without properties.

Matter Is Phenomena

Vedic philosophy solves the identity problem by adopting an approach opposite to that taken in science. In Vedic philosophy, matter is not a substance, an individual thing, or even reality. Matter is just phenomena, on similar footing with sensations and concepts, although more objectivized than sensations and concepts. Sensations and concepts are defined in relation to an observer's senses and mind, but matter can also be defined in relation to other objects. This constitutes the basis of current theories of science that are formulated in terms of physical properties measured against other objects. But, unlike science that treats these objects as real, Vedic philosophy does not. Material objects in the Vedic view are not immutable, unchanging things because objects are created and destroyed. Even fundamental objects are known to be spontaneously created and destroyed from the energy field in atomic theory. Matter is therefore not reality. Matter is a phenomenon like sensations.

Then what is reality? Only consciousness is real, as it is immutable and unchanging. It is real because it is never created and will never be destroyed, it always exists individuated, and the individuality of consciousness never changes. Consciousness creates phenomena through choices but the person or individual underlying those phenomena remains unchanged. Sensations, concepts and the body are all phenomena in this view; the Vedas state that the senses are produced from the mind and the body is further produced from the senses. The body is also the experience of consciousness, and it is therefore just like a sensation or a concept, although more objectified. Now we might ask: If the body is a phenomenon, then who perceives this phenomenon? There cannot be phenomena without perception. And reality—we believe—is not perceivable. Then how can reality be a phenomenon? This goes straight to the problem of realism in science which arises because reality cannot be perceived.

In Vedic philosophy, however, reality is perceived by another type of sense called *prāṇa* on which I will elaborate in the next chapter. *Prāṇa* allows us to perceive that there is something "out there" even when we can't see, hear, touch, taste, smell or think about that. In the West, this phenomenon is known as clairvoyance which is defined as the ability to gain information about an object without sensing it. Martial artists are taught to perfect their *prāṇa* (or *Qi* as it is called in Chinese) to perceive the enemy without sensing them. *Prāṇa* is extra-sensory perception, and it acts as another kind of sense that can create and perceive reality. In Vedic philosophy, there are two kinds of extra-sensory perceptions—(a) the mind, intelligence, ego and consciousness, which are beyond the senses, and involve the perception of meaning that sensations don't provide, and (b) the *prāṇa* that perceives matter because matter too cannot be sensed. But, this matter is not reality as believed in current science, because material objects are not eternal. They are created and destroyed, but they exist, just like sensations and concepts. *Prāṇa* can perceive and modify objects without senses and mind. These objects exist in the ether which is the basis of other elements.

The short answer to the problem of scientific realism in Vedic philosophy is that material objects are not reality. They are phenomena that exist beyond the sensations, and to perceive these phenomena another kind of sensory capability is needed. This capability perceives objects as they exist prior to being *sensed* by the senses and the mind. In that respect, the nature of things as they exist prior to being sensed and known exists in Vedic philosophy.

Realism and the Brain

The problem of scientific realism creates difficulties in understanding the mind. The mind sees the world in terms of ordinary concepts. It can also understand fundamental concepts, but most of the everyday transactions with the world involve the use of ordinary concepts. But if the mind uses the brain to interact with the world (or even if the mind is the brain, as modern materialistic theories hold) then we have the problem that reality is fundamental concepts and, at the same time, the mind is capable of holding both fundamental and everyday concepts. If everyday concepts can exist in the brain, then why can't they exist in reality? The solution of this problem needs a rethink on the distinction between fundamental and ordinary concepts. Specifically, fundamental concepts cannot be more 'real' than ordinary concepts, especially since both types of concepts, and the objects to which they apply, are phenomena.

The same problem exists for sensations as well. Scientists believe that the sensations of length, mass, momentum, energy, etc. are real but the sensations of color, taste and smell are the observer's creation. Assuming that the brain helps us perceive the sensations of color, taste and smell, these sensations must somehow exist as properties of the brain. But if they can be properties of the brain, then why can't they be properties of external objects in reality?

The major issue in studying the observer scientifically today arises because matter and the observer are described by two different *languages.* The language of science includes words like position, energy, momenta, mass, etc. which is different from words like color, taste, smell, etc. which are used to describe sensations. To map these words, there has to be some scheme in which sensation words are reduced or converted into matter words. Unfortunately, such a scheme has not been found. And many philosophers now argue that this reduction will never be possible, because the qualitative aspects of sensations and the semantic aspects of concepts cannot be reduced to the physical properties being used by current science.

In Vedic philosophy, the problem is solved by describing reality by the same *words* as sensations and concepts. Thus, if I sense an apple to be of red color, the redness is not just in my mind, but can also be applied to reality. Western philosophy calls this view *naïve realism* because properties in the observer are applied back to reality. But the Vedic view is not *naïve realism* because it does not say that sensations and matter are identical. Sāṅkhya philosophy distinguishes between senses, *tanmātra*, and material elements. In naïve realism, matter is identical to sensations or *tanmātra,* but that is not the case here. Material elements are rather created from *tanmātra*, which is information about sensation. During sensation, the information is present in the senses, but the same information existed earlier in material objects. The sensation, matter and information are described by the same words, but they are distinct things. Vedic philosophy can therefore be called *naïve linguistic realism* because it applies the same words back to reality, without equating physical properties with sensations. This idea rests upon the notion of information which can exist both in matter and in the mind.

When the brain represents a sensation, it encodes the same information as the object to which that sensation is ascribed. Thus, the apple is red, the brain is red, and the sensations are red because they all have the same information about redness, which has an independent existence even outside matter, the brain and the senses. That information can exist as concepts, sensations and objects. Therefore, sensations, matter and concepts are not identical even though they can all be described by the same word. The problem of describing the knower and the known using the same language is thus solved by mapping the language of knowing to the language of the known. This allows us to describe the brain state in a way that is correlated to the state of reality, avoiding the problem of having to reduce the meaning of science to the meaning of perception.

Vedic philosophy describes matter in terms of properties and concepts that we can *directly* relate to our native abilities to sense and understand. This means that the Vedic theory uses a view about matter that describes objects directly in terms of sound, touch, sight, taste and smell. The world is meant to be known, and consciousness is not an afterthought. Matter therefore is intended to facilitate experience, and reality conforms to the manner in which consciousness can experience. To better understand this view, we need to ask not only what matter is but also *why* matter must exist at all. In other words, why is there something rather than nothing?

We have seen earlier that the reason for the existence of matter is that consciousness needs to know and express itself. To fulfill this need, matter must conform to capabilities in consciousness through which a soul can express his inner meanings and know the world as those meanings. Matter must thus be formed in such a way that everything in the universe would always be knowable and usable by the abilities in consciousness. If something was unknowable or not usable, it would be redundant for the purposes of consciousness. If, on the other hand, the capabilities in consciousness would far exceed the ones in matter, then there would be some meanings that we could never know and express through matter. A difference between the native capabilities of matter and consciousness would limit or hinder the purpose for the existence of matter in the first place, namely to facilitate self-knowledge and self-expression.

The Problem of Communication

Current approaches to the study of reality focus on *what* matter is but do not ask *why* matter must exist. What philosophical or scientific purposes does the existence of matter fulfill? This question is not asked in Western philosophy and the nature of matter is, therefore, derived from observation rather than questions about necessity. We can however ask: Why does matter exist? What are the *justifications* for the existence of matter? The notion of matter given in Vedic philosophy is an outcome of trying to answer this question.

Matter helps us climb out of the prisons of our own experiences;

if our experience corresponds to matter, then we are not alone in the world; there are other people and things that can also perceive what we perceive. Of course, this appears to be a human reason for postulating the existence of matter: we postulate matter to overcome our loneliness in the world. Is there a scientific problem over and beyond these needs? The modern philosophy of science denies the existence of any such need for reality. Science, it claims, is exhausted by discovering predictive laws, and predictive laws correlate state preparation with measurement experiences, neither of which is concerned with reality. The philosophy of science view is that as long as laws make correct predictions, we don't need reality. But this is where philosophy makes a mistake. Science is not an individual activity but a collective one. If I as a scientist made some implements and found them working for me, the assumption is that they should work for every other individual. The state preparations done by me should be observable by another individual. In other words, to practice science, we must be able to agree with others on the outcome of measurements based upon state preparations.

The problem of science is preeminently one of *communication*. When one scientist carries out a state preparation that is observed by another scientist, they have communicated information from one consciousness to another through state preparation and measurement. To communicate, there must be: (a) an objective reference to talk about and (b) a bridge that connects observers. The first overcomes ambiguity in knowledge and the second facilitates a channel for information to pass through. A thesis of matter must then come forth as filling the above two needs. The real need for matter is that it fulfills the need to communicate and gives an objective reference for that communication. The objective reference allows us to know if the meaning indicated in communication is true. Communication can be seen as overcoming loneliness, but it is also a scientific need to agree upon experiments and communicate results in the scientific community. If I find scientific results, they are not valuable unless other scientists can reproduce them. Communication is necessary in science because science is a social activity. While science aims to explain the world, it presumes the existence of the world to communicate observed results. If we can communicate, we must *explain* how communication is possible. Meanings can pass from one mind to another. How do they transcend somebody's awareness?

Communication cannot survive ambiguity, so there must be an unchanging reference. Communication also needs a message path that transports meanings from one consciousness to another. If communication is real, then messages must be real. Philosophers have generally emphasized the reference aspect of knowledge; they believe that to communicate there must be objective things about which we can talk. If there is no reference, the *truth* of the communiqué cannot be verified. They somewhat ignore the fact that there must be a *connection* between observers to transport meanings. A message connects experiences across individuals. Without a communication channel observers cannot communicate. It would be moot to think about the *truth* of what is communicated, because this truth depends on the other party receiving a message. While questions of truth and reality are justified, these questions must also address the possibility of communication. After all, one may merely be communicating ideas, feelings or experiences that do not yet have any external reference. Though the truth of these cannot be verified, it seems erroneous to deny that such communication is possible.

In fact, these two aspects of communication (an external reference and a channel for transport) can be combined if we say that *matter* is both the objective reference and the channel of communication. It leads us to the view that *matter is a communications channel*. In this view, when some meanings have to be communicated, they must go through matter. When a meaning originator sends a meaning to a receiver, he or she must use matter to encode his message; at this time, matter is a communication channel. When this message is received, the receiver uses matter as an objective reference to decode the meaning out of the message; at this time, matter is an external reference or reality. That is, the receiver decodes meaning out of a message as if it were a *property* carried by matter.

This view is in line with everyday intuitions about the world in which we create artifacts (books, music, pots, etc.) for communicating meanings. When this idea is extended, even ordinary artifacts of this world—e.g., tables and chairs—can be regarded as communicative acts of semantic construction. So a table or chair is a message that someone created by encoding information into matter. When others receive this message, they see information encoded in a table or chair as the *property* of the matter that constitutes these objects. The two views about matter (a) that it is a communicative medium and (b) that it is an external reality, are reconciled as two phases of a communicative paradigm in encoding and decoding a message.

Communication takes place correctly when shared conventions are followed and common knowledge is used in encoding and decoding messages. Miscommunication happens when messages are not interpreted according to the rules by which they were encoded. These ideas can be extended to an understanding of reality. In science, the outcome of measurement experiments depends upon prior state preparations. Communicatively, state preparations encode a message which is decoded during observation. Matter is both objective reality constructed by state preparation and the medium used to pass messages. The idea of science and the idea of communication are simply that state preparations and measurements can be carried out by different individuals. When I prepare a state that is measured by another observer, I have encoded a message that is decoded by him or her. Matter is a medium that transports messages without distortion[28]. Communication works if we share the conventions involved in interpretation. When knowledge used in interpreting a message differs between the sender and receiver, messages will be misconstrued. The world is now a combination of medium and message, the message being carried in a material medium. The medium is matter and the message is the information in it.

This idea has a parallel from Greek times. Greek philosophers Plato and Aristotle distinguished *matter* from *form*. The Greek idea was that there are a few substances—which Greeks called Earth, Water, Fire and Air[29]—that constitute the medium. But how do these few substances give rise to a huge variety of objects? The Greek answer was *form*. Form adds onto the substance and converts it into an object. The form here is the message. *Matter* or substance is thus the medium and *form* is the information carried in that medium. A lump of clay can be shaped into many kinds of pots. The difference between these pots is not in the substance that constitutes them but in the *form* that *informs* the clay into pots. A pot is therefore not merely clay, which is the substantial ingredient of the pot. The pot involves an additional level of reality, which is information. When information is added to substance, an *object* is created. This object is a complete message that can be transported. Another person can look upon the pot and know that it is a pot, can appreciate its beauty, and can use it to barter for other things. But substance and form cannot be experienced in isolation. The substance cannot be experienced because it has not been organized into an object; it is amorphous. *Form* cannot be known because it does not have any sensual properties; it is abstract. So we have two things—one that is physical but amorphous and the other that is conceptual and abstract. When we combine the amorphous with the abstract we get an object that can be sensually perceived and conceptually known.

Serializing Information

When ideas exist in the mind, or in the senses, they are generally grasped as a unit. The idea of a man or woman, or ideas of yellowness or circle exist in the mind and senses as a single concept and percept. But, when this information has to be communicated, it cannot be transferred as unit. To communicate, the ideas have to be *serialized*. An artist serializes a form into a painting through incremental strokes of the paint-brush. A musician serializes his insight through notes and words of a song. An author serializes his ideas through words, sentences, paragraphs and chapters in the book. The perception of a circle must be serialized by defining an origin and a radius as two separate values. The perception of a color must be serialized by defining relative proportions of RGB color hues. What is perceived as a single idea, color or form, may need many symbols.

To serialize information, a physical space and time are required. Many ideas can be serialized simply through static shapes in space. Words in a book are examples of how information can be serialized simply by forms extended in space. Extension is therefore a basic *requirement* for matter, because to objectify information we need to represent information as extended forms. When elementary forms have to be combined to create complex propositions, serialization includes time. Symbols are ordered in time to create propositions. The need for the existence of space and time arises from the need for communication. The external material world must be extended as space because information has to be objectified as forms, which require space. It must be extended as time to create complex propositions from elementary symbols. Space and time are now the medium in which we can encode and represent ideas. These ideas may be observed by others, enabling communication. Descartes also defined matter as something that is extended; he called matter as *res extensa* as opposed to the mind called *res cogitans*. But Cartesian extension was stipulated as a matter of fact, not as a necessity arising out of needs for communication. The extended substance objectifies and serializes ideas and percepts within a thinking substance.

Forms in space will not have a causal efficacy if there was no energy in them. This energy exists in objects as vibration, rotation and spin. The existence of energy, therefore, implies the existence of time[30]. There is, however, a difference between the time needed for vibration, rotation and spin and the time needed to serialize the symbols as propositions in time. In a sense, the time required for vibration, revolution and spin is 'within' the symbol, while the time needed to serialize symbols into complex propositions is 'in between' the symbols. Similarly, there is a difference between the space 'within' a symbol that represents its extended form, and the space that exists 'in between' the symbols to make them distinct objects. There are thus two notions about space and time needed to represent meanings—to denote extension and distinction.

In classical physics, the distinction between these two types of space and time is collapsed as the objects are point particles which don't have any extension and hence no ability to denote meaning. Space and time are thus treated as containers of objects and not carriers of information. Sāṅkhya philosophy treats space and time as carriers of information. Meanings can be encoded in space and time because extension, location and directions can themselves represent meanings. The extended form in space-time is a vibration which can denote a phoneme. The spatial distance between such phonemes can represent their meanings and the temporal order amongst phonemes represents a proposition that joins the symbols. Spatial distances amongst propositions represent the logical consistency of propositions and the temporal durations between propositions represents the evolution of meaning or computation. In this way, space-time is the most fundamental reality. Its forms, locations, distances and durations represent various types of meanings.

In modern physics too, the most fundamental reality is space-time, but this reality is non-semantic. Matter in this space is a modification of the space-time vacuum. But since space-time is non-semantic, matter in the space-time is also non-semantic. Space-time is, therefore, a medium of physical but not semantic communication. Additionally, since objects are a modification of space-time, the objects are not real. We can only claim that objects emerge from space-time and dissolve back into it. This raises fundamental questions about causality: What causes the objects to emerge and dissolve? In classical physics, change was caused by physical properties which impacted objects through force and the objects were persistent. Now, matter itself is created and destroyed. The classical notion of causality is totally lost when matter is reduced to space-time.

But, in another sense, with the semantic view, a new notion of objectivity is born, one which physicists don't yet recognize. In this notion, space-time forms are symbols. Everything we perceive is produced from this objective information. The reality behind sensations is not a material substance, it is not an object, and it is not eternal. We can say that behind the ordinary phenomena of everyday sensations is the phenomenon of vibrations in space-time.

Five Material Elements

The Vedic view of matter is that all objects are created from space-time, when *tanmātra* are added to space-time. Forms are added by the senses, under the control of the mind, which is controlled by the intelligence, which is controlled by the go, and ultimately under the control of consciousness. Consciousness too is, in turn, under the influence of Time which governs the unconscious body of the living being. This influence of Time should be seen as serializing information in the unconscious body by bringing out ideas that are latent in the *chitta*. The serialization proceeds from the *chitta* all the way into the Ether. The Ether itself should be seen as serializing the *tanmātra* as vibrations. Space-time is therefore the channel of communication and information is exchanged between observers through space-time. Science that began as the study of matter ends in space-time forms. These forms can be understood if the idea of information is separated from its physical expression as a vibration. In other words, forms in space-time should be seen as *symbols* that objectify information which originally existed in the observer.

To encode various sensations (taste, touch, smell, sound, sight) we need to find methods of objectifying these sensations as space-time forms. Ordinary shapes are used to denote meanings in language. The vibration, contraction, expansion, rotation, translation and revolution of these forms can further represent meanings. Once these meanings can be understood, they need to be classified as meanings that represent the sensations of taste, touch, smell, sound and sight. The vibrating space-time forms will correspond to the Vedic material elements. These forms can be thought of as representing information about sensations. In Vedic philosophy, the information that corresponds to the sensation and cognition of smell is denoted by the element *Earth*. Information that corresponds to the sensation and cognition of taste is denoted by the element *Water*. Similarly, the information for form, touch and sound are denoted by elements called *Fire, Air* and *Ether*, respectively. These elements are not substances (unlike Greek philosophy) and they are not things (unlike naïve interpretations). These elements are created by objectifying *tanmātra* and they encode them as symbols.

Space and time are the medium and their modifications are the message. A space-time form is therefore a message in a medium. The message is created from the medium and disappears into it. Every sense brings with it multiple types of sensations. The sense of sight for instance helps us see color, shape, brightness, distance and directions. Other senses similarly encode different types of sensations. Information about various types of sensations therefore also involves a hierarchy where first the type and then the value of information must be encoded. Earth, Water, Fire, Air and Ether are generally described as encoding the types as sensed by smell, taste, sight, touch and sound respectively. These elements, therefore, are not monolithic entities but can be highly differentiated as information about different sub-types and sub-sub-types are added.

Because they provide the medium on which information can be superposed, each of these carriers of information can be character-ized by the lack or void of the kind of information superposition it supports. Thus, Earth is the smell of odorlessness; Water is the taste of tastelessness; Fire is the form of formlessness; Air is the touch of touchlessness; Ether is the sound of silence. The senses, mind, intel-ligence and ego are also subtle material elements characterized by the lack or void of information. The sense of smell, taste, sight, touch and sound are respectively void of information of smell, taste, sight, touch and sound. The Mind is the state of meaninglessness, Intelli-gence the state without judgment (called *svāpah* or sleep) and ego the state devoid of intention. These may appear self-contradictory, but the contradiction is only apparent. Each kind of matter is a different type of medium that encodes a different type of information. In the exter-nal world, information creates space-time forms. Within the observer, information creates sensations and meanings. A particular smell is a sensation generated from information superposed on a type of space-time form called Earth from where it can be extracted by the organ nose. A particular taste is the sensation generated from the infor-mation superposed on a type of space-time form called Water from where it can be extracted by the organ tongue. A particular color is the sensation generated from information superposed on a type of space-time form called Fire from where it can be extracted by the organ eye. And so forth. The medium and the information together constitute a message. The information in this message is extracted by organs and represented in the brain. When this message is grasped by the senses, then sensations are created.

The material carriers therefore do not carry sensations and the Vedic view is not the same as naïve realism. Earth does not hold the sensation of smell, because, if this were the case, these objects would have to be described as sensations. The element instead holds infor-mation *corresponding* to smell which is *perceived* by the senses as smell. This information can be perceived differently by different observers creating interpretations of reality. Furthermore, different interpretations of reality by different observers (or even the same observer) can be explained on the basis of the difference in how the observer's senses interact with the information.

In Locke's empirical thinking, each object is directly a collection of certain sense-data. For example, an apple is the collection of a certain kind of taste, form, color and size put together. But this gives rise to two kinds of problems: (a) what an apple is prior to being sensed as sensations of taste, smell, color, etc., and (b) why different individuals perceive the same object differently. Locke said that the notion of objectivity of an apple is just a *word* we associate with the sensation of taste, smell and color. There is nothing objective corresponding to an "apple" over and beyond these sensations. When this idea is extended, it leads to positivism, namely that there is nothing real about electrons, protons, quanta, etc. All these are simply words that we associate with sensations. This leads to the view that there is nothing real apart from sensations. In the Vedic view, instead, there is a reality underlying the sensations of apple. This reality is that which *informs* space-time into an object, which is also a space-time form. While Earth, Water, Fire, Air and Ether are different forms that make an apple, the *objectivity* of *apple* is not in space-time. It is rather in the information that makes the medium into a message.

The objectivity of an apple is the information about an apple. Earth represents the part of this information that corresponds to the smell of an apple. Water is the part of this information that corresponds to the taste of an apple. Fire is part of the information that gives rise to the color and shape of an apple. Air is the part of the information that gives rise to the texture of an apple. Ether is the part of the information that creates the name 'apple' by which the object can be distinguished. The apple is a space-time form. The mind and the senses can pick up information from the material elements and generate concepts and sensations from those forms.

It should be noted that everything that can be smelt can also be tasted, seen, touched and heard. Everything that can be tasted, can also be seen, touched and heard. Everything that can be seen can also be touched and heard. Everything that can be touched can also be heard. Therefore, when the sense ear interacts with Earth, Water, Fire, Air or Ether it obtains sound, but the matter corresponding to that sound is different each time. In the case of Earth, it will obtain a sound-sensation of smell words (e.g., sweet, pungent, sour, etc.). In the case of Water, it will obtain a sound-sensation about taste words (e.g., hot, sweet, sour, bitter, etc.). In the case of Fire, it will obtain sound-sensation about words of color and form (e.g., redness, square, long, etc.). In the case of Air, it will obtain sound-sensation about words of touch (e.g., rough, hot, hard, etc.). In the case of Ether, it will obtain sound-sensations about words of sound (e.g., notes, phonemes, etc.). The same information can therefore be perceived in different ways, each time creating different types of sensation. The information in Earth when perceived by the nose gives the sensation of smell. The same information when perceived by the tongue gives a taste, which is a mapping of smell into taste. That information when perceived by the eyes gives rise to color and form, mapping the smell into sight. The same information when perceived by the skin creates a touch sensation, mapping the smell into touch. When perceived by the ear, the same information leads to a sound, mapping smell into a sound. Thus, when we smell good food, we are also able to imagine its color, taste and textures. Similarly, in a neurological condition called synesthesia, patients may associate colors with sounds, or personalities with numbers.

This presents two interesting possibilities: (a) that without sensations, we may obtain a conceptual knowledge of the world by reading information in matter, and (b) there may be sensations generated by the senses that interact with this information unmediated by sense organs. An example of the first possibility is a book that gives conceptual knowledge of reality and may describe the world as touch, smell, taste and color even though sensations corresponding to these descriptions are not present. An example of the second possibility is that the organs of a person may be defunct, but the person can still see, hear, taste or smell by interacting with the world through senses, without interaction through the organs.

An interesting question at this point is that if all the information is already present in the elements and can be read by the senses, then do we even need organs to collect this information separately? The answer to this question is that even though all the information is present in the elements, our senses are not that developed to directly interact with matter. Nature has therefore given us organs which are specialized in reading one particular form from one specific type of material element. Thus, skin is specialized to read information about touch, and eyes are specialized to read information about color. Even if the senses cannot read everything from the elements, these organs extract the information from different material elements and store them as symbols of reality as chemical elements within the brain. The neural circuitry in the body and the brain is designed to use the organs to collect this information.

But this doesn't eliminate the possibility that someone could actually read all the information directly from the elements and still have the same sensations and understanding about reality as gained through organs. Then it would be possible to taste food without putting it on the tongue, see color without opening the eyes or when the surroundings are completely dark, or feel the texture of an object even without touching the object. Someone who can do these things has no need for the gross body of sense organs. His subtle body of senses together with the elements would suffice. Such a person would extract information through the interactions of senses with elements. In fact, if the senses are developed, they can sense the information in objects and convert it into sensations without bringing the gross body in physical contact with the objects of these sensations. Such a person can have unlimited sensations uninhibited by whether his bodily organs can actually contact those objects.

Symbols in Matter

If all knowledge is based upon communication, then all communication depends upon symbols. Semiotics—developed in parallel by Saussure and Pierce—pioneered the idea that everything in the world is a symbol. Semiotics argues the universality of symbols based upon the observed fact that nothing in the world has meaning by itself unless interpreted so. This, however, incorrectly leads to the view that the world cannot be known as it exists because all knowledge is *interpreted*. It implies that the universalizing tendency in science is incorrect: there is no objective reality that can be known because all knowledge is interpretation. This extreme position is false because even if the world is symbolic and amenable to interpretation, these symbols were originally *intended* in some particular way by the message encoder. So a message *can* be variously interpreted, but that does not eliminate the possibility that there is indeed a uniquely valid interpretation[31]. On the other hand, the scientific construal that every scientific measurement reveals objective *a priori* properties of the world just because laws of science are successful is also wrong. The properties that science measures were originally put into the world by state preparations. The success of science can be compared to the correlation between the encoding and decoding procedures in a communicative act. By state preparation we encode symbols in matter which are revealed during measurement. The order in science tells us how to encode symbols so as to detect them in measurement. It does not preclude a possibility of someone encoding different messages and then finding different results in measurement procedures. A semantic interpretation cannot be *post-facto* added upon a subject-independent conception of reality. Rather, the concepts of reality must accommodate the interaction between subjects and objects to arrive at a semantic interpretation. While semioticians believe that this so-called subject is a living human being, it applies equally well to measurement devices which are designed to decode information from the physical world. The meaning generated in a measurement procedure depends as much on the measuring device as on the measured system.

The ideas leading from symbols to contextual interpretation are part of semiotics, although semiotics does not treat meanings naturalistically. Semiotics believes that the symbolic domain is created by humans. Semiotics thus treats tables, chairs, books and culture as human symbols, but it does not take a radical leap to treat the objects of science also as symbols, requiring interpretation and understanding. This radical leap is made in Vedic thinking which does not distinguish between human-made and natural objects as far as their symbolic status is concerned. In fact, the Vedic argument for symbolism is deeper than a human need to interpret. The world is symbolic because matter can be used for communicating. Communication requires channels and channels carry symbols for someone to sense and know them, as we might put a parcel on a train expecting it to reach its destination. This argument—for semiotics—is stronger than the argument from a human need of interpretation. It implies that symbols are not just things that are created by human beings for human consumption but even natural objects are symbols, including the ones that the physical sciences study.

In the Vedic view, symbols can be understood in various ways corresponding to each channel of communication. The symbol can be heard, tasted, smelt, seen and touched, depending upon how the information is represented and extracted. Based on a hierarchy of channels of communication, the symbolic information communicated through these channels is also hierarchical. The symbols that can only be heard correspond to the information carried in Ether. Symbols carried in the Air element can be heard and touched. Symbols carried in the Fire element can be heard, touched and seen. They are followed by symbols that can be heard, touched, seen and tasted because they are carried in the Water element. Finally there are symbols that can be heard, touched, seen, tasted and smelt as they are carried in the Earth element. Since carriers are hierarchical, a carrier has the properties of the previous carriers. Thus, symbols are not special types of objects; rather, all objects are symbols.

Matter encodes information symbolically prior to interpretation. This symbol is created by gradually objectivizing the properties of consciousness. Information or language originally begins in the choices of consciousness. In consciousness, they represent the search of personal meaning and pleasure. Gradually the personal meanings and pleasures are objectified into intents, propositions, concepts, sensation and, finally, space-time forms. The objectivized symbol in space-time is different from the sensation, proposition, intent and morality. It has reached a point where every property in consciousness is removed. This matter is totally unlike consciousness and there are no further steps to objectify the symbol (objectification being defined as the process of stripping consciousness of the properties of consciousness one at a time). Matter is thus created by removing subjectivity from consciousness. This is the opposite of what scientists currently believe—namely that consciousness is created by adding complexity to matter. At the very least, we must recognize that matter and consciousness are not the only categories needed; there are several categories in between that connect them.

Epistemological Problems

The informational view described here requires us to think of the world as symbols. A symbol is anything that can be tasted, seen, touched, smelt and heard. Since matter doesn't exist as sensations, but as space-time forms, converting them to sensations involves an act of interpretation by the senses. That is, the senses must be able to extract and represent the space-time form as information in the senses. This interpretation may, however, be flawed, leading to misperception and errors of judgment. Even if the symbol is sensed correctly, it may still not be understood correctly. This is because the meaning of a symbol is not identical to its physical properties; a sign like 'red' denotes the meaning of redness, but is not red itself. The conversion of sensations to meanings requires acts of interpretation as well, which are also context-sensitive; in this case, for example, the meaning depends upon the language used to encode meaning. Further levels of meaning from concepts—such as judgments by intelligence, intentions by the ego and the perception of pleasure by consciousness may also be mistaken because they rely on the interpretations of some prior level of sensation which may be mistaken.

Today, philosophers of language recognize that there are no objective means to decipher meanings other than to interpret them from sensations, which are also interpretations of reality. The Vedic epistemology is, therefore, based upon hearing from the perfect source, which can transmit information directly to consciousness, instead of objectifying it through layers of phenomena and then subjectivizing those phenomena into ideas. When information is transmitted directly between two souls—and the Vedas are replete with descriptions of such occurrences—this situation does not suffer from the problem of interpretation of phenomena into reality. Such information is not objectivized and subjectivized through layers of matter. It is rather directly transmitted as meaning between souls.

In physical communication, the same meaning can be communicated in various ways through different media: a book can be printed on paper or imprinted on a magnetic disk. Today, communication relies exclusively on matter. But there can be communication that relies on concepts. Communication is the act of sending and receiving symbols. These symbols are encoded in matter. But in the way science is practiced today, concepts cannot be encoded because present science is based upon the manipulation of matter and not that of concepts. In modern science, when we communicate meaning, we exchange matter, not concepts. Concepts are *interpreted* from these sensations, and this is fraught with problems. How can a person ever be sure that they interpreted the meaning correctly? The Vedic notion of *śabda* is pure sound and it exists in consciousness as choices. Information transfer unmediated by the senses, mind, intelligence, ego, and other unconscious instruments is *śabda*. The perfected soul is capable of pure communication and he can impart the eager listener information without encoding it in matter.

7

The Systemic Cause of Creation

Power is the faculty or capacity to act, the strength and potency to accomplish something. It is the vital energy to make choices and decisions. It also includes the capacity to overcome deeply embedded habits and to cultivate higher, more effective ones.

—Stephen Covey

The Problem of Causality

We saw in the previous chapter how the notion of matter in science leads to the problem of causality. The problem arises because causality in science was traditionally associated with objects, which had physical properties, which exerted forces, and which caused changes to the state of other objects governed by the universal laws of science. However, if objects and their properties are reduced to forms in space-time, then the question of causality also shifts. Earlier, the question of causality was about how an object causes another object to change. But, now, since objects can be created and destroyed from space-time, causality is that which causes an object to be created or destroyed. The effect of an object on other objects (which was so far considered as causality in science) is now subordinate to the question of how objects themselves are created. While causality earlier dealt with the influence between objects on each other, the reduction of objects to space-time changes the notion of cause. The effect of an object on another object is simply the dissolution of one object and the creation of another one. The real question now is: What causes the *synchronized* creation and dissolution of objects? This question is essentially unanswerable in science except by supposing that there is a causal agency outside space-time.

In Vedic philosophy, space-time is the 'field' of activities where events are created and destroyed. This field of activity is however orchestrated by Causal Time and *prāṇa*. The Causal Time (with a capital T) and the phenomenal time (with a small t) are different in Vedic philosophy. The Causal Time is the script of the universe which pre-decides which events will occur when. The phenomenal space-time is created as events. The past, present and future are simultaneously real in the Causal Time, but only the present is real in the phenomenal time. The script of Causal Time, however, does not decide who will enact or participate in the events. Participating in the events has to do with the choices of consciousness. The choices of consciousness are conditioned by their *karma* and personal predispositions (the Personal and Efficient Causes), and Time acts on them to impel a living being to take advantage of opportunities created in the phenomenal space-time. The script of Causal Time represents *roles* in which living beings can participate. The cosmic drama is fixed by Time, but the participants in that drama are not.

Living beings are free to choose to participate in the cosmic drama, subject to the availability of roles and their *karma.* However, a living being can reject a role, even if the role is being offered by Time and their individual *karma* allows them to fulfil it. This rejection is ultimately the expression of a living being's free will.

The connection between a living being's subtle body and the gross material situation is made by another element called *prāṇa* which is the entity that connects the senses of a living being to a material body and its physical situation. *Prāṇa* converts sensations into space-time forms, and space-time forms into sensations. The choices of consciousness are eventually expressed in *prāṇa* which is said to carry the subtle body of the living being. When a living being dies, *prāṇa* carries the subtle body to a new gross body. *Prāṇa* also carries the subtle body from one gross body to another within the present life. This is because the bodies at two different locations in space or instances in time are different bodies. Recall that material objects are produced from space-time and they dissolve into space-time. A

living being's body therefore appears and disappears from moment
to moment. *Prāṇa* represents the sense of *continuity* that we
feel even though the consciousness hops from one gross body to
another.

Prāṇa solves the problem of causality of how matter transforms
from one state to another. The transformation is essentially the dissolution of one form and the creation of another. The body therefore
does not *move* from one point to another or from one state to another.
Rather, one body is destroyed and another one is created. The subtle body of the living being is also not fixed, because all our thoughts,
intentions, emotions and sensations are changing. All these changes
are *discrete*. *Prāṇa* connects the discreteness of the changes in the
subtle body to the discreteness in the gross body.

You might now ask a question: If the gross body changes because
there is a subtle body, then why does the gross body decay when the
subtle body leaves the gross body? If the *prāṇa* has left the body at the
time of death, then the changes to the body must stop. To understand
the answer to this question, we must first understand what we mean
by a body. The body is, essentially, information. This information has to
be maintained by the presence of a subtle body. When the subtle body
leaves the gross body, the information is gradually destroyed. Inherent
in this destruction is the fact that Time always destroys information.
Time is said to be the representation of Lord Shiva who is the destroyer
of the universe. When the subtle body is present, this destruction
manifests in the conversion of *karma* into activities, whereby *karma*
is destroyed. Of course, when the subtle and causal bodies are present and the living being acts under the influence of Time, new *karma*
is automatically created. This *karma* is new information created by
the presence of consciousness which partakes in activities impelled
by Time. But when the subtle body is absent, Time still destroys the
information in matter although new information is not being created anymore. The gross body therefore decays when the subtle
body is absent.

Time thus constantly destroys information and the living being
creates it. Whatever the living being creates will eventually be destroyed by Time. Since the destruction and creation
occur through the same activity, the living being persists in the

cycle of changing bodies, within one lifetime or from one life to another.

The Five Life Airs

The actions of *prāṇa* on space-time cause different types of effects which are described as different types of *prāṇa*. These are collectively called *pancha-prāṇa* or five airs. The term 'air' represents a particular type of process. These processes are named after their effects within the human body, although *prāṇa* is not limited to within the body. These five airs are called—(a) *prāṇa* which performs the activity of ingestion, (b) *apāna* which performs the activity of elimination, (c) *samāna* which performs the activity of digestion, (d) *vyāna* which performs the activity of circulation and assimilation, and (e) *uḍāna* which performs the activity of creativity and the production of useful things by using some matter. Together, the five airs constitute everything that a system must do, because they cover ingestion, digestion, elimination, circulation and creation. Imbalance in the role of these five airs leads to diseases. The notion of *uḍāna* or creativity as a process is somewhat unique to Vedic thinking because it connects one living being to others. The creative products from one system are inputs to other systems, and this inputs and outputs aggregates to create larger and larger systems.

It is important to see how this process description of a living system complements the description in terms of material elements. There are five material elements in Vedic philosophy, called Earth, Water, Fire, Air and Ether. The *prāṇa* air is the cause of ingestion and is related to the element Air. The *apāna* air is the cause of elimination and is related to the element of Earth. The *uḍāna* air is the cause of expression and creativity and is related to the element of Ether. The *vyāna* air is the cause of circulation and is related to the element of Water. The *samāna* air is the cause of digestion and is related to the element of Fire. The five elements constitute the material description of a system and the five airs represent a causal description of the same system. If matter is present but airs are not present, then the body is dead because it does not perform the activities of ingestion, digestion, elimination, circulation and production. At the time of death, the five airs leave the material body and carry the subtle body comprised of senses, mind, intelligence, ego, consciousness, and the unconscious to the next body. This means that out of the six causes, five causes persist. Only the sixth—the material cause—is left behind. Thus, not only is consciousness eternal, but five out of six material aspects of a living being also persist in the face of death, although they are changing and are not eternal.

In the new life, the five airs gradually build a new body, subject to and influenced by the nature of a living being's desires, self-image, unconscious faculties and abilities, and the subtle body of mind, intelligence, ego and senses. This is easily understood because *prāṇa* is the causal agency between sensations and objects, and the gross body is therefore affected by *prāṇa*. By perfecting and modifying the *prāṇa* one can, therefore, modify the working of the body. Large portions of the Vedic practices on *hatha-yoga* and *prāṇayāma* are designed to alter and fix the workings of the five airs. Simple practices of breath regulation give very good results in terms of controlling a disturbed mind, and can be successfully used by people even when they are not aware of the philosophy and science of *prāṇa*. These practices can also be used to treat chronic illnesses.

Prāṇa and the Nature of Life

The Vedic theory of *prāṇa* illustrates the big gap that exists between a materialistic view of the material body and the living individual view of the same body. In the semantic view, the gross body is manifest based on a subtle body—i.e. senses, mind, intelligence, ego and consciousness. The connection between gross and subtle bodies is made by *prāṇa* which maps sensations, concepts, judgments, intents and pleasures into the physical body. When *prāṇa* leaves the body, the body loses perception because the gross to subtle mapping depends on *prāṇa*. Many documented reports about people having out of body experiences are narrations about *prāṇa* leaving the gross body and carrying the subtle body of senses, mind, intelligence, ego and consciousness with it. In the out-of-body experience, the person sees his body from the outside. Since the subtle body has left the gross body, the gross body is seen as unconscious. The reports of out-of-body experiences illustrate that the perceptive capability is not in the gross body but actually in the subtle senses and the mind. The gross and subtle bodies are, however, connected by the *prāṇa*.

The activities of *prāṇa* form the basis of the science of reincarnation where *prāṇa* carries the subtle body to a new gross body, and under the influence of *prāṇa* the gross body is developed based on the subtle body. The Yogi who has perfected the control of *prāṇa* can choose the time and place of his death. He can also choose the type of body he wishes to enter after leaving the present body. The control of *prāṇa* therefore constitutes the basis of a science by which a person can control his body and manipulate matter, unmediated by the senses and the mind. Those who do not understand the science underlying the use of *prāṇa* will generally consider these actions as miracles and may confuse it with spirituality. However, in Vedic philosophy, *prāṇa* is a material energy by which consciousness can control matter, but it is not spiritual. It can however purify the consciousness of its attachment to matter, because the Yogi can see that he is not the body, but only connected to the body by *prāṇa*. The Yogi can also see all associations to the body—material possessions, relationships, stature in society, etc.—are irrelevant as compared to the ability to remain detached from the bodily concerns.

The Vedic view shows that the gross body is created by choices, because there is no causality in matter. The laws of matter are about the effects of one choice on other choices, because objects are created due to choices. The idea that objects act automatically on other objects is a view that predates the reduction of matter to space-time properties. Unfortunately, this physical view continues in chemistry and biology because the scientific and philosophical implications of advancements in physical theories have gone unnoticed by the mainstream scientists working in other fields.

The distinction between living and non-living systems is a matter of hot debate in biology. Of particular interest is the point at which a bag of chemicals becomes a living body. Many people treat life as something sacred, and wonder whether they should apply the ideas that they apply to living beings also to cells, viruses or other rudimentary forms of life. Is an embryo living? Diverse opinions on the distinction between the living and the non-living exist today. These include the idea that a living being must have the ability for sensations, emotions, thoughts and creativity. In the Vedas, in addition to consciousness, the mind and the unconscious, the ability of matter to function as a living system—i.e. ingest, digest, eliminate, circulate and produce—is also a difference vis-à-vis non-living matter. These activities convert a dead body into a living body, although they don't exhaust the fact that a living being is conscious. The five airs represent the first and important distinction between living and non-living systems, although the five airs are also material.

The Cycles of Consumption

The Vedic view of *prāṇa* creates the basis of studying matter in terms of systems that input raw materials and output useful products and waste. The output of one system becomes the input of another system, creating cycles of consumption within matter. The cyclic view of material transformation differs from current science in two ways. First, the cyclic view of matter creates a cyclic appearance of time based on repetitions of events of ingestion, digestion, circulation, assimilation, elimination and creation. Second, it reinforces the idea that waste eliminated from a system must be regenerated back into useful raw materials that can be consumed by other systems. The systems view of matter is an ecological view of nature rather than an inorganic approach generally used in physical sciences. The ecological view is physical although it differs from the physical views where matter evolves randomly or linearly. In the ecological view, the evolution is neither random nor linear. The evolution depends on systems that produce and consume. These systems are interconnected in a way that the output for one system is the input for another and thus matter circulates in cycles.

We are systems and we live within systems—be it society, organization or family. A system is an interrelation of activities overlaid on matter. If we look at an individual's body, for instance, we will find that the matter in the body is always changing but the system remains intact. All systems follow a similar process: they intake ingredients to build themselves, then break down ingredients into basic useful components and remove what has become redundant or undesirable for that system. A system can be described in two ways—(a) as matter that builds up a system and constitutes all its internal components and (b) as systemic *causes* that sustain a system as a living entity. The term 'living' here may not necessarily be identified with a living being's body but any system whatsoever. Of course, the living body is a prime example of a living system, although we could apply the same principle to an economy or a city.

All living systems exist in a cycle in which the system consumes and excretes matter but also uses the ingested matter to produce (ideally) useful things. They are called useful because these things are ingested, consumed and then excreted by a living system, while producing consumables useful to other systems. No living system lives in isolation. They are interlocked into complex cycles of give and take, which are structured into more and more complex higher-level giving and taking. For instance, there is a cycle of give and take between people within an organization, and a higher level cycle of give and take in between organizations. The organized world *circulates* matter in many ways through these levels of organization, such that matter enters and exits the boundaries of systems. Beginning with the living cell that ingests food, oxygen, water, etc., and excretes waste, there are many complex levels of organization such as organs and systems in the living body, an economy that circulates raw materials, goods and money, a society that circulates cultural artifacts and an ecosystem where one living being is the food of another living being. In all these cases, the principles of functional organization of the system remain relevant to a system's working.

Scientific reductionism reduces these complex functional processes to the *steps* that make them up. Each step involves a small physical transaction, such as a chemical reaction, electron impulse transfer or the motion of molecules. The reductionist claims that the complex processes of matter circulation in the living body, economy, society and ecology as a whole are nothing but the individual physical transactions strung together in a meaningful sequence. The reductionist further claims that these things came to be interconnected as a matter of chance, but stayed connected because it facilitated the survival of all living beings. This view of matter is incorrect on two counts. First, it still assumes that objects are acting according to mechanical forces, which is false in atomic theory because we can predict the probability of a change but not its cause. The probabilistic description only says which changes are possible without saying what cause selects amongst the various possibilities. Second, it doesn't see a role for semantics and mind within matter. The biological view discards meaning and choice from our vocabulary, which must play a central role in fundamental theories of matter. These two problems can be solved by attributing causality to choices. Matter only stipulates its possible uses and ways in which it can change. These possibilities are actualized by choices of consciousness.

There is another problem in thinking of interconnected cycles as being tuned by evolution. The problem is that a small change in one of the outputs will cascade through the entire system and create large scale impacts even for small changes, because interconnected systems are governed by non-linear dynamics. We see that interconnected cycles maintain coherence in the face of ongoing change. Many thinkers have suggested that the ability in living systems to maintain their form is because there is some higher level control that sustains it. But what is the nature of this higher-level control?

We are not aware of or consciously control various mechanisms in cells or in the body. We automatically feel hungry, the blood circulates without our knowledge, and we continue breathing even during deep sleep. Digestion is an unconscious process and so is immunity. The body appears to function on its own even in the face of continuous adversity. Postulating higher level controls for things that are happening without our knowledge would seem incorrect because the control isn't conscious. Of additional importance is the fact that the processes sustaining a system are distributed and not centralized, although we think of control systems as centralized entities. We cannot thus attribute the systemic organization only to control systems although there is certainly control involved through the use of choice in all living systems. What we need instead is an understanding of the nature of cyclic processes of matter circulation that sustain systems in the face of change.

Life Air and Vitalism

The theory of *prāṇa-vayu* is not unique to Vedic thinking and it has been articulated in the past as the notion of *vitalism,* which is the idea that there is some kind of vital force which makes the living being different from non-living things. The problem is that vitalism was identified with properties of organic versus inorganic matter, rather than as a distinction between object and process. When it was shown that organic compounds can be synthesized in ways similar to the inorganic compounds, vitalism fell into disrepute. In the Vedic view, vitalism is a process view of the living body different from its objective division into parts. The process view is needed because matter by itself cannot transform. The processes of change must now be overlaid on the material distribution to evolve the states of the material objects. The process view differs from the dynamical view because in the process view, processes are a separate type of reality different from the material objects. In the dynamical view, processes are created by the motion of the material particles, and there is no separate existence for the processes themselves.

Classical theories of science dealt with individual particles, whereas all modern physical theories deal in systems. In atomic theory, the behavior of an individual object depends on the ensemble it is part of. The holism in atomic theory has a counterpart in functional systems in biology that perform processes of ingestion, digestion, circulation, elimination and production. The idea of functions in biology therefore is not the *vitalism* that existed centuries ago. It is rather a necessity in modern science that can be used to fix the problems of incompleteness and indeterminism in the theories.

The key missing ingredient now is to think about how a collection of parts becomes a whole. That is, how do we draw boundaries that constitute the parts into a *system*? Once we have drawn these boundaries, known laws of science can help us better appreciate the manner in which these parts play complementary roles to fulfill a complete function. The role of *vitalism* is not therefore in describing how a non-living system becomes a living system, but how a collection of parts becomes a *system* of interrelated and interdependent parts. In classical physics, for instance, which reduces the whole into *independent* parts, this must never happen; as each part acts independently, there is no boundary between systems. Modern theories of science, however, are faced with the problem of how we can divide nature into systems of interconnected and related parts.

The idea that the world is divided into systems is needed not just for living systems but for every type of meaning cognition as meanings arise only within the context of a system. To know that something is a table, we need to draw a boundary that relates the table to other objects such as books or computers, differentiates it from objects such as beds and chairs, and connects the object to its users. Are these boundaries imaginary constructs in our experience, or do they correspond to something in reality? In modern science, there is no analogue to our perception of boundaries. And this leads us to the conclusion that all macroscopic objects—and the everyday object-concepts and action-concepts we associate with them—are actually convenient fictions. When, therefore, my intelligence judges something to be a table, the judgment is illusory, because there are no boundaries that separate the table from the rest of the world. However, without the notion that there are actual boundaries, the notions about ordinary semantics and meaning become suspect.

In Vedic philosophy, boundaries that separate material particles into systems exist as *forms* in the ether. These boundaries are not just imaginary constructs, but they create real physical effects in nature. For instance, parts of the system become logically distinct, just as people in a closed team take on different roles. These logical distinctions are of two types: conceptual and functional. That is, parts within the whole are conceptually different types of things, and play functionally different types of roles. This idea can be understood in analogy to a house, where parts of the house are conceptually distinct types of things (e.g., kitchen, bedroom, study, dining, bathroom, etc.) and they play functionally different types of roles (e.g., cooking, sleeping, studying, eating, bathing, etc.). The important idea needed to study functional and conceptual properties in nature is that matter divides into ensembles, and there are subtle, invisible boundaries in space that divide matter into systems.

Systems, however, only represent the *potentials* about how we can conceive and use them. To actualize the use, choices are necessary.

For instance, a gun can be used to shoot, but whether or not we shoot the gun is a choice. The interaction between the gun and our body is through the senses of action. But the activity within the body, which causes the body to move the gun, is triggered by *prāṇa-vāyu* or life air. The life air carries the choices of consciousness through which atomic matter is altered and the energy that exists as a potential of activity is transformed into activity. For the body to continuously engage in activity, the body must be restored to its former state—i.e. again in the state of potential for activity. This is achieved through the *cycles* of energy flow performed by the life air. *Prāṇa-vāyu* is therefore understood in terms of the cycles of activity rather than linear motion described by classical physical theories.

Functions and Intelligent Design

Many modern creationists argue against evolution using arguments from design. They assert that because nature has complex processes that make a system, we must presume that these were created by an intelligent creator—God[32]. From a Vedic view, while this argument is not entirely wrong, there are several levels at which we need to clarify it. First, there are forms in nature because God as creator reflects the meanings in His consciousness into nature. The understanding of these meanings requires a new semantic study of nature, different from the current materialistic approaches. In the new approach, material objects can describe other material objects, and objects have meanings besides physical properties. Second, the design in nature is not just due to God, but also due to the desires in the living beings who wish to know themselves in different ways. The study of design need not immediately refer to meanings in God, although doing so would not be entirely wrong. Desires in the living beings are carried in the *prāṇa-vāyu* which causes the material body to act like a living being— i.e. perform functions of ingestion, digestion, circulation, elimination and production. The gap between creationism in religion and physicalism in science has to be bridged by a new study of living beings in which causes are attributed to choices. The study of matter without incorporating the choices effected by *prāṇa-vāyu* cannot explain how randomness leads to order. This is a well-known problem not just in living systems but also in non-living things. The order in non-living things is created by the actions of living beings. But the activity in the living being is itself effected by the choices of consciousness. The order is created by a consciousness that structures matter, and is thus not randomly generated.

While arguments from design using God as a source of meaning are transcendent, the design created by *prāṇa-vāyu*, mind, intelligence and ego represents a naturalistic argument. The mind creates semantic effects in nature and *prāṇa-vāyu* converts these semantic possibilities into actions. *Prāṇa* as a functional description of a body can also be scientific, although such a science requires a different conceptual foundation than the one employed in current science. In this new paradigm, both space and time can be closed. The closure in space represents ensembles and systems which create semantic effects. The closure in time creates cycles of change which appear as functional systems. In current science, space and time are viewed as open and infinitely extended axes. When space and time are seen in a different way, scientific theories will also have to change. These theories will be able to account for semantic and functional effects in matter using new material concepts. These concepts are closer to concepts of consciousness and God and by formulating theories that explain material phenomena in a new way we will be able to understand how consciousness and God actually control material objects.

Prāṇa is adaptive and it changes not just through the course of our lives, but many times during the day. These changes affect our bodily and mental functioning. The derangement of *prāṇa* is responsible for physical and mental diseases and the restoration of its normal functioning can therefore be used as an alternate form of therapy. Indeed, practices of Yoga teach the control of *prāṇa* for a healthy body and mind. These don't require a direct intervention from God, but these are also not effects that will happen deterministically. The classic design argument often fails in the face of adaptation: Why are living beings adapting to environments if God created everything perfectly at the start of creation? A more naturalistic account of design and adaptation is therefore needed and the Vedas provide that naturalistic account in the theory of *prāṇa-vāyu*.

8

The Nature of God's Power

The external potency Māya who is of the nature of the shadow of the cit potency, is worshiped by all people as Durga, the creating, preserving and destroying agency of this mundane world.

—*Brahma Samhita*

The Role of Śakti

We have seen how the six causes relate to various aspects of conscious experience, and how they are controlled by *prāṇa* which works under the choices of individual consciousness. However, in Vedic philosophy, the individual living being is not the only controller. Rather, nature is primarily controlled by God acting as Time. The manner in which God controls material nature is called His *śakti* or power. Matter can be controlled by an individual living being's will, but it can also be controlled by God's will. God's will creates possibilities of *what* can happen in nature, but not *who* will do it. The universe is *what* deterministic but *who* indeterministic. Living beings are free to choose from what is possible in the universe, subject to their capabilities and *karma* which limits the possible choices they can make, but does not eliminate choice. A living being's choices are therefore first limited by what is possible in the universe at a given time and then by what they are individually capable of based on their *karma.* The living being is however free to use their *karma* in different ways, pursuing different meanings and objectives in life, based on their capabilities and afforded possibilities. The living being inhabits the material body and mind, but he is not the only controller of this body. The body is controlled by God's will, which is present in the universe as Time which creates possibilities from which the living being can choose. This power of creating possibilities is called *śakti*, and it determines which choices in consciousness can be realized. In a sense, all six causes are under the control of the choices of consciousness, but consciousness itself is, in turn, under the control of Time. In this chapter I will first summarize the discussion of the six causes so far and then relate these six causes to the nature of God's *śakti*. Let's begin by summarizing the causes.

The six causes can be best understood through the types of possible experiences. As mentioned before, the Vedas tell us that all experience can be classified into four stages—(a) waking, (b) dreaming, (c) deep sleep, and (d) transcendent. The waking state pertains to observations of the external world. In the dreaming state, we have thoughts and sensations and the senses are active, but the gross body is inactive. In the deep sleep state there is neither perception of the external world nor experience of emotions, concepts and sensations. This state is the unconscious, which exists when we have a dreamless sleep. The transcendent state pertains to how consciousness exists prior to material experience. Scientific research shows three types of EEG patterns observed in a body, which correspond to waking, sleeping and deep sleep states. Beyond these three stages there is a transcendent and pure state of awareness unfettered by matter.

The four levels of consciousness are also sometimes equated with the four types of ether in Vedic philosophy. These are respectively called *vaikhari, madhyamā, paśyanti* and *parā*. The *vaikhari* ether corresponds to the external space of objects that we observe during the waking stage. The *madhyamā* ether corresponds to the senses, the mind, the intelligence and the ego, which are active even when the gross body is not active. Their activities lead to the experience of dreaming, which feels just like the waking stage, although the external world is missing. The *paśyanti* ether corresponds to the unconscious repository of impressions, a person's nature, our worldview, and hidden capabilities in the form of *karma*. This unconscious realm becomes visible to the mystic during meditational states by which a person can experience their past life experiences and *karma*. Hypnotists also can put a person in deep sleep and dig out a lot of information about a person's past lives from that state. The *parā* ether corresponds to the pure consciousness that is not conditioned by unconscious and conscious instruments. This stage is transcendent because it is beyond matter and because it exists even when material conditioning is removed. Spiritual practices are needed to attain the pure state from the current condition.

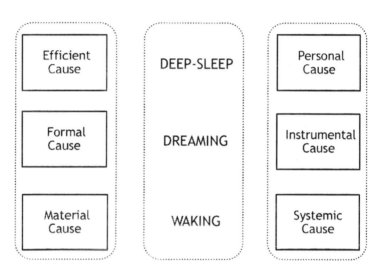

Figure-7 Six Causes and Their Relation to Consciousness

The relation between the six causes and the three conditioned states of consciousness is shown in Figure-7. The systemic and material causes are associated with the waking state, as in this state we engage with the external world and use the gross body to do that. The formal and instrumental causes are related to the dreaming stage, because they are active even when the external world is switched off. The formal and instrumental causes are active when the external world is present, but they are active even during the dreaming stage, because when the external world is absent whatever we experience can be attributed to the activity of the senses and the forms they produce. In deep sleep the senses and their sensations are absent and therefore most of us consider that a silent stage. But at this stage the unconscious can be observed. Mystics practice awareness during the deep sleep stage so that they can see their past lives, hidden *karma*, hidden aspects of their personality and other unconscious tendencies of which we are unaware of during the waking and dreaming stages. While these are all unconscious as far as waking and dreaming stages are concerned, they play an important role in shaping the conscious world, as the study of the unconscious by Western psychologists like Freud and Jung has shown.

One of the reasons why the Vedic theory is difficult to understand is that only one-fourth of the Vedic descriptions consist of things that we are familiar with through science—i.e. the waking stage. Even here, science limits itself to the study of gross matter—the material cause—while leaving a functional and systemic description out. Within that material cause, only objects, or things-in-themselves are described and symbols or things-about-things are not. Vedic philosophy is much more encompassing. It covers not just the waking stage but also dreams, deep sleep and the transcendent stage, the last two of which we know very little, if anything at all, from modern science. The four stages can all be part of conscious experience but at present they are not. To know these stages requires a development of abilities in consciousness, because we will not be able to delve into the unconscious through the waking experience, although we can see *effects* of the unconscious in the waking experience. Similarly, we cannot find the nature of the conscious experience from the body, although we can see the *effects* of conscious experience in the body. One reason why scientific descriptions are limited is because science tries to describe all experience in terms of the waking stage alone. Vedic philosophy is based not just on the waking experience but upon everything that can be experienced, including three stages beyond the waking stage.

Śakti and Prakṛti

God's energy has two aspects: *prakṛti* and *śakti. Prakṛti* (literally that which is created) is that aspect of God's energy which becomes the six causes of creation. This energy is said to encapsulate God's *seed,* which is information about God being reflected into matter. The second aspect of God's energy, called *śakti,* is His power of free will by which God constrains the possibilities in the manifest universe. The third aspect of God's energy is the living being itself whose choices select from amongst the possibilities in the universe. While God is the completeness of the six categories, the energy of God called *śakti* applies constraints on the six categories to reduce the possibilities. The constraints define what experiences are possible. Individual living beings can now choose from amongst possibilities to create their experiences, subject to capabilities and *karma.*

The Vedas state that there are three types of *śakti* based on the three aspects of consciousness, namely *sat, chit* and *ānanda,* which respectively define the possibilities for existence, action and enjoyment. These are called *bhūti-śakti, kriyā-śakti* and *māya-śakti,* respectively. These three aspects of God's energy represent three aspects to God's will, by which He defines the nature of His existence, the nature of His activity and the nature of His pleasure. Since the material creation reflects God's personality in matter, God's choices become the constraints for existence, activity and pleasure in the material creation. God's will is 'coarse-grained' in the sense that it leaves room for individual living being's choices, although the living being's choices are considerably limited by God's choices.

Each of these three types of *śakti* comprises three modes—the mode of goodness (*sattva*), the mode of passion (*rajas*) and the mode of darkness (*tamas*). We can thus speak of a body in the mode of goodness, passion or ignorance, work in the mode of goodness, passion or ignorance and pleasure in the mode of goodness, passion or ignorance. The modes of nature pervade everything and while they are distinct from the six causes, they influence these causes. Sensations, thoughts, and judgments are conditioned by the modes, and a person's conscious and unconscious existence is tuned according to the mode they are in. Thus, sweet taste and smell are in the mode of goodness, sour and hot are in the mode of passion and bitter and pungent are in the mode of darkness. What this means is that a person in the mode of goodness would enjoy sensations, thoughts, emotions, actions and pleasure in the mode of goodness. He will do actions in the mode of goodness and he will exist in the mode of goodness. Sensations, thoughts, emotions, actions and pleasure for a person in a specific mode will thus have a specific flavor to them.

The three modes mutate and combine over and over to create an infinite variety, but in each case one of the modes predominates over the other two modes. Owing to this domination, it is possible to see each type of existence, activity and pleasure as primarily governed by one mode. The mode of goodness is seen in the pursuit of knowledge, detachment and the performance of duties. The mode of passion is seen in working for profit, love and creativity. The mode of darkness is seen in laziness, inertia and various forms of addictions. The Vedas urge us to rise through these modes—from ignorance to passion to goodness—and then be situated in unmixed goodness. A living being advances in spiritual life by moving through the modes, and then being situated in unmixed goodness.

In the Vedas, all living beings are identical as far as their native capabilities of consciousness are concerned. They are all eternal and they have similar needs to know and express themselves and enjoy through that knowledge and expression. But individuals are not identical in *how* they wish to know and express their individuality. There are many possible schemes governed by the three modes of nature. Since the modes are graded, different schemes to know and express the self are also graded due to the modes. A consciousness that chooses a *higher* level of existence sees significance in a different type of experience. These levels are stages of progression of conscious existence; a consciousness alters the kinds of experiences it seeks as it finds newer and more meaningful kinds of experiences.

The Vedas describe that as a living being elevates his consciousness, he becomes eligible for different kinds of bodies. Different bodies have different kinds of organs, senses, mind, intelligence and ego, and play different roles in society by which the mind experiences different meanings and intelligence cognizes the world differently. The unconscious nature and tendencies are modified differently according to the different kinds of bodies and the living being seeks to know itself in diverse ways and derives pleasure from different types of self-knowledge. In other words, as the living being upgrades his consciousness, the combination of the six categories is altered and the living being has a different, body, mind, intelligence, unconscious, ego, relationships, pleasure and meaning in life. Thus, ultimately, the causal, subtle and gross bodies of a soul are manifest based upon the desires of that soul. The *śakti* only helps create these bodies, although the choices behind these bodies are in the soul. *Śakti* is called the Divine Mother because she gives birth to the soul as an embodied existence, conditioned by different types of choices.

The variety in the six causes is produced as a possibility through the combination of the three modes. The living being chooses from amongst the possibilities and the choice that selects a particular combination of modes is also under the same modes. Regardless of whatever choices a living being makes, they are always a subset of God's choices. But, since God does not completely preclude an individual's choices, the responsibility ultimately rests on the individual. When a specific mode of *śakti* predominates in a living being, it automatically selects a combination of the six causes in that mode, which creates a type of experience. Thus if the mode of goodness predominates, it will automatically select a corresponding type of experience across all the six causes. In this sense, *śakti* is all-powerful and controls all the other causes. The Vedas describe that the modes are always in a flux, as long as a living being has not transcended his consciousness to a point beyond the material modes. At any given time, one of the modes predominates while the other two become subordinate. That in turn shapes the types of experiences.

The Role of Time

The relative strength of the modes of nature is controlled by the influence of Time, which controls, through the modes, everything in the universe. Time is, in a sense, the script of nature, the predetermined history and future of the universe. As Time unfolds, the relative dominance of the three modes of nature is altered and the combination of the modes changes experience. Time is a type of consciousness in Vedic philosophy and an aspect of God. It is called *Mahā-Kāla* or *Mahā-Śiva*. This aspect of God is not a seeker of knowledge and pleasure, but acts as a controller and administrator. The knower and controller aspects of God play complementary roles in creation. The knower aspect becomes the essence of the universe, and the meanings known in creation are the meanings that God wants to know Himself as. The expanse of all meanings spread throughout the universe is a byproduct of the semantic variety in God. The controller aspect orders these meanings into events, and causes different meanings to be manifest and unmanifest.

Time makes the world temporary. The meanings exist eternally in God, but the objects created by combining and mutating these meanings are temporary. While matter is eternal and forms in this matter have an eternal origin in God, the combination and reflection of the originally eternal forms in God into matter is temporary. An example that illustrates this idea is that of an object reflected in a water stream. If an object is reflected in moving water, the ripples in the water give the impression that the reflected object is changing. Actually, the reflected object is still, and forms appear moving because of the ripples in water. In a similar fashion, the form of God is reflected in matter and while this form is eternal, Time causes matter to churn like ripples in water. Individual consciousness identifies with these changes, and imagines these changes to be caused by its choices and causing changes to it, when the causality is actually in the predetermined script of Time that controls changes to matter.

We may wonder that if Time preordains events in the universe then how are we free? If some form of God predetermines events then we obviously have no choice. How can individuals be responsible for their actions and thereby be made to suffer or enjoy? The answer to this dilemma is very interesting because it represents the classic conflict between choice and determinism. The answer is that free will and determinism are responsible for different aspects of choice. Time determines *what* will happen in the universe but not *who* will do it. Consciousness, with its unconscious tendencies, *karma*, ego, mind, intelligence and senses, determines whether it wants to participate in the events preordained by Time. The events in the universe are fixed, but their doers are not fixed. Events, as we see them in the universe, will happen regardless of whether a particular individual participates in them. However, the decision to participate in those events makes the consciousness responsible for them.

The controller form of God is considered the first emanation of the enjoyer form. While both enjoyer and controller forms are supreme, the Vedas treat the enjoyer form to be the original form, and the controller form to be a subordinate manifestation of the original need to enjoy. The controller form emerges as consequence of the need in God to know and enjoy. This is sometimes difficult to grasp, because the controller form of God controls all experiences—including those of the enjoyer form of God. Different aspects of Vedic literature therefore emphasize the relative importance of these two aspects of God. *Viṣṇu* in the material creation represents the knower and enjoyer form of God and is the ultimate essence and purpose of the creation. However, *Śiva* represents the controller form of God. Different sects in Vedic philosophy argue about which form of God is ultimate. The truth is that *Śiva* is the supreme controller and *Viṣṇu* is the supreme enjoyer. The need to control arises from the need to enjoy, and in that sense, *Viṣṇu* is superior to *Śiva*. Nevertheless, *Śiva* controls the universe. There is actually no conflict, if we can see the different roles played by *Viṣṇu* and *Śiva*.

Each of the two forms of God exercise different powers, and their energies are called by different names. The energy of the *Viṣṇu* form is called *prakṛti*, which can be roughly translated as *nature*. *Prakṛti* is a name for the combination of six causes, which are the aspects of the knowing and enjoying form of God into the 'mirror' of material nature. *Śakti*, on the other hand, is the combination of three modes of nature that are controlled by the consciousness in the controller form of God. They are sometimes regarded as different energies and sometimes as aspects of the same energy. The Vedic view does not treat God as a monolithic person, although the Vedas are, in the ultimate analysis, monotheistic. The Vedas treat God as the sum total of existence, activity and pleasure, but God also takes on many forms that predominate differently in different types of existences, activities and pleasures. These different forms of God are not different persons, although they are different personalities! An analogy to explain this idea is that of a person who puts on different guises to play different parts in a play, although he is the same person across all his different forms of expression. The analogy, while useful to understand the basic idea of multiplicities, is insufficient for two reasons. First, a person in a guise cannot play many different parts simultaneously, although God does play many parts simultaneously. Second, we assume that the 'real' person is different from the guises he wears and the roles he plays, but that is not the case for God. The forms of God are different complementary moods or personalities that exist in the same Supreme Person and He manifests these moods as different individuals with different forms.

The Nature of Māya-Śakti

The first feature of *śakti* is called *māya-śakti*. *Māya* literally means *that which is not*, and the term implies a negation. When *māya* acts on consciousness, it creates a sense of inadequacy, incompleteness or imperfection in the soul. The search for self-knowledge and pleasure is the quest for completeness. Something is pleasurable and meaningful if it gives consciousness a sense of completeness. Every individual feels incomplete and imperfect, regardless of their situation in the world (which may be exalted or deprived). In fact, each individual feels incomplete in a different way and we seek to obviate that sense of incompleteness through pleasure and self-knowledge. An individual's incompleteness makes him search for particular kinds of pleasure and knowledge, by which consciousness can be complete. The experience of completeness can come from things that complement consciousness' sense of incompleteness.

For instance, some people perceive perfection in compositions of artistic works while others seek to know the world through science and philosophy. The manner in which we seek completeness depends on the manner in which we feel incomplete. The living being seeks to unite with objects that complete it and the experience of completeness gives rise to pleasure. Why then is consciousness not always blissful? What makes it feel incomplete and inadequate? The Vedas describe that incompleteness is created as limitations for consciousness. Consciousness feels inadequate by identifying with these limitations. There are five kinds of limitations that consciousness experiences in this world. These limitations drive it towards a quest for different kinds of pleasure and self-knowledge. Given these limitations, a living being is forced to seek pleasure in ways that will compensate his or her perceived sense of incompleteness.

The limitations are called *niyati, kāla, rāga, vidya* and *kalā*. *Niyati* is the condition that consciousness is in a particular place and that it cannot be in all places. The limitation of *kāla* is the condition that consciousness is in a particular time and cannot be in all times. The limitation of *rāga* is the condition that consciousness can like only certain things and that it cannot like everything. The limitation of *vidya* is the condition that consciousness knows only a few things and cannot know all possible things. The limitation of *kalā* is the condition that consciousness has certain capabilities and cannot have all capabilities. Together, these five constraints constitute the *forms* of personal understanding, or the modes in which a person understands himself. The significance of this Vedic idea is that a consciousness always sees itself as a limited individual; the individuality of consciousness is the constraints of place, time, likes, knowledge and skills that make it a different and specific entity.

When a living being perceives that he is limited in several ways, he finds himself incomplete. The effect of *maya* on the living being therefore impels him to act in ways to obviate this sense of incompleteness. For instance, a person who feels he is in a limited space wants to learn about the universe at large or travel to different parts of the world, physically or even mentally. A person who feels he is limited by time develops the urge to do things faster and acts frantically. He may also be interested in history and the future. A person who feels he is limited by his personality of likes and dislikes is likely to be tempted to experiment to do new things. Individuals who believe they have limited amounts of knowledge develop a hunger for knowledge. And individuals who feel that they have limited capabilities try to learn new skills to complement their sense of incompleteness. *Māya* thus creates an urge in living beings to pursue things that they perceive themselves to be lacking in.

We know the world in terms of certain *forms* of worldly understanding such as taste or color or smell, which were presented extensively in previous chapters. *Māya* however creates the *forms* of personal understanding, which are the ways in which consciousness perceives itself. While sensations define the modes in which we know the world, *māya* defines the modes in which we try to know ourselves as limited beings in space, time, knowledge, preferences and capabilities. These forms of personal understanding create a view of the self that accompanies the perception of the world. Senses aid perception of the world and *māya* creates a view of the self. Each view of the self is related to a view of the world; a certain view of the world implies a related view of the self and both views arise and exist simultaneously. We may call them objective and subjective interpretations of experience. Subjective limits create the idea that a consciousness is an individual; that it is not present in all space and time, that it does not prefer everything and that it has limits on knowledge and abilities. This perception is similar to the sensation of taste and touch, but it is much more subtle and personal.

The experiences of pleasure and self-knowledge depend upon the ways in which *māya* constrains consciousness. In the Vedas, this covering aspect and individuating principle is called *āvaraṇātmika* (covering energy)[33]. *Āvaraṇātmika* causes a sense of inadequacy. When a living being feels inadequate in a certain way, he or she also desires certain kinds of knowledge and pleasures. Adequacy, inadequacy and neutrality are the three modes of *āvaraṇātmika* which are accompanied by pleasure, unhappiness and neither pleasure nor unhappiness. They are also accompanied by self-knowledge, self-ignorance and neither knowledge nor ignorance. There is thus a relation between how we know ourselves and the pleasure derived from this knowledge. This relation is like that between the taste of sweetness and the pleasure of sweetness or the difference between knowing that one is skilled and enjoying that knowledge; different people may or may not enjoy sweetness; even the same person may not always enjoy sweetness. It is also the relation between the perception that an individual is a limited personality and the pleasure or pain associated with that perception. Because of a certain type of constraint, a living being finds sensations pleasurable. When these constraints are removed, the same sensations become painful.

Due to *māya* a person sometimes feels happy that he is a limited individual (as opposed to and different from other individuals) and sometimes he laments his limitations. Another person with the same individuality may feel happy with it; indeed, the same person can find his individuality pleasing and depressing at different times. The world by itself is just perceptions; these percepts become sources of happiness or distress based upon the action of *māya*.

The meaning of *māya*—literally *what I am not*—varies from one context to another depending upon its action. Sometimes, *māya* creates the sense of inadequacy, which results in unhappiness. At this time, *māya* or not-self means "I am not such-and-such (and I want to be such-and-such)." When the living being unites with the intended objects, that unity leads to a sense of happiness and fulfillment. At this time, *māya* or not-self means "I am different from others (and superior to them)." When the action of *māya* ceases, the living being feels that "I am a unique individual although neither superior nor inferior to anyone (I relish my individuality without comparison)." Freeing oneself from the influence of *māya* is the most basic goal of spirituality in Vedic philosophy because freedom from *māya* makes a living being happy, content and self-satisfied perpetually. Without *māya*, a person sees himself as an individual, who is eternal and unique and doesn't need to feel inadequate or incomplete in any forced way. This is the true nature of the soul.

Inadequacy is the most prominent effect of *māya*. Under its influence, a person feels that he is not whole or complete; that they need something before they can be complete and whole. Such a person develops the need for uniting with something other than his self to bring about that sense of unity. The search for pleasure and the need to know oneself is the search for this unity. Consciousness experiences pleasure when it temporarily unites with something that can provide it a sense of completeness. Consciousness also engages in activities that create artifacts, in order to give consciousness a sense of completeness. Different individuals find different things pleasurable because they experience the limitations of fragmentedness in a different manner, conditioned by various kinds of *māya*. The perception of pleasure is experienced when someone reaches a sense of unity as he finds what seemed to have been missing.

Māya defines both suffering and pleasure. It defines suffering by prescribing ways in which consciousness finds itself incomplete. It also defines pleasure because incompleteness determines the things to be enjoyed. *Māya* is the sense in which something complements our internal sense of disunity or incompleteness, or the reason why we think it can give us pleasure. *Māya* is the sense in which a thing is partially complete. In the Vedic theory, the living being is conditioned by *māya* because it chooses a certain kind of limited identity. The living being now chases various types of experiences in the world to compensate for the perceived incompleteness of consciousness. And consciousness never comes out of its endeavors of pleasure because *māya* continuously conditions it with newer forms of incompleteness. When one form of incompleteness is resolved by uniting with a worldly object, another one is created by *māya*. Psychologists often say that inadequacy is one's own mental creation. They suggest that the sense of inadequacy can be overcome by mental adjustments, such as cultivating a "positive attitude" towards life. In the Vedic view, however, *māya* is not an artificial creation of the living being and there is no way it can be avoided. Even the most successful people also experience inadequacies.

God and Māya

Everything in the world is incomplete or imperfect in some sense. Only God is complete in all respects because He is free from the influences of *māya*. Indeed, God feels Himself as the completeness of space, time, character, knowledge and abilities. The Vedas state that the quest for completeness is satiated when a living being unites with God, because God is not conditioned by *māya*. Free from the influence of *māya*, a person is free from feelings of superiority and inferiority. A person stays free from the influence of *māya* only when he unites with God. This unity is not the act of *merging* into God, as an impersonalist portrays. The impersonalist says that we must free ourselves from the influence of *māya* and stay free. The personalist instead says that a living being is *aṇu* or very small and therefore the sense of inadequacy is not an imagination. It is very real. To overcome this sense of incompleteness, the living being must not stay free of *māya*, but unite with God—who is the most complete—in a way that complements his own sense of incompleteness. This unification with God is not merging, but is *yoga*.

The impersonalist incorrectly interprets the term *yoga* as an act of merging into God. When a living being merges in God and gives up his sense of individuality, he imagines himself to be the whole of existence even though he is still an individual ontologically. By giving up individuality, the living being frees himself from the influence of *māya* but also loses the self-knowledge and the pleasure which characterize all consciousness. The personalist takes a different route in which he remains an individual and feels incomplete, but overcomes this sense of incompleteness by uniting with God in meaningful relationships. Therefore, *māya* in Vedic philosophy is not just a negative term. It also denotes a positive aspect where the sense of inadequacy in the living being propels them towards God.

By giving up individuality one imagines oneself to be the entire existence. But a living being falls again into the material world because he is in fact very small and is therefore ontologically incomplete. The Vedas state that to avoid repeated falldowns the living being must enter into a *relation* with God in which the living being constantly feels deprived of God and finds pleasure in meeting Him. Unity with God is the act of entering into this *relationship* with Him. God is the highest pleasure object because He is the most complete; He presents the greatest unity in diversity. God is the principle that reconciles diversity because the diversity is His creation.

God is perfect because He does not feel inadequate. The Vedas state that when living beings leave the association of God—the most complete person—they come under the influence of *māya*, which conditions them with inadequacies. Every living being is incomplete without God and conditioning by *māya,* as the evidence of this inadequacy, constantly haunts the living being. Living beings refuse to accept it; they concoct self-images that complement the inherent feelings of incompleteness and try to actualize them. When this self-image is realized, the type of conditioning by *māya* changes and the person feels inadequate in a different way. The view that inadequacy is an artificial creation of our minds is wrong. *Māya* is imposed on everyone and cannot be avoided by mental adjustments.

If *māya* conditions every living being, why does *māya* not condition God? Vedic philosophy says that even God can come under the influence of *māya* and He feels inadequate, although He is not inadequate. The influence of *māya* on God, therefore, is not real because God is actually complete but feels incomplete. This sense of incompleteness influences God in different ways, which become the source for different kinds of desires for self-knowledge and pleasure in Him. These desires then lead to different types of creation, called the creations of matter, spirit and consciousness. The Vedas proclaim that beyond the present material world there is another spiritual creation. All these creations are under the influence of *māya*, although *māya* acts differently in these creations. Correspondingly, it creates different kinds of pleasure and inadequacy in these three types of creations. Different types of creations represent different ways in which God feels conditioned by His own energy *māya*.

There are three ways in which God feels inadequate, that lead to three types of self-knowledge: to know Himself (1) as He is, (2) as He is not and (3) as He can be. The material creation arises out of God's need to know His Self as He is not. Here, God's actualization is effected as His self-denial or self-negation, also called God's austerity: God wants to know what He is not and He engages in self-abnegation. The material creation from His self-image is like someone looking at a picture of oneself from a time that one does not identify with anymore (say when someone was very ugly or very poor). In such a case, one does not acknowledge the picture to be one's true self, although in some sense it is that person's picture. Similarly, when God engages in self-denial He creates the material world, which is everything that God is *not*. It is still God's image, although the image is vitiated. God does not identify with this vitiated self-image as His true self, and so the image is about what He is not. This self-denial is God's conception of not-self and constitutes the material form of *māya*. The material *māya* does not directly affect God because God does not identify with this not-me image. He rather looks upon it as something alien to Him; He regards the material creation expelled from His true Self. In other words, although *māya* exists, God does not lose His Godliness because of it. However, the living beings who want to be away from God quickly adopt this *māya*. They *interpret* the idea of a world that is not-God as something that is free of God's control, where they can be independent.

By adopting the material world, the living beings believe that they have become independent of God. They don't realize that God is completeness and by adopting something that is not-God, they will also suffer from incompleteness. The material *māya* therefore operates differently on God and on the living being. In relation to God, it creates the idea of what God is *not*. This negation is not inadequacy, but self-denial; God wants to know Himself as what He is not and He obtains that knowledge by creating a world that He does not identify with. However, living beings think of *māya* as the domain where God does not exist, or where they can be independent of the subordination to God. This apparent freedom from God, however, conditions one with other kinds of incompleteness.

Māya also conditions God in the spiritual creation. Under the influence of spiritual *māya* God thinks of Himself as inadequate, or as not-God (as someone who is not full in all respects). But in such a condition, God does not seek completion by reinventing His Godliness. This is because He is conditioned to the extent where He loses all *notions* of Godliness as even a remote possibility. When He has forgotten His Godliness, He completes Himself in association with other living beings, quite like we engage with other fellow human beings in society. These relationships arise because God thinks Himself as not-God. Though He is complete, the conditioning makes Him feel inadequate without the association of His devotees. This arrangement of *māya* is for the mutual satisfaction of God and His devotees. Just as devotees of God feel inadequate without God, God feels inadequate without His devotees. Both God and His devotees are conditioned to feel inadequate by the same spiritual *māya*. This spiritual *māya* ties God and His devotees together. When *māya* conditions God, it makes Him feel not-God, or an ordinary living being. When *māya* conditions living beings, it also makes them feel not-God, and inadequate without God. *Māya* therefore acts both upon God and the ordinary living beings, although in different ways.

The spiritual *māya* is not forced on the living being like material *māya*. Rather, in the spiritual creation, one voluntarily adopts a certain type of *māya* to feel inadequate in a particular manner. The sense in which one feels inadequate without God and misses Him is said to be the living being's eternal form or *svarūpa* in relation to God. All living beings are similar as consciousness. They are different in the kind of *māya* they adopt, the sense in which they miss God and feel incomplete without Him. Unless a living being feels incomplete he will not seek anything to complete himself. Unless a living being seeks this completeness, he cannot enjoy. In a spiritual relationship God and the living beings voluntarily adopt *māya*.

The term *māya* thus does not denote one thing. There are many meanings of *māya* and they arise originally in relation to God. Each of these meanings is a different interpretation of the term "not God." Depending upon the viewpoint, negation means different things to different living beings. In the spiritual creation: (a) *māya* for God implies that God is not-God; that he is an ordinary living being and must therefore conduct Himself as ordinary beings (b) for the living being, *māya* implies that the living being misses God and therefore finds satisfaction only in uniting with God. In the material creation: (a) *māya* for God implies the vision of self-denial that God sees (b) for the living being *māya* means a supposed freedom from God but a concomitant conditioning by other kinds of limitations. Ultimately, the Vedas describe that *māya* and God are closely associated. This is because to say something is not-God, one must have a prior conception of God. The different kinds of *māya* are ultimately one, although they are interpreted in various ways. The material world can change into the spiritual world, provided *māya* is interpreted differently.

Māya and Māyavāda

This relation between God and *māya* has parallels with Hegel's conception of Being and Nothingness[34]. In Hegel's view, originally God existed as pure Being. However, when this Being attempted to think Himself (i.e. know Himself), He ended up with Nothingness, since pure Being is unthinkable. So by thinking Himself, God distanced Himself from His own essence. Hegel calls this God's self-alienation and it can be compared to the Vedic notion of *māya*[35]. God's attempt to think Himself is His attempt at self-knowledge. However, this is where the similarity between Vedic and Hegel's thinking ends.

Hegel claims that Being and Nothingness are opposite forces constantly clashing to create the diversity of the world. In the Vedic view, *māya* and God are not clashing. *Māya* rather aids in God's self-realization by helping God define what He is. There is however a clash between the three modes of nature, *sattva*, *rajas* and *tamas*, which are aspects of *śakti* and play a different role than *māya*. The three modes of nature can be compared to Hegel's categories of Being, Becoming and Nothingness. The state of being called *sattva* is a material state of existence and not the existence of God. The key difference is that in Hegel's view Being itself becomes the world, whereas in Vedic thinking, Being impregnates matter (Hegel's Nothingness) with information which then manifests the world. Hegel's view resonates with the *advaita* Vedanta view where *Brahmān* becomes the world and the embodied individual—called *puruṣa*—struggles with *prakṛti*. The *advaita* view is right in that the individual living being struggles to overcome his feelings of inadequacy but it is wrong in applying this struggle to God. *Māya* facilitates God's self-knowledge as His energy to feel inadequate and desire Himself. It is wrong to suppose that a person's own energy overpowers the owner of that energy. Hegel's philosophy, like *advaita* Vedanta, believes in God's victimization, although other personal theistic forms of Vedanta do not accept such an impoverished view of God.

In the *vaiṣṇava* Vedanta view, God derives self-knowledge from the creation and is not struggling with the creation. God is related to the creation as an object is to its reflection or an author is to his book. God does not become the creation, as does the clay that becomes a pot. When the pot is broken, formless clay remains. But, when a mirror is smashed the original object having form remains. The form of the world in the case of the mirror has its origin in the reflected objects; the world has a hidden meaning. The form of the world in the case of the pot has no explanation; the world has no meaning at all. The Hegelian or *advaita* position comes when we conflate the individual consciousness as the original Being that created Nothingness. In the *vaiṣṇava* Vedanta, there is a basic difference between individual and supreme living beings. God as the supreme consciousness creates the universe out of matter. The individual consciousness looks at this universe and considers it his own reflection—the living being has the tendency to identify with the products in the creation as images of his personality. The correct view instead would be to see the world as God's reflection. The worldly changes must then be seen as God's play with matter. But when the living being thinks the world is his reflection, he is caught in the tangle of constantly trying to prove his superiority over matter. Individuals struggling with matter are not God, but they have chosen to be away from God and imbibed a material domain that is not-God. The equation of self with God implies that *māya* is not-self, giving rise to inadequacy.

Incompleteness and Values

Each of the five notions of incompleteness of a conscious being can be classified by the six kinds of values: knowledge, beauty, renunciation, power, fame and wealth. Consciousness is made to experience not only that it is limited by space and time but also that it has a limited availability of the six values. The living being thus aspires to not just complete itself by being in different places and times, having different kinds of knowledge and skills, but also by having perfect power, beauty, renunciation, fame and wealth in every possible space, time, liking, knowledge and ability. It does not matter how much knowledge, beauty, renunciation, power, fame or wealth a person already has, since *māya* still makes them feel incomplete in some respect. A person strongly conditioned by the need for wealth, for example, is not satisfied unless he or she can own all possible wealth in all possible places and times. Even an extremely rich person can still be unhappy due to perceived deficiencies of poverty artificially created within him by the actions of *māya*.

In the material creation, *māya* forces a living being into the pursuit of various pleasures, each temporary, driven by a sense of inadequacy. In the spiritual creation, *māya* creates in the living being a sense of separation from the ultimate pleasure object, God. A spiritual being lives under the idea "I am not God, and I miss God as the source of my completeness;" He or she also thinks, "I can be complete by being in touch with God;" This *māya* too creates the feelings of separation and meeting, but its evolution does not change the object from which one feels separated—God. In this sense material *māya* is temporary (because its objects change) but spiritual *māya* is eternal because its objects are constant. The height of intensity of separation from God characterizes the limit to pleasures experienced in relationship with God. The spiritual practices of the Vedas are designed to move a living being from a changing *māya* to a permanent *māya*. This is different from the *advaita* view that considers freedom from *māya* as the ultimate goal of spirituality.

The Vedic notion of *māya* is similar to Kantian categories that condition our experiences, with one important difference. Kantian categories[36] condition the view about the world but *māya* conditions the view about the self. Kant thought that space and time are forms in terms of which we view the world. In Vedic thought, however, *māya* as space and time is categories in terms of which we see ourselves as embodied. The notion of space and time in Kantian thinking defines the *form* of the world. In Vedic thinking, notions about space-time as *māya* define the *form* of the self, which is an individual soul conditioned due to material influences in the world. Because we see ourselves as limited, we seek various means by which we can complete ourselves. Of course, this does not mean that in the Vedas there isn't a space and time that pertains to our worldly phenomenal experience. It just means that the phenomenal space and time is different from the space-time constraints that make consciousness feel that it is embodied in the world. Indeed, the view of the world and the view of the self are derived from the same sensation. The phenomenal space-time pertains to the objective interpretation of sensations[37] and the personal space-time pertains to their subjective interpretation. However, the constraints of *māya* are prior to sensations: one seeks sensations because one feels incomplete; one does not become incomplete because of sensations. It is thus incorrect to claim that if we stopped seeking sensations, we would become complete (free of the view that we are limited by space and time). Closing the eyes and restraining the senses can rid us of phenomenal space-time that Kant construed, but not from space-time limitations that arise from *māya*. The only way to free oneself from *māya* is to revive one's relationship with God.

Three Types of Existence

The *māya* in the material world is also sometimes called the *external* energy because it directs consciousness in the external world in search of objects that can help it gain completeness. The material world is external because it is a creation of what God is not; it is a creation that has been evicted or thrown out of God. The *māya* in the spiritual world is called *internal* energy because it is created from aspects that God is. The spiritual *māya* directs the living being towards God. This external-internal distinction is sometimes misunderstood by philosophers who treat spirituality as discarding of the "external" world in favor of "inwardly" directed meditation. A true spiritualist or *yogi* meditates not on the individual self but on God. Those who advocate meditation as the means to realize the self are confused about the nature of the internal-external distinction by treating the terms *internal* and *external* as applying to the living being, when they are actually applied in relation to God. *Internal* and *external* denote energies in relation to God (by defining His self-knowledge positively and negatively, respectively). Both energies create a world that is "external" to individual consciousness and hence observable and empirical. Such a world can be publicly spoken of and involves shared experiences. This means that the goal of religion is not a private, internal and subjective world but a world that is common and shared. Science-religion reconciliations based upon an internal-external duality are thus based upon a mistake.

There is also a *marginal* energy in which consciousness derives pleasure not from material objects or from God, but from itself. That is, consciousness finds itself to be complete, by freeing oneself from the influence of the external or material *māya*. This stage is called *liberated* because a person is free from the misery of incompleteness, and this existence is sometimes called *vaikuntha* or freedom from misery. This pleasure however is considered miniscule in comparison to that derived from being under the influence of the *internal* energy in which the living being always feels incomplete and overcomes it by unity with God. In the marginal state, the living being can experience itself to be complete and perfect, but this sense of completeness or perfection fades in comparison to the perfection in God. The pleasure from gaining God is far greater than the pleasure from gaining one's self, although gaining the self is far greater pleasure than gaining a material object. The pleasure gained from internal energy is the highest because it relates one's self to God. Next is pleasure gained from marginal energy that relates to one's self in which one realizes oneself as a conscious being distinct from both matter and God. Finally, the pleasure gained from material objects is both small and temporary.

It is small because it is caused by a limited degree of unity present in each material object. It is also temporary because the *external māya* is always changing.

The Nature of Kriyā-Śakti

The next aspect of God's *śakti* is called *kriyā-śakti*. This *śakti* defines the possible activities within the creation. Living beings can choose from amongst the activities that *kriyā-śakti* permits at any time. The Vedas classify actions into five types called *creation, destruction, maintenance, hiding* and *revelation*. An act is called a *creation* if it adds knowledge, beauty, renunciation, power, fame and wealth. An act is called *destruction* if it removes knowledge, beauty, renunciation, power, fame or wealth from an object. *Maintenance* sustains values and keeps the world in an operational state. In science, we think of matter as something that is never created or destroyed. But creation and destruction in Vedic philosophy refer not to matter or energy but to information. While matter and energy are conserved, information can be created and destroyed. Knowledge, beauty, power, fame, renunciation and wealth are different kinds of information, which can be encoded in matter as its structure and order. To understand this order and structure as information, we have to describe matter semantically. Creation or destruction pertains not to matter (which is indestructible) but to order, which consciousness creates and destroys. For instance, in a clay pot, we distinguish between the clay and the pot. The destruction of the pot does not destroy matter, although it destroys value. The above three aspects of *kriyā-śakti* are associated with three deities—*Brahmā, Viṣṇu* and *Śiva. Brahmā* creates, *Viṣṇu* maintains and *Śiva* destroys.

But what is hiding and revelation? This is a key point of departure between scientific and Vedic views. In science, order is created out of random chance events. In the Vedic view, order always exists, but it is alternatively hidden and revealed. A key element of Vedic philosophy is the idea that the universe exists in an unmanifest state prior to creation. In this state, the phenomenal world of distinctions has not been created, and the universe is unknowable because the world cannot be distinguished into objects. The universe is *hidden* because it has not yet been thought, felt, willed, known or created. Before a thought, feeling, will, knowledge or action is manifest to us as creation, destruction or maintenance, it appears to us as a *possibility*, which is also a subtle state but different from other subtle states such as thinking. The stage of possibility lies intermediate between manifest and unmanifest states. In the Vedas, knowing possibilities is also knowledge, which is a progression from a stage in which we don't know anything at all. Before a consciousness thinks, feels, wills, knows or acts, it experiences the *possibility* of thinking, feeling, willing, knowing and acting in some way. This possibility is produced by the action of Time which converts the impossible into the possible. Creation is revealed but not manifested in this stage of knowing possibilities. When this possibility is converted to actuality, the thought, feeling, will, knowledge or action is completely manifest[38]. The stage of revelation is sometimes called *about to manifest*. Knowing the world as possibility allows visionaries to intuit things that in some sense existed outside them and were inexplicably "perceived." The history of scientific ideas shows that they arose in times made conducive by cultural, political or economic factors. Most social revolutions succeed after there is a growing dissatisfaction with the current situation and the revolutionaries can *see* a new kind of future for their society. The appearance of an idea is highly probable before someone sees that possibility. The appearance of things as possibilities for creation is therefore a subtle level of reality described in the Vedas. A deterministic world has no room for possibility since everything is predetermined. But in a consciousness friendly world, possibility appears before reality.

The five stages of manifestation are applicable to both *primary* creations (creations of knowability by God) and *secondary* creations (creations of knowledge by living beings). In the case of *primary* creation, the divisions of *creation, destruction, maintenance, revelation* and *hiding* refer to the ingredients of knowability. The same terms pertain to knowledge in the case of *secondary* creations performed by the living beings. This is yet another sense in which creation by God can be understood similar to the creativity of other beings.

Since creation, maintenance and destruction are tied to a living being's personal images, a living being often considers himself or herself created or destroyed through the creation of the objects that reflect his personal image. A person who considered himself rich because he owns properties would consider himself poor if those properties were destroyed in accidents. Thus, although consciousness is eternal and undergoes neither creation nor destruction, it perceives itself in various states due to its identification with material objects. A living being considers himself created when he grows in material assets that signify knowledge, beauty, fame, etc. A living being considers himself destroyed when those assets are lost or diminished. A consciousness considers the creation of values in the world as changes to its own self-image, and considers itself created or destroyed when the creation actually is in matter. This means that the self-image is physically connected to the objects in the world and a consciousness defines itself through that self-image.

The Modes of Nature

Śakti is the power of choice residing in God through which He creates possibilities in the creation. This power converts the unmanifest material universe into a collection of events which individual living beings can choose to participate in. The free will of consciousness picks these possibilities and enacts things, actions and pleasures from the possibilities. The events in the universe are therefore the products of choices by God and the individual living being. God mandates *what* will happen while the living being chooses from those possibilities. The three modes of nature are a decomposition of God's and the living being's choices. Each choice can be comprised of one or more modes. *Śakti*, *prakṛti* and the living being are all therefore said to be imbued with the three modes. *Śakti* defines the possibilities of the three modes; the living being chooses these possibilities under the influence of the modes to create experiences which are called *prakṛti*. To better explain the modes of nature and how they combine, I will take a short detour into the role choices play in logic. This detour illustrates shortcomings in current logic, which helps us see the need for a different view of choices, given in the Vedas.

In logic, there are three aspects of choice called mutual-exclusion, identity and non-contradiction. These are *logical* in nature and they are identical with the manner in which logic itself is decomposed into distinct principles. The principle of identity represents the fact that a claim or choice is identical with itself. This is the positive aspect and it says what the choice represents. To choose in the world, the world must be built of distinctions. This is the negative aspect of choice in which the world is defined by opposites and we choose one side of the distinction while rejecting the other side. When we draw a distinction of opposites, and we need to make a choice, the distinctions must be logically orthogonal. That is, there must be nothing in between true and false in the distinction. In logic, this is called the principle of mutual-exclusion where something can be either true or false, but there cannot be grades of truth or falsity. Note that probabilistic logic or fuzzy logic contradicts this principle. The third principle of logic tells us that something and its opposite cannot be *simultaneously* true (although they could be true one after another or in the context of a different set of choices being made).

When we make a choice, generally we invoke all three principles simultaneously. We must mean something by the choice, which stands for what we are choosing, given by the principle of identity. The choice must deny the opposite logically. That is, logically we must know that if X is chosen then anything not-X must be false due to the principle of non-contradiction. And, we must know that X and not-X are the only possibilities to be chosen because the form of the choice is given by the mutual opposition between X and not-X.

Note that while choosing it is not necessary to always know the form of choice and the opposites that have been rejected. For example if we choose 'black', we know what 'black' stands for—the identity of the choice. But we may not know that by choosing black we automatically rejected 'white' through the principle of non-contradiction. We may know what we have chosen but we may not know what we rejected. So knowing identity does not guarantee knowing non-contradiction. We may also not know that black and white are the only choices available for us (the choices could include red, blue, green, etc., in which case the choice is not governed by mutual exclusion between the chosen and rejected alternatives).

In classical logic, all choices are governed by duality because binary distinction defines knowledge. Hence choosing something means rejecting its opposite and the choice implies a binary opposition between two and only two opposite meanings. Of course, this also depends on the nature of distinctions in the universe and could be violated if knowledge were not binary distinctions. Suppose for the moment that distinctions are not binary oppositions; for example, distinctions could be ternary or quaternary relations, although we do not always know upfront what kind of relation (binary, ternary or quaternary) governs our choice. In this case, choosing one of the alternatives in the relation would not tell us how many and which other alternatives were automatically rejected. This would violate the principle of *mutual-exclusion* since we do not know for sure which possibilities were left out. Knowing the identity is therefore not the same as knowing the *mutual-exclusion*. Similarly, if we have higher order distinctions (ternary, quaternary, etc.) and we are not constrained by a single choice—that is, we could choose two out of three or three out of four possibilities—then it would violate the principle of non-contradiction, because knowing that we chose one amongst the three or four possibilities does not automatically imply that some of the others were not also chosen at the same time.

The three logical principles of *identity, non-contradiction* and *mutual-exclusion* thus tell us that (a) we can choose from amongst a set of possibilities and this is called *identity*, (b) the set from which we choose comprises only two elements, and this is called *mutual-exclusion* and (c) we can choose only once from the set and multiple choices are forbidden, and this is called *non-contradiction*.

Having seen how classical logic uses the three principles, it is easy to also see when these principles could be violated. If the set from which we are choosing comprises more than two alternatives, then the principle of *mutual-exclusion* would be violated. If, further, we are allowed multiple choices at once, then the principle of *non-contradiction* would be violated. Now it makes sense for us to identify not just what is chosen, but also what is rejected and how many alternatives are simultaneously selected or rejected. That requires us to represent choice in three ways but these ways are different from the three principles of classical logic. One mode of choice must now represent those things that have been chosen, and this is called *rajas.* Another mode of choice must represent all those things that have been rejected and is called *tamas.* The third mode must represent possibilities not yet selected or rejected, although these were possibilities for selection or rejection and this is called *sattva.*

Accordingly, in a set with more than two alternatives, and more than one choice, the principles of classical logic must be tweaked to allow for selection and rejection of multiple alternatives such that some alternatives may neither be selected nor rejected. The Vedic theory of the three modes of nature portrays a picture of how reality emerges from possibilities through choice. Nature in this theory exists in an unmanifest form in which objects have not yet been created because nature consists only of various possibilities. Choice converts this unmanifest nature into objects. In the unmanifest stage of matter, objects have not been distinguished and cannot be known or used. This is the *sattva* stage of matter, in which the universe is in the potential stage without any change. As choice selects some possibilities, the unmanifest becomes manifest and real. This is the mode of *rajas* and the universe is said to be created. Through rejection of what is created, we destroy what is created and it merges back into the unmanifest and becomes a possibility. Destruction of reality into the unmanifest is called the mode of *tamas.*

The Vedic philosophy is interesting because it says that everything that we know or don't know—everything that was in the past, present or future—always exists at least in the unmanifest form. Selection and rejection as choices make the unmanifest manifest and vice versa. Selection identifies a possibility that always existed in an unmanifest form and makes it real. Rejection takes what is real, destroys it and puts it back into the possibility stage. There are things never created or destroyed which always exist as possibility.

In the beginning of the creation, the six causes are created from the unmanifest by God as the conditions of knowability. These six causes combine to create the possibilities of events in the universe, and subsequently, living beings choose these events to manifest their real experiences. Matter is thus the possibility for events, and Time restricts this possibility to *what* will happen but not *who* will do it. The individual living being converts these possibilities to reality. *Śakti* is the agency between the material elements and the experience of a living being. This *śakti* creates the universe as a possibility under the influence of Time, from which the living being can choose.

9

The Nature of Consciousness

Let my skin and sinews and bones dry up, together with all the flesh and blood of my body! I welcome it! But I will not move from this spot until I have attained the supreme and final wisdom.

—*The Buddha*

Consciousness-Matter Interaction

We have seen the material categories responsible for experience, how these experiences are constrained by the influence of Time, and that consciousness chooses from amongst the possibilities. In this chapter, I will focus on how consciousness chooses. These choices are limited to what is made possible by Time and a living being cannot go beyond the control of Time. But, within that control, a living being can still choose to enjoy or renounce, indulge or refrain, and experience or abstain. How does consciousness choose? In the Vedic view, matter and consciousness are separate categories. This leads to the interaction problem: If matter and consciousness are separate then how do they interact? In Vedic philosophy, consciousness does not interact with matter. Rather, as earlier described, creation proceeds in the *presence* of consciousness. In this sense, consciousness as a cause differs from other forms of causality. Consciousness is a cause in whose *presence* creation happens although consciousness is not directly involved in the creative act itself. This idea of cause can be illustrated through everyday examples.

Consider, for example, how proceedings of law are carried out in a court. While lawyers, the judge, defendants and witnesses play an active role, the court is merely an incidental presence. Nevertheless, the court must be available for law proceedings to occur. In this sense, the court is necessary as it affects legal proceedings by its presence. Consciousness similarly must be present for the universe to be created, although consciousness does not physically cause the universe. We can call consciousness a cause by its mere existence. This type of causality is often seen in the everyday world in people who play supervisory roles. Think of the examiner who stands watch over students while they write an exam—although the examiner does not write the exam, the examination cannot be conducted in the absence of an examiner. Imagine a tennis match referee who watches the tennis match on the side of the court and announces the results. Although the referee does not play the match, the match cannot be played in her absence. Consider a factory floor supervisor overseeing production. Although the supervisor may not participate in manufacturing in the factory, he is responsible for the actions of subordinates under his supervision. The Vedas similarly state that consciousness is responsible for the actions of the material body even though it does not perform those actions.

In everyday life, before something is done, we ask why it should be done. The question of why seeks justifications for actions. When justifications are available, we then find ways in which it can be achieved. In a similar way, the first step in the creation of the universe involves the *justification* why the universe must exist. Questions about justifications are often different from questions of causality. As an example, we can say that John is hurt because Peter punched him. The act of punching is a cause of someone being hurt. But this explanation is often not enough. We must also ask why Peter punched John, because we seek a *justification* for the action; we assume that Peter is a rational person so he must have a valid reason and a morally correct reason to hurt someone. Science uses causal explanations but consciousness seeks justifications. The existence of the world is not justified unless the purpose behind the world is well-known. The Vedas say that the world exists because consciousness needs it to know and express itself. Consciousness must therefore be present for the universe to come into existence because consciousness provides the *justification* for its existence.

This existential causality in consciousness is an important consideration to solve the mind-body problem, which involves deciphering how a conscious being controls the material body. In the Vedas, consciousness is a spectator but not an active controller of the bodily actions. As long as consciousness is in the material world, it remains a spectator. But, if consciousness is only a spectator, does it mean that it is not responsible for the actions of the body? How can consciousness be responsible if it is only a spectator? The Vedic view is that consciousness is responsible for actions under its supervision, just as a department head is responsible for all deeds that happen under her supervision. Consciousness is a witness of the actions in the body. Although it does not carry them out, these actions will be attributed to consciousness just as the actions of a department are attributed to the head of the department. After all, consciousness is the *justification* for why these actions happen. If consciousness did not exist, the actions would not either.

Besides being the witness, consciousness is also the *approver* of the actions. If consciousness would not approve of actions being carried out under its supervision, the actions would not exist. Consciousness does not move matter but it controls actions by approving or disapproving them. The actions themselves are manifested through multiple stages of efficient causes beginning with thoughts that are created from the *chitta*. Consciousness does not generate thoughts but it controls their *continuation* by approving[39] or disapproving their existence. At each stage of the creation and subsequently, conscious approvals are required for actions to proceed to the next stage. Consciousness must provide these approvals for actions to be carried forward to the next level of maturity. It thus becomes responsible for actions by approving their existence.

The Existential Role of Consciousness

Typically we get both good and bad thoughts and we *consent* to both kinds of thoughts. The Vedas however urge the living being to *reject* bad thoughts and approve only good ones. Consciousness selects and rejects thoughts by *applying* and *withdrawing* itself to and from these thoughts. When consciousness is applied, thoughts are accepted. If consciousness is withdrawn, thoughts are rejected. The approval of thoughts by consciousness is its association with those thoughts. This association is passive in the sense that consciousness has not actively created the thoughts. But by associating and watching over the thoughts, consciousness accepts those thoughts and they continue to develop. When consciousness is withdrawn, thoughts automatically disappear. This is because thoughts need consciousness to be present (the existence of consciousness is needed for their existence). By applying and withdrawing itself, therefore, consciousness becomes the selector or rejecter of thoughts. Like previously mentioned consciousness does not create thoughts; these are automatically[40] generated by *chitta* under the influence of Time. But the acceptance and rejection of these thoughts depends upon consciousness. We are not free to determine which thoughts are generated, but we are free to accept or reject generated thoughts.

This philosophy will seem familiar to practitioners of *yoga*, who aim to control the urges of the *chitta* or the unconscious mind. While it can appear that *yogis* control their mind by actively generating certain thoughts, the truth is that consciousness does not direct the body and thoughts (particularly in the sense that philosophers of the mind-body problem envision). Rather, the thoughts are automatically produced based upon past impressions. Consciousness cannot force wanted thoughts or prevent unwanted thoughts no matter how hard one tries[41], because these thoughts are created without an active participation of consciousness. Anyone who has tried to control their thoughts quickly finds that thoughts are not under the control of their will. Rather, thoughts are automatically created, often against conscious "wishes." So how is a *yogi* expected to control his mind? The answer is by *choosing* to dwell upon or ignore thoughts that are automatically created from the *chitta*. Consciousness cannot directly determine what thoughts are created, but it can reject unwanted thoughts and withdraw from them.

The ability to select and reject thoughts depends upon a distinction between *chitta* and consciousness. *Chitta* is the repository of impressions that leads to new thoughts. Consciousness decides to dwell upon or ignore the thoughts. That is, consciousness can *choose* whether to be conscious of these thoughts or not. Thoughts or actions are conscious when consciousness chooses them. So, while the production of thoughts cannot be controlled (thoughts are subtle material objects), *consciousness* of these thoughts can be. Consciousness being the justification for the creation, only conscious thoughts will continue; thoughts from which consciousness turns away will fade away. This is evidenced by the fact that when awareness withdraws from a thought, the thought ceases to be. Because thoughts lead to actions, thoughts for which consciousness is present will be enacted in the body. Lack of awareness for the rejected thoughts implies that these thoughts will not lead to actions.

Of course, consciousness can withdraw not just at the thinking stage, but at the stages of feeling, willing, knowing or acting as well. A person may think thoughts and like them due to his *prakṛti* but withdraw his consciousness at the willing stage. The development of a thought into action is arrested at the stage at which consciousness withdraws. A *yogi* controls the mind by selecting and rejecting thoughts that are being automatically created by *chitta* and not by generating other thoughts. Consciousness is present for the selected thoughts and absent for the rejected thoughts. The rejected thoughts cease to exist (after they have been created in the *chitta*).

While most of us are surrendered to whatever thoughts are automatically produced by the *chitta*, a *yogi* learns to examine, analyze and actively select or reject these thoughts. When a *yogi* practices this *control* over a period of time, the virtuous cycle of thoughts and actions alters the type of thoughts being automatically created. If, through mind control, only virtuous thoughts and actions are permitted, over a period of time the control of the mind leaves behind only virtuous impressions from which only virtuous thoughts will be produced. Therefore, after a certain period of practicing thought control, a *yogi's chitta* only generates virtuous thoughts. At this time, the *yogi's chitta* is said to be purified. Now the *yogi* dwells in peace because he does not need to reject unwanted thoughts and all thoughts are virtuous. Analytic philosophy in the West since the time of Descartes has spoken of critically examining all assumptions and questioning premises to find the truth. But it does not close the loop with an everyday uncritical stance. If we are always critical, how do we ever become happy? In the Vedas, spirituality begins with a critical approach but if the practice of the critical approach is perfected through consistent practice, the approach is discarded in favor of an uncritical, yet purified and perfected consciousness.

It is likely that a spiritual beginner finds it hard to jumpstart good thoughts, because *chitta* only produces bad thoughts. A person may continuously reject unwanted thoughts, but if only unwanted thoughts are produced by the *chitta*, then it can be hard for anyone to even start thinking pure thoughts. This is a hindrance to the spiritual practitioner, and the practice of yoga suggests the use of external implements such as beads, *yantras,* physical exercises, Vedic rituals, etc., to reduce the production of unwanted thoughts. However, aids in the spiritual practice have a limited use when the *chitta* has been purified and only produces good thoughts. Notably, external implements aid in the reduction of unwanted thoughts but not in the sustenance of spiritual thoughts. Not all Vedic rituals or practices are therefore regarded permanent although some of them are.

An extreme case of a *chitta* conditioned by bad thoughts is illustrated in the legend of the sage *Vālmīki* who was a robber prior to turning to spiritual life after a chance meeting with the sage *Nārada*. Upon seeing his piteous condition, sage *Nārada* advised *Vālmīki* to chant the holy name of Lord *Rāma* as a method of purifying his *chitta*. *Vālmīki*, however, expressed his inability to chant the holy name because of his long association with murderous activities (his mind could not produce the sound of *Rāma* even though *Vālmīki* wanted to). Sage *Nārada*, therefore, revised his instruction and asked *Vālmīki* to chant *Mara* (death) instead of *Rāma*. Continuously chanting *Mara* produces the same sonic effects as the chanting of *Rāma*, and *Vālmīki* could purify his *chitta* by chanting *Mara* instead of *Rāma*. This legend shows that *chitta* and consciousness are different but they need each other. Consciousness needs *chitta* since the schemes of self-actualization come from *chitta*. *Chitta* similarly needs consciousness for a continued existence of thoughts. When *chitta* cannot produce good thoughts, external implements may be needed to purify the *chitta*. An expert spiritual master is adept at giving instructions specific to various types of *chitta* conditioned by past activities. By following those specific instructions, a person can slowly use the causally influenced *chitta* for its own purification.

In conclusion, the Vedic answer to the mind-body problem is that consciousness never comes in direct contact with the material body and never directly effects the changes in the world. Rather, the presence of consciousness is crucial to the creation of the world because consciousness plays an existential role in the creation. This existential role is also the personal cause as described earlier. When a living being identifies with her body, she approves all the thoughts arising in the *chitta* and essentially no choice operates at this point. Consciousness is just a spectator at this time and identifies with the actions of the body. When, however, a living being is detached from the bodily identification, she scrutinizingly selects and rejects thoughts and choice begins to operate. A living being gains her freedom by detaching herself from the bodily identification. At this time, she is both the knower and approver of her thoughts. So, true choice is effected when a living being distinguishes self-awareness from bodily awareness by ceasing bodily identification. Now, consciousness becomes free of the cyclical chain of actions and thoughts.

On the other hand, when consciousness identifies with the thoughts in the *chitta*, no selection actually takes place. Though appearing to be a free thinker, such a person is conditioned by past actions. In both cases, consciousness is a spectator and approver of bodily actions, which are automatically created by the material machinery. When a person realizes that he is not the body—that actions carried out in the body are not carried out by him but by the material machinery, and he is a spectator in these worldly schemes—he comes to the point of knowing that he is the *existential* or personal cause of the body in which he resides. The living being realizes that the body will cease if he is not present in it although because he is not directly involved with it, he will not perish with that body. The existential role played by a consciousness in the material world is the point from which a number of spiritual discourses, including the famous one in the *Bhagavad-Gītā* begin. Detachment from the body and realizing that consciousness only plays an *existential* role in the material body (and the material world) is therefore a crucial starting point in progressive self-realization.

Is Free Will an Illusion?

The existential role played by consciousness has also been empirically demonstrated through neuro-scientific experiments by Benjamin Libet[42]. These experiments show that thinking precedes our conscious reports of that thinking. In one experiment, for instance, a subject is shown objects and then reports of their conscious thinking are compared with the neuronal firings in the brain. Libet found that the conscious reports by subjects always follow neuronal firings. This led a number of scientists and philosophers to conclude that our view that consciousness makes a decision through free will is an illusion. They instead postulate that decisions are already made automatically in the brain and at some point we become aware of such automated decisions. In other words, consciousness is an afterthought to automated unconscious brain processing.

Libet himself did not interpret his experimental results in this manner. His interpretation is instead remarkably close to the Vedic viewpoint and Libet called the nature of conscious choices *free won't* rather than *free will*. The idea is that consciousness is not free to create these thoughts because they arise automatically. But consciousness is free to reject the thoughts, if it doesn't like them. If thoughts are rejected, they cease to exist and the subsequent development of these thoughts into feelings, wills, etc., is arrested at the thinking stage itself. Libet called this the *power of the veto* in which a consciousness has the ability to veto thoughts that it did not itself create. Libet's experiments are radical because they illustrate a view of consciousness quite different from how Descartes thought about it. Descartes said: "I think therefore I exist," thereby equating thinking with existence. Under this view, consciousness and thought are the same faculty. In Vedic philosophy, consciousness is different from both unconscious and conscious thought instruments. Consciousness is free to choose thoughts but it does not itself think. Under the Cartesian equation of thinking with consciousness, Western philosophy has continued to believe that the mind must generate thoughts *consciously*. Libet's experiments show that thought generation and consciousness are two different things. Thought generation is unconscious and automated, while consciousness selects or rejects these thoughts by continuing to observe or withdrawing away from those thoughts. The creation of these thoughts is automated but the continuation of the thoughts depends on consciousness.

The Vedas and Existentialism

There is a great deal of similarity between the Vedic idea that consciousness seeks meanings in life and the philosophy of Existentialism as described by Sartre, Nietzsche and Kierkegaard. The quest for personal significance is at the heart of existentialism, which seeks to understand the nature of the self, as it is left over after consciousness has been stripped of experiential content. The idea of existentialism takes off from Kant's philosophy where the order in the world is not native to the world but an imposition of the mind in its attempt to cognize the world. Existentialism similarly contends that although content is gathered from the world, a subject accords it significance, which becomes the reason that the subject continues to experience the content. What significances consciousness accords to the worldly content is the freedom of consciousness. If consciousness sees a "book," it can choose to experience it or not, depending upon what meanings it finds in it, although these meanings are different from the *content* of the book. The significance of the "book" depends upon the kinds of purposes that can be fulfilled by owning or reading the book. The purposes aren't, however, non-material. They are a deeper and subtler level of material reality. We might argue that this significance is nothing more than perceived benefits gained from experiencing. So, in this case, consciousness would experience a book because it wants to gain knowledge. But why do we want knowledge? And we may say: "Because we wish to enhance our abilities to carry out newer actions. " But why do we want to carry out these actions? The point is that we find reasons and causes for doing things in the world, up to a certain point. Ultimately, rationality ends not in reasons and causes but in justifications, which are self-evident grounds. We don't forever keep questioning *why* something must be done. We rather question until a point that we find a *justification* that makes sense to us. The same justification may not appeal to another person and although he appears to be looking to find reasons and causes, he may be unconvinced about a deeper meaning in life represented by some reality. No amount of reasoning can bring them to acceptance, because reasoning itself has no conclusion. Logic terminates when we find self-evident grounds, and we find them in life. The search for self-evident grounds makes the freedom of conscious choice *rational* to us. Consciousness chooses to act because it accepts those *choices*.

Epilogue

Consciousness in Vedic philosophy consists of three aspects: *sat* (existence, eternity), *chit* (consciousness, activity) and *ānanda* (pleasure). These three aspects make up both the individual's and God's consciousness. *Sat* is existence and *ānanda* is pleasure. To obtain pleasure, the living being develops a desire, which represents activity and is also called *chit*. *Chit* is God's energy of consciousness. This energy develops into three parts: *jñāna* (knowledge), *kriyā* (activity) and *iccha* (free will). *Jñāna* and *kriyā* represent the power by which God knows and expresses Himself. The energy called *iccha* further develops into *māya-śakti, kriyā-śakti* and *bhūti-śakti* and they represent three kinds of choices. God creates to know and express His personality and He uses His three kinds of *śakti* to manifest the creation. The need to know and express divides into three parts, each under the influence of the *śakti* to create the six causes we have discussed in this book. The need for knowledge becomes the Personal Cause or personality, the Instrumental Cause of knowledge and its associated forms (i.e. *tanmātra*), and the Material Cause (i.e. the five gross material elements). The need for expression becomes the Efficient Cause that develops the personality into causes, the Instrumental Cause of action that converts the causes into actions, and the Systemic Cause within the gross material body that converts the actions into forces of change.

The hallmark of Vedic philosophy is that subtle forms manifest into gross forms. Thus the personality comprising six values (knowledge, beauty, power, fame, wealth and renunciation) manifests into sensations which then manifest into objects. Matter in Vedic philosophy is devoid of value. However, matter is imbued with six kinds of values—knowledge, power, fame, wealth, beauty and renunciation—by God whose personality comprises these six values. Similarly, matter in Vedic philosophy is inert and it is caused to move by the will of God. This will first becomes the cause in the unconscious; these causes become actions of the conscious which then manifest as forces with gross matter that modify the state of objects. Thus, matter, which is devoid of value and activity, inherits the values from God's personality and activity from God's will. When God withdraws His consciousness, He abstracts values and activities from matter. Modern science studies how objects are created and how they undergo natural change, objectivity in Vedic philosophy originates from six values, while activity emerges from His free will.

This is the inverse of the worldview in modern science where gross matter and material forces are the ultimate reality; material particles combine to create the body, which acquires representational abilities to create the mind, the mind automatically becomes conscious and this consciousness creates a personality, which develops individual choices. Science assumes about half a dozen transitions that develop gross matter into living bodies with conscious abilities. For instance, matter forms complex structures, these structures acquire semantic properties and become symbols, the symbols can refer to other objects, these references become conscious and lead to knowledge of the world, consciousness creates an individual's personality and then personality creates free will. Each such transition represents an explanatory gap, which is yet to be filled by any empirical or theoretical advance. The people who think that science is complete while religion has explanatory gaps need to recognize that science has yet to explain the majority of our conscious experience, which is not religious in nature.

Before we set out to compare science and religion, we need to recognize that they have completely different conceptual foundations. Science aims to build consciousness from elementary material parts, while Vedic philosophy builds matter from consciousness. Within the scientific explanation, however, the need for consciousness arises because science cannot explain the origins of knowledge, beauty, power, wealth, etc. Today we believe that these are merely human constructs and have no natural counterpart. Therefore, additional scientific effort is needed to show that the laws of nature—even within gross matter—are laws of knowledge, beauty, etc. That is, matter is a semantic reality and material objects are symbols that carry meaning. Scientific effort is also needed to show that causality in matter is based upon choices of consciousness, as current forms of causal laws in science cannot explain how our choices control matter. This problem is recognized in science through various types of incompleteness, incomputability and indeterminism[43]. Hence, there are avenues within science where new ideas about causation and objectivity are necessary. The pursuit of such alternative forms of causality and objectivity can benefit from an understanding of Vedic philosophy and how layers of matter gradually embody the choices in consciousness into ever more objective types of matter.

Endnotes

WHY CREATIONISM?

1   In this book, by evolutionists I mean those who believe that life has spontaneously arisen from chemicals and then further diversified via undirected natural processes, such as natural selection acting on random mutations in the genetic material of living beings.

2   Proponents of the Intelligent Design (ID) theory purposely exclude God as a creator from the scope of their theory, although they may privately believe in God. In as much as they promote their theory, they distinguish themselves from creationists. Their idea is that, empirically and rationally, it can be proved that life was created by a mind that is similar to the human mind, but more intelligent, without referring to the identity of that mind as being God. In this book the term "design creationist" or "creationist" refers to those who state that God is the designer.

3   All physical properties pertain to objects themselves and not to other objects. An object in current physics cannot be a symbol of another object.

4   Gödel's incompleteness theorem forbids incorporating symbols that describe other objects as part of first-order logic.

5   The distinction is important because most empiricists also tend to be materialists.

6   Western philosophers equate phenomena with sensations. Here, the term phenomenon includes both sensations and concepts in the creation. I will show later the need to distinguish the world through sensations and through concepts.

7   This *diksha* is mystical and different from the ceremonial initiation. *Diksha* is the act of a *guru* imparting information about God and can take place without the ceremony. Sometimes, the semantic act may not happen even after the ceremony (especially in cases when the ceremonial spiritual master is ignorant about God's personality). The genuine spiritual master knows the scientific process of conveying information about God, after which godly qualities automatically begin to manifest in the disciple.

8   I will describe later that the knowledge of the self consists of three parts—what we are, what we are not not and what we could be. Matter represents God's knowledge of what He is not. This is knowledge by elimination or exclusion, and while this is not the complete knowledge it is part of knowing what God means. Vedas thus sometimes describe God as *neti-neti* or not this and not that. This is knowledge by elimination, similar to the *via negativa* of Christian theology, and not knowledge of what He is.

9   For example, to reflect extended objects, the mirror in which they are reflected must be extended as well. Ordinary mirrors merely reflect shapes, but the mirror of nature must reflect all kinds of knowables including taste, touch, sight, sound, etc.

THE PERSONAL CAUSE OF CREATION

10 The mind and intelligence are *internal* but they are also accessible. Internal realities such as perception by mind and other mental phenomena make this internal world equally a part of the universe as external things.

11 Istvan Meszaros (1970), "Marx's Theory of Alienation," Merlin Press Ltd.

12 This is an important point, often misunderstood. Impersonalists speak of freeing consciousness from the "contamination" of the world. They fail to recognize that the world is necessary for consciousness to know itself. Spirituality is not about freeing consciousness from the world but embedding it into the right kind of world.

13 However, God, in His other aspects is still aware and active in the spiritual creation. In the Vedic view God's unique feature is that He can

simultaneously take as many forms as He wants, each time embodying a different kind of desire, personality and activities.

14 Wegner D., 2002. The Illusion of Conscious Will. Cambridge, MA: MIT Press.

15 I will describe in a later chapter how matter itself can be directly perceived by the *prāṇa* unmediated by the mind and senses.

THE EFFICIENT CAUSE OF CREATION

16 Positivism was the attempt in early 20th century philosophy to eliminate everything that cannot be *sensually* experienced. Examples of such notions included occult substances, morality, 'good', God, and notoriously, the 'knower' or mind.

17 A.H. Maslov, "A Theory of Human Motivation," Psychological Review 50 (1943):370-96.

18 In the Vedas, God is averse to the material creation, favorable to his devotees and neutral towards all other living beings. These three kinds of attitudes in God are discussed in detail in chapter 8 as the sources or seeds underlying the three kinds of creations.

19 The Vedic notion of *mahattattva* is comparable to the notion of "design" used by Intelligent Design (I.D.) proponents. However, unlike I.D. theory, where design is a logical principle, in the Vedas, it is a level of physical reality that assists creation. The Vedic view can give a realistic grounding to claims such as "such-and-such thing conforms to so-and-so method of design" because we can now assert that design is *in the object* and not just in the behaviors of the creator. Indeed, in the Vedic approach, God does not explicitly add design to roses, trees and the universe. Rather, He wills the creation and everything else is automatic. Design principles are not therefore in the behavior of God but in a level of physical reality itself. Of course this physical reality is a reflection of God; so, design originates in God, although not in His behaviors.

20 This ego is different from another ego which is the identification with

the objects of the world (the "I" and "mine" of experience). The identification ego will be encountered as part of actual cognition of objects when such experiences have to be related to the cognizing self. Both these Egos are not "personalities" as the word is often used in the Western psychological sense. The ego being discussed here is the knowledge to perform procedures. The Sanskrit word *ahaṃkāra* here translates literally into the individual (*aham*) procedure (*kara*).

21 The collection of all *chitta* is called *pradhāna* or collective unconscious, although the collective unconscious in the Vedas is distinct from same term as used by Carl Jung. The Vedic collective unconscious is the collection of all individual unconscious memories. Jung further thought that the collective unconscious has patterns of commonality across individuals that transcend cultures, eras and societies, which is more than the collective unconscious that I am talking of here. I will explore the Jungian unconscious later during the discussion on rituals and their deities that transcend cultures.

THE INSTRUMENTAL CAUSE OF CREATION

22 The *chitta* here is different from the efficient cause called *chitta*. The sense that senses pleasure and the repository of past experiences are both called *chitta*.

THE FORMAL CAUSE OF CREATION

23 For further details on this and other kinds of paradoxes in mathematics, the reader is referred to my book *Godel's Mistake*.

24 One example is the sentence "I saw a man on a hill with a telescope" which has many possible meanings, depending on how noun phrases are formed in the sentence. In one case, the noun phrase just consists of the word "man." In another case, the phrase is "man on a hill." And in yet another case, the noun phrase is "man on a hill with a telescope." In these cases, the remaining words form verbs and verb-phrases drastically altering the meaning of the sentence.

25 It is worth bearing in mind that judgments can also involve moral issues. But the sense of intelligence is not responsible for these judgments. Rather, the *mahattattva*—also sometimes called consciousness—judges whether

actions are morally right. For instance, charity is, generally speaking, a legal action. But charity to criminals is considered aiding and abetting crime and morally incorrect. Charity depends on the capacity of a person to contribute, and a small act performed by a person who has a huge capacity would not be considered morally right. The judgment of right and wrong involves several such complex considerations. This judgment is important in the Vedas because the reaction to a person's action depends on whether these actions are right or wrong. The Vedic theory of *karma* dictates that a person must understand their role and responsibility in society and perform right actions according to those considerations.

THE MATERIAL CAUSE OF CREATION

26 The Vedic ideology contrasts with science in this respect as I will shortly show. In the Vedas, matter is created before objects are created and a distinction between matter and objects is paramount to understanding the nature of material reality.

27 Actually, in classical physics, this connection is made through continuous trajectories. That is, if a particle's immediate next position is infinitely close to the previous one, then, we might suppose that these two positions correspond to the same particle. This is no longer possible with atomic theory where changes are discrete.

28 This is a non-trivial assumption as far as communication in the real world is concerned. It is well-known that communication is affected by noise and interference. But when we are building a conception about matter, we can make this assumption. The effects of noise and interference must later be accounted for through the superposition of additional information on a message carrier.

29 Although Vedic thought uses the same words as the Greeks did, they are meant quite differently. In Greek terminology, Earth denotes solidity and Water denotes liquidity which is how we phenomenally interpret these words. In the Vedic view these terms denote noumenal reality and not phenomenal experiences.

30 In classical physics, the conservation of energy is due to the homogeneity

of time and energy implies the existence of time.

31 Deconstructionists argue that a reader has no access to the author's intents because even an understanding of those intents is subject to inter-pretation. This is false because all information—including the intent of a long dead author—is objectively present in the Ether and can be picked up from there by anyone familiar with the process of reading the Ether.

THE SYSTEMIC CAUSE OF CREATION

32 Intelligent Design theorists do not refer to the creator, although they might privately believe in the presence of a creator.

THE NATURE OF GOD'S POWER

33 We will discuss later another 'pleasure energy' which makes a liv-ing being enjoy this limited sense of individuality. This energy is called *prakṣepātmika* (enjoying energy).

34 Hegel wrote in an obscure style and the best way to get an understand-ing of his work is to read scholarly accounts such as Beiser, Frederick C., *The Cambridge Companion to Hegel*, (Cambridge: Cambridge University Press, 1993).

35 Christian theologians have interpreted this differently. They interpret God's self-alienation as the creation of Satan, who is regarded as a fallen angel.

36 Kant's revolutionary idea was that science is not merely the fortuitous activity of collecting facts but also their organization through categories of understanding which transcend individual consciousnesses and are neces-sary conditions of any experience. These categories constitute the unavoid-able goggles through which we must see the world. They include the notion of space, time, causality, etc. The idea here is that space and time are not things that we sense from the world but categories that the mind applies to external sensations in order to organize them into experience. Refer to Kant's *Critique of Pure Reason*, Dover Publications; new edition (2003).

37 Kant's ideas on space and time are similar to the Vedic notion of senses

that measure the world to generate a phenomenal sense of space and time. Kant drew a distinction between phenomena and noumena. In Vedic philosophy, this is the distinction between the Formal Cause and the Material Cause. Kant's theories are helpful in explicating some Vedic ideas that are touched upon throughout the book.

38 The manifestation first takes place as a creation, then as maintenance and finally as destruction.

THE NATURE OF CONSCIOUSNESS

39 Vedas describe two aspects of consciousness—*dṛṣta* and *anumanta*. In being the observer, consciousness is the *dṛṣta*. In approving the experience, it is the *anumanta*.

40 Actually, this automatic generation of thoughts is not a random phenomenon. Rather the generation of thoughts is controlled by Time, which causes thoughts to arise, as inspirations to individuals to act in a certain way. When consciousness accepts these thoughts, it can be said to have been "inspired" by Time, although consciousness can equally well reject the thoughts and assert its independence from Time.

41 This "trying" is in consciousness and not in the mind. A succession of thoughts in the mind can be connected generatively although intents in consciousness cannot be connected in this way. So when we say that "someone wants to do such-and-such" we have to distinguish between when this desire is in the mind and when it is in consciousness.

42 http://en.wikipedia.org/wiki/Benjamin_Libet

43 For a detailed discussion on the problems of incompleteness in physics, please refer to my book *Quantum Meaning: A Semantic Interpretation of Quantum Theory*. For a detailed discussion on the incompleteness in mathematics, please refer to *Gödel's Mistake: The Role of Meaning in Mathematics*.

Acknowledgements

The inspiration behind this book lies in the writings of His Divine Grace A.C. Bhaktivedanta Swami Prabhupāda. He spoke about matter and science with as much ease as he did about soul and God. From his work I first came to believe that there is indeed an alternative way of looking at the material world, different from how it is described in modern science. I am deeply indebted to him in more ways than I can express here in a few words.

The book in the current form would have been impossible without the tireless efforts of Ciprian Begu. He has been my friend and partner in bringing this to life. He read through drafts, edited, did the layout and helped with the cover design. He has tried to teach me the nuances of English grammar, although I haven't been a good student. He figured out all the nits on publishing—something that I did not have the time, energy or the inclination for.

My sincerest gratitude and thanks to Ankur Sethi for editing a draft version of this book and suggesting many improvements in style and flow. His interest in the content of the book and innumerable suggestions made me aware of how the book could be significantly improved and made relevant to the current debates.

I would like to thank my long-time friend Rukesh Patel. His exuberance, encouragement, patient hearing and drive have helped me in innumerable ways. We have laughed so much together—often at our own stupidity and ignorance— that simply thinking of him makes me smile.

My immense gratitude also goes to my parents, who taught me honesty, hard work and simplicity. They gave me the values and upbringing for which I am deeply indebted. My heart also reaches out to my daughter, whose affection and kindness inspires me everyday to become a better person. My wife has been the leveling force in my life. She keeps me grounded to reality, distills complex problems into a succinct bottom-line, and manages the relationships that I would not.

And finally a big thank you to all my readers who have, over the years, written (and continue to write) showing a deep sense of excitement about these books. Their encouragement continues to instill confidence in me that there is a need for these types of books.

My Story

I have always had a great curiosity for the inner workings of nature, the mysteries of the human mind and the origins of the universe. This naturally drew me towards pure sciences. My father, a more practical man, saw this interest as pointless; he was upset when I chose a 5-year program in Chemistry at IIT Kanpur rather than one of the engineering programs, which stood to offer me a better career.

When I started at IIT Kanpur, I believed that my long-held curiosities about the inner workings of nature would be satisfied by an understanding of science. But as I scraped through the coursework and scoured through nearly every section of IIT's extensive library looking for answers, I found that, contrary to my belief, many fundamental and important questions in science remained unanswered. That prompted me to turn towards other departments—since chemistry pointed towards physics which in turn pointed towards mathematics, it seemed that the answers lay elsewhere. However, as I sat through courses offered by other departments—mathematics, physics and philosophy—my worst fears began to materialize: I realized that the problems required discarding many fundamental assumptions in science.

That started me on a journey into the search for alternatives, which has now been spanning 20 years. It was not uncommon in India for students in elite institutions to spend a lot of time discussing philosophy, although often in a tongue-in-cheek manner. My intentions were more serious.

I studied Western philosophy—both classical and modern—as well as Eastern ideas (such as Zen and Taoism) before turning towards Vedic philosophy. I was primarily interested in the nature of matter, the mind and the universe and only Vedic philosophy seemed to offer the kind of synthetic detail I was looking for. I suspected that if the ideas of reincarnation, soul and God in Vedic philosophy were connected to a different view of matter, mind and the universe, then I might actually find an alternative view that could solve the problems in modern science.

At the end of my 5 years at IIT Kanpur, I knew I wanted to pursue the alternative, but I wasn't quite clear how that could work.

I anticipated the pursuit of an alternative in mainstream academia to be very hard. The development of the alternative would frequently run into opposition, and would not fit into the publish-and-tenure practices. A reasonable understanding of ideas often requires longer discussions which may not fit into 3000-word papers. Alternatives often require stepping outside the parochial boundaries of a single field and the journals that accepted such multi-disciplinary articles did not exist at that time—they are more common now.

I therefore faced a difficult choice—pursue a mainstream academic career and defer the search for alternatives until I had established a reputation through conventional means, or pursue a non-academic career to finance my interest in academic alternatives. I chose to separate academics from profession. It was a risky proposition when I started, but in hindsight I think it has worked better than I initially imagined. This and my other books are byproducts of my search for answers to the problems in science, outside mainstream academia.

My career is that of a computer engineer and I have worked for over 17 years in multi-national corporations on telecommunications, wireless and networking technologies. I have co-authored 10 patents and presented at many conferences. I live in Bangalore, India, with my wife and 10-year old daughter.

Connect with Me

Has this book raised your interest? You can connect to my blog or get involved in discussions on www.ashishdalela.com. For any questions or comments please e-mail me at adalela@shabdapress.net.

Other Books by Ashish Dalela

Is the Apple Really Red?

10 Essays on Science and Religion

Conventional wisdom on science and religion says the former is based on experiment and reason, while the latter is based on faith and belief. Is the Apple Really Red? discusses how the notions of soul, morality and afterlife in religion can be scientific. But for this to be possible, a new science that studies meanings instead of objects is needed.

The clash of ideologies between science and religion—this book argues—is based on an incorrect understanding of matter, disconnected from consciousness, and an incorrect notion of God, disconnected from matter, space and time.

A revision of the current views on religion and science is needed, not only to settle the conflict but also to deepen our understanding of matter (and its relation to consciousness) and God (and His relation to matter, space and time)

Written for the layperson, in 10 essays, the book delineates the Vedic view of matter, God, soul, morality, space and time. The author shows how the existence of the soul and God implies a new view of matter, space and time which is empirical and can be used to form new scientific theories.

Such theories will not only change our understanding of matter but will also change our outlook on religion. Readers interested in the science and religion debate will benefit significantly from the viewpoint described in Is the Apple Really Red?

Sāṅkhya and Science
Applications of Vedic Philosophy to Modern Science

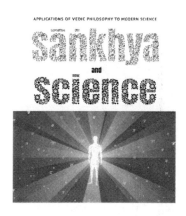

Since the time of Descartes, science has kept questions of mind and meaning outside science, and in recent times materialists aim to reduce mind and meaning to matter. Both approaches have failed. There are problems of meaning in mathematics, computing, physics, biology and neuroscience. A new view of nature is needed, one that integrates matter and meaning more directly.

The Vedic theory of matter—called Sāṅkhya—shows a path fruitful to the resolution of modern scientific problems. In Sāṅkhya, material objects are created when the mind transfers meanings or information into space-time. These objects are not meaningless things, but symbols with meanings.

The book shows how a symbolic view of nature can be used to solve the problems of incompleteness and indeterminism in atomic theory, chemistry, biology, mathematics and computing. In the process, the book builds a new foundation for science, based on a semantic or symbolic view of nature.

The book will be of interest to both scientists and philosophers, especially those looking to integrate mind and matter without stepping outside the rational-empirical approach to science.

Quantum Meaning
A Semantic Interpretation of Quantum Theory

The problems of indeterminism, uncertainty and statistics in quantum theory are legend and have spawned a wide-variety of interpretations none too satisfactory. The key issue of dissatisfaction is the conflict between the microscopic and macroscopic worlds: How does a classically certain world emerge from a world of uncertainty and probability?

This book presents a Semantic Interpretation of Quantum Theory in which atomic objects are treated as symbols of meaning. The book shows that quantum problems of uncertainty, indeterminism and statistics arise when we try to describe meaningful symbols as objects without meaning.

A symbol is also an object, although an object is not necessarily a symbol. The same object can denote many meanings in different contexts, and if we reduce symbols to objects, it naturally results in incompleteness.

This book argues that the current quantum theory is not a final theory of reality. Rather, the theory can be replaced by a better theory in which objects are treated as symbols, because this approach is free of indeterminism and statistics.

The Semantic Interpretation makes it possible to formulate new laws of nature, which can be empirically confirmed. These laws will predict the order amongst symbols, similar to the notes in a musical composition or words in a book.

Gödel's Mistake

The Role of Meaning in Mathematics

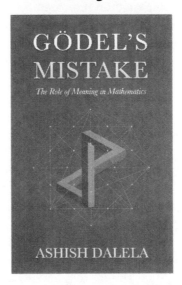

Mathematics is the queen of sciences but problems of incompleteness and incomputability in mathematics have raised serious questions about whether it can indeed be used to describe nature's entire splendor. Proofs that demonstrate the incompleteness and incomputability are respectively called Gödel's Incompleteness and Turing's Halting Problem.

This book connects Gödel's and Turing's theorems to the question of meaning and shows that these proofs rest on what philosophers call category mistakes. Ordinary language contains many categories - such as names, concepts, things, programs, algorithms, problems, etc. but mathematics and computing theory do not. A thing can denote many concepts and vice versa. Similarly, a program can solve many problems, and vice versa. A category mistake arises when we reduce one category to another, and this leads to logical paradoxes because these categories are not mutually reducible.

The book shows that the solution to category mistakes requires a new approach in which numbers are treated as types rather than quantities. This is called Type Number Theory (TNT) in the book. TNT requires a hierarchical theory of space and time, because it is through a hierarchical embedding that objects become symbols of meanings.

Hierarchical notions of space and time are well-known; for instance postal addresses and clock times are hierarchical. A formal theory of hierarchical space-time will also be a theory of symbols and will address problems of incomputability in computing and incompleteness in mathematics.

Signs of Life
A Semantic Critique of Evolutionary Theory

This book challenges the fundamental ideas in the Neo-Darwinian theory of evolution from the perspective of mathematics, physics, computing, game theory, and non-linear dynamics.

It argues that the key ideas underlying evolution—random mutation and natural selection—are based on notions about matter, causality, space-time, and lawfulness, which were supposed true in Darwin's time, but have been unseated through 20th century developments in physics, mathematics, computing, game theory, and complex system theory. Evolution, however, continues in a relative time-warp, disregarding these developments, which, if considered, would alter our view of evolution.

The book illustrates why natural selection and random mutation are logically inconsistent together. Separately, they are incomplete to account for biological complexity. In other words, the theory of evolution is either inconsistent or incomplete.

The book, however, does not deny evolution. It presents a new theory of evolution that is modeled after the evolution of cultures, ideologies, societies, and civilizations. This is called *Semantic Evolution* and the book illustrates how this new model of evolution will emerge from the resolution of fundamental unsolved problems of meaning in mathematics, physics, and computing theory.

Moral Materialism
A Semantic Theory of Ethical Naturalism

Modern science describes the physical effects of material causes, but not the moral consequences of conscious choices. Is nature merely a rational place, or is it also a moral place? The question of morality has always been important for economists, sociologists, political theorists, and lawmakers. However, it has had almost no impact on the understanding of material nature in science.

This book argues that the questions of morality can be connected to natural law in science when science is revised to describe nature as meaningful symbols rather than as meaningless things. The revision, of course, is entailed not just by issues of morality but also due to profound unsolved problems of incompleteness, indeterminism, irreversibility and incomputability in physics, mathematics, and computing theory. This book shows how the two kinds of problems are deeply connected.

The book argues that the lawfulness in nature is different from that presented in current science. Nature comprises not just *things* but also our *theories* about those things. The world of things is determined but the world of theories is not—our theories represent our free will, and the interaction between free will and matter now has a causal consequence in the evolution of scientific theories.

The moral consequences of free will represent the ideological evolution of the observer, and the correct theory represents the freedom from this evolution. Free will is therefore not the choice of arbitrary and false theories; free will is the choice of the correct theory. Once the correct theory is chosen, the observer is free of natural laws, since all phenomena are consistent with the correct theory.

Uncommon Wisdom
Fault Lines in the Foundations of Atheism

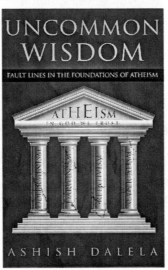

The rise of militant atheism has brought to fore some fundamental issues in our conventional understanding of religion. However, because it offers science as an alternative to religion, militant atheism also exposes to scrutiny the fundamental problems of incompleteness in current science.

The book traces the problem of incompleteness in current science to the problem of universals that began in Greek philosophy and despite many attempts to reduce ideas to matter, the problem remains unsolved. The book shows how the problem of meaning appears over and over in all of modern science, rendering all current fields—physics, mathematics, computing, and biology included—incomplete. The book also presents a solution to this problem describing why nature is not just material objects that we can perceive, but also a hierarchy of abstract ideas that can only be conceived. These hierarchically 'deeper' ideas necessitate deeper forms of perception, even to complete material knowledge.

The book uses this background to critique the foundations of atheism and shows why many of its current ideas—reductionism, materialism, determinism, evolutionism, and relativism—are simply false. It presents a radical understanding of religion, borrowing from Vedic philosophy, in which God is the most primordial idea from which all other ideas are produced through refinement. The key ideological shift necessary for this view of religion is the notion that material objects, too, are ideas. However, that shift does not depend on religion, since its implications can be known scientifically.

The conflict between religion and science, in this view, is based on a flawed understanding of how reason and experiment are used to acquire knowledge. The book describes how reason and experiment can be used in two ways—discovery and verification—and while the nature of truth can never be *discovered* by reason and experiment, it can be *verified* in this way. This results in an epistemology in which truth is discovered via faith, but it is verified by reason and experiment.

Did You Like Six Causes?

If you enjoyed this book or found it insightful I would be grateful if you would post a short review on Amazon. Your feedback will allow other readers to discover the book, and can help me improve the future editions. If you'd like to leave a review then go to the website below, click on the customer reviews and then write your own.

http://www.ashishdalela.com/amazon-sc

Find Out in Advance When My Next Book Is Out

I'm always working on the next book. Currently, I'm writing *Signs of Life*, which is a semantic critique of evolutionary theory and *Moral Materialism*, a book about the Vedic science of choices and their consequences, both to be released in 2015. You can get a publication alert by signing up to my mailing list on www.ashishdalela.com. Moreover, If you want to receive advance copies of my upcoming books for review, please let me know at adalela@shabdapress.net.

CPSIA information can be obtained
at www.ICGtesting.com
Printed in the USA
LVOW11s1659260117
522285LV00004B/790/P